Super Six Comprehension Strategies: 35 Lessons and More for Reading Success

Super Six Comprehension Strategies: 35 Lessons and More for Reading Success

Lori Oczkus

Christopher-Gordon Publishers, Inc.
Norwood, Massachusetts

Credits

Every effort has been made to contact copyright holders for permission to reproduce borrowed material where necessary. We apologize for any oversights and would be happy to rectify them in future printings.

All children's work used with permission.

Chapter One: "Super Six Artful Expressions" adapted from work by Mario Penman.
Chapter Two: "Find Someone" adapted from work by Judith A. Williams.
Chapter Two: "Journal Writing Connections 'This reminds me of . . . .'" adapted from work by Jodi Queenan.
Chapter Three: "One Word" adapted from work by Susan Page.
Chapter Four: "Pull a Passage" adapted from work by Candace Cease.
Chapter Four: Idea for dinner party adapted from, Chapter 5, "Active Learning: Dramatic Play in the Content Areas," by MaryEllen Vogt in Maureen McLaughlin and MaryEllen Vogt, Editors, *Creativity and Innovation in Content Area Teaching*, Copyright © 2000 by Christopher-Gordon Publishers, Inc.
Chapter Five: "Question Sort" adapted from Ozzie Allenberg.
Chapter Six: "Famous Last Words" adapted from work by Janice M. Karels.
Chapter Seven: Idea of story telling hand and rewriting familiar tunes adapted from Linda Hoyt, *Revisit, Reflect, Retell*, Copyright © 1999 by Heinemann Publishers.
Chapter Seven: Summarizing Synthesis adapted from workshops by George Gonzalez and work by Jon Bindless.
Chapter Seven: Tunes for Retelling, in "Choose a Quick One" (p. 181) adapted from Maureen McLaughlin and Mary Beth Allen, *Guided Comprehension: A Teaching Model for Grades 3-8*, Copyright © 2002 by the International Reading Association.

Christopher-Gordon Publisher, Inc.
Bridging Theory and Practice
1502 Providence Highway, Suite 12
Norwood, Massachusetts 02062
800-934-8322
781-762-5577
www.Christopher-Gordon.com

Printed in the United States of America

10 9 8 7 6 5 4 3   08 07 06 05

ISBN: 1-929024-69-X
Library of Congress Catalogue Number: 2003113677

To my own "Super Six"

Mark, my husband

and our three precious readers

Bryan, Rachael, and Rebecca

and to my parents, Bruce and Barbara Dutton

Table of Contents

8 Evaluating

Appendix

Acknowledgments

Although crafting a book demands a certain amount of solitude, a project such as the one you are holding also takes a "village" of caring friends, colleagues, and family members to support the author in rising to the arduous task. I would like to take the opportunity to acknowledge and thank all the people who so graciously shared their honest feedback, emotional support, and practical ideas to the making of this book.

Thanks to Sue Canavan at Christopher-Gordon Publishers who listened intently as she always does to my ideas, believed in my project, and carefully maintained my voice in my writing. Thanks to Kate Liston for her attention to detail and caring nature.

Without the ground work of some very special researchers and teachers, this book would not exist. The comprehension research of P. David Pearson, Laura R. Roehler, Janice Dole, and Gerald Duffy (1991) provides the foundation that this book is built upon. Ellin Keene and Susan Zimmerman's landmark book *Mosaic of Thought* (1997) brought comprehension strategies to life for tens of thousands of teachers. Their work also continues to inspire my thinking and teaching.

My own little band of reviewers spent hours reading and responding to every word of this manuscript during its progress. Thanks goes to my readers Audrey Fong, Ellen Osmundson, Joan Masaryk, Liz Irwin, and Lynne Gurnee, whose suggestions made a difference in communicating my message and whose kind emails kept me going. Thank you to my friend, Regie Routman, who suggested I run chapters by trusted teacher friends during the writing process. This is a most practical recommendation that made the process of writing so much easier and more enjoyable.

Many talented classroom teachers and educators contributed ideas to the the lessons in this text including; Mario Penman, Nancy Whistler and Judy Williams, Glorianna Chen, Jodi Queenan, Karen Thompson, Susan Page, Candy Cease, MaryEllen Vogt and Maureen McLaughlin, Ozzie Allenberg (student), Jan Karels, Jill Hope, Sandy Buscheck, Kristi Webster, Linda Hoyt, Lori Falchi, Kit King, Debra Le, George Gonzales, Jon Bindloss, and Krista Koch. Also thanks to the staff at each of the following schools, Epiphany in San Francisco, Randall in Milpitas, Washington in Berkeley, Wilson in San Leandro, Palmecia in Hayward, Melrose in Oakland, and Hester in San Jose.

Special thanks goes to Nancy O'Connor and her colleagues at OWL for their long time support of my work in classrooms, staff development, and writing. Judy Herns also inspired me to go forward with writing this book.

Most of all, I appreciate the support, love, and blessings of my family. Thanks to my husband, Mark, for picking up the slack and listening to my constant chatter about the book. And thanks to my children for teaching me the fine art of multitasking. Some days I wrote with two children under my desk and one climbing on my back. Bryan, Rachael, and Rebecca supply me with daily inspiration and joy!

Foreword

Lori Oczkus has written a marvelous book for teachers. *Super Six Comprehension Strategies: 35 Lessons and More for Reading Success* is the right book at the right time. Perched as the profession is on a precipice facing two sharp descents—one the steep face of a cliff of constructivist, student centered reform of the early 90s and the other the face of an even steeper cliff into a world of basic skills, direct instruction, scripted lessons, and accountability to rest—we need the sort of balanced guidance that a book like this can provide.

This is evidence-based practice at its best. The strategies recommended for teachers to teach in their classrooms exhibit a clear link to the 25 year history of research on reading comprehension strategies. The key strategies—the Super Six as Oczkus calls them—are Connecting, Predicting/Inferring, Questioning, Monitoring, Summarizing/Synthesizing, and Evaluating. While they are not precisely the same as those recommended in the National Reading Panel report or in the research reviewed by Pressley (2000) or Duke and Pearson (2002), they are certainly drawn from the same literature and bear a strong family resemblance to those reviews of research. A teacher who employs these six strategies in his or her classroom can argue compellingly that they are based on current scholarship about effective strategy instruction.

This is also evidence-based practice at its most useful. Oczkus does not stop at a reporting of what the research says about these six strategies, leaving it up to each and every reader to invent ways of engaging students in the use of these strategies in the classroom. Instead, she relies on her extensive work in schools to offer us vignettes about how various teachers with whom she has worked implement these strategies with real live kids (Or sometimes she relates her own experiences teaching these strategies within the classrooms of fellow teachers). When she discusses how to implement the strategy, she also provides *guidelines for implementing it in various instructional contexts* defined by both the degree of scaffolding (e.g. guided reading, literature circles, independent work, or cross-age tutoring) or the population of readers (e.g., English language learners or struggling readers); this is important because (a) instructional contexts and populations vary between schools and classrooms, and (b) so do implementation guidelines. She does provide a *generic framework for strategy instruction* (introduce the strategy, model it, guided application in pairs or small groups, independent practice, and reflection), but she also shows how that generic framework has to be adapted to each strategy. Finally, she shows how the strategy can be applied at *various points in the "flow"* of a lesson—before, during, and after reading.

Another feature that teachers will find useful and engaging is the "teachers as readers" coda at the end of each chapter. This is a place where Oczkus encourages teachers to reflect on how each strategy enters and makes a difference in their own lives as readers. This is an essential understanding and experience for teachers because, as we have learned from the past 20 years of research in becoming an expert teacher of writing, it is hard to teach about a process strategically and reflectively unless one has engaged in serious reflection about one's own use of strategies in negotiating "the tricky bits" of the process, be it writing, reading, or thinking critically about either. Oczkus encourages teachers to share with their students, no matter how young, the ways in which they as readers use the very strategies they are teaching to help them over those tricky bits they inevitably encounters while reading.

I cannot close without singling out the material on professional development, found on the CD-ROM, primarily because my own experience working with schools to generate reform in curriculum and teaching tells me that Lori is right on target in her suggestions for developing effective professional development programs. One-shot-bring-in-the-outside-expert approaches don't work. Nor does the flitting butterfly model where a staff moves from topic to topic each session, pretending that the sheer mention of a topic, approach, or strategy (which is about all you can hope for in a single session) will somehow magically transform what goes on inside classrooms. We know that does not work. We know that sustained effort and emphasis—where a staff stays with a topic long enough to unpack it, look at it up close and personal, develop plans to implement it, try it out, and then re-examine it to reshape it for another tryout—provides our best hope for making lasting change on what happens inside classrooms. Yet, we are still more likely to see the "topic of the month" than we are a sustained program of work that we ought to wonder about our collective commitment to instructional change and building cultures of improvement within schools. Well, Lori Oczkus has provided us with a cornucopia of examples of sustained professional inquiry and learning, along with some principles to guide us as we attempt to build our own professional development programs.

This book fits nicely into a growing "library" of books that attempt to help teachers develop an "inside view" of what good strategy instruction can and should look like and how to actually carry it off. It fits into the same family as its predecessors, *Mosaic of Thought* by Keene and Zimmerman and *Strategies that Work* by Harvey and Goudvis, but differs from these recent ancestors by providing a more specific set of implementation guidelines and tools. A person wanting a richer treatment of the research underlying these strategies would do well to couple it with a reading of Janice Almasi's new book, *Teaching Strategic Processes*; a person wanting a richer treatment of the theory of teaching underlying the work would do well to pair it

with Gerry Duffy's new book, *Explaining Reading*. Teachers who take seriously the idea that it is a solemn responsibility to help students develop a reserve of cognitive and metacognitive strategies that they can use when the going gets tough, when things don't just happen naturally, will find much in this book to get them started on meeting that responsibility. I know it is a book that I will recommend to all teachers who share this goal with me and with Lori Oczkus. Happy reading!

References

Almasi, J. (2003). *Teaching strategic processes in reading.* New York: Guilford.

Duffy, G. (2003). *Explaining reading.* New York: Guilford.

Harvey, S., & Goudvis, A. (2000). *Strategies that work: Teaching comprehension to enhance understanding.* York, ME: Stenhouse.

Keene, E., & and Zimmerman, S. (1997). *Mosaic of thought: Teaching comprehension in a reader's workshop* . Portsmouth, NH: Heinemann

Introduction and Overview:
Comprehension Strategies for Success

The Need for Improved Comprehension

Do these students and scenarios sound familiar to you?

Fourth grader, Cecily reads during silent sustained reading (SSR) but only selects comic books and magazines to read. She says books are "boring."

Brandon can't read the fifth grade social studies text alone and reads with a partner.

Seven students in Mr. Simon's fourth grade are reading at the second grade level at the beginning of the year. They have difficulty reading the grade level anthology.

Mrs. Lee has students in her sixth grade class who read from the third grade level to high school level.

Sixth grader, Ana came from Mexico three years ago and now reads texts fluently in English but has difficulty understanding what she has read.

Perhaps some of these students are just like the ones that fill your classroom. Most likely your students vary greatly in their reading levels and abilities to comprehend. Some students you work with decode well but do not understand what they have read. Other students simply aren't engaging in the reading. Even the most proficient readers sometimes have difficulty understanding nonfiction texts. Improving reading comprehension while at the same time motivating and inspiring students to love to read is one of the most difficult challenges we face as teachers.

Now, with the added pressure of meeting standards and raising test scores, the need for explicit instruction in comprehension is increasing every year. It is no wonder comprehension remains a popular and sought-after topic on the International Reading Association's "What's Hot, What's Not" list (Cassidy & Cassidy, 2003). Teachers are asking for more help in meeting the diverse needs in their classrooms and for reaching high expectations for students' reading and comprehension.

Good reader research

Even though comprehension is a concern, in the past 25 years research has provided us with some excellent strategies to guide the teaching of reading comprehension. Thanks to the "proficient reader" or "good reader" research, as it is often called, we have a proven list of strategies that good readers rely on and that can be taught (Dole, Duffy, Roehler, & Pearson, 1991). These strategies include predicting/inferring, making connections to background knowledge (Keene & Zimmerman, 1997), self-questioning, monitoring, visualizing (Pressley, 1997), summarizing/synthesizing, and evaluating.

Comprehension is strengthened when the proficient reader strategies are scaffolded with an explicit description of the strategy, teacher modeling, collaborative use, guided practice, and finally independent use of the strategy (Duke & Pearson, 2002). By also including time for reflecting on strategy use, students become more metacognitive and in control of their use of the strategies (Pressley, 2002). For example, a teacher may ask students after a prediction activity to reflect on how predicting helped them better understand the reading.

The need for more lessons: strategies to improve comprehension

In addition to research that points to a list of consistent strategies for improving comprehension, there are many valuable resources for teaching comprehension strategies. When I work with school districts and staffs we read and refer to the following books: *Mosaic of Thought* by Keene and Zimmerman (1997); *Strategies That Work* by Harvey and Goudivis (2000); *Guided Comprehension* by McLaughlin and Allen (2002); and *Scaffolding Reading Experiences, Second Edition* by Graves and Graves (2003).

So, how does this book fit into what is "out there" already? My intent is not to reinvent the wheel, but rather to build on and extend the foundation set by the researchers and teachers who have published before me. Perhaps you are actively basing your comprehension instruction on the good reader research and are using the above-listed resources. This book is a natural extension of these proven strategies and is filled with more lessons to further strengthen your students' comprehension. If the good reader research is new to you, this book will also support you in your journey into improving your students' comprehension.

The ideas and lessons can be used with your existing materials whether you use an anthology or novels to teach reading. *Super Six Comprehension Strategies* is more than a collection of lessons; it is a resource that provides meaningful ways for putting the proficient reader strategies into the heads, hearts, and hands of students.

Super Six Comprehension Strategies includes the following unique features that can assist you in strengthening comprehension in your classroom.

Super Six Comprehension Strategies provides:

- Thoughtful overviews of the research and current thinking around each of the "Super Six" strategies;
- Engaging lessons that motivate students to comprehend better and to love to read;

- Lessons organized around the strategies proficient readers consistently use;
- Scaffolded instruction that includes teacher modeling, cooperative and guided practice, and reflection on strategy use to develop metacognition;
- Applications for teaching the strategies in a variety of classroom structures including
  - small groups for struggling readers and English language learners;
  - guided reading groups;
  - literature circles;
  - cross-age tutor pairs;
  - independent work;
- Reproducibles to use in guiding students in their use of the strategies;
- Classroom vignettes for primary and intermediate examples and ideas;
- Teachers as Readers feature to assist teachers in reflecting on their own use of strategies and using those experiences to enhance their teaching; and
- An extensive chapter on staff development that includes an inquiry model for studying comprehension related topics as a staff.

How to Use This Book

This book is designed to be a desktop reference that you can use in any order based on your teaching style and your students' needs. There is no one right way to use these lessons. It would be helpful to look over the lessons in the first chapter to decide how you might provide opportunities throughout the school year for students to see how the strategies work together. You may find it beneficial to either hang the posters found on the CD-ROM that come with the book or to have your students create their own. This way you will have a handy, kid-friendly wall reference for the strategies to use throughout the year. After briefly introducing students to the Super Six through the first lesson, you may select any strategy or strategies from Chapters 2-8 to study in-depth while returning to the comprehending with the Super Six lessons in the first chapter periodically to give students the big picture.

I hope that you will at some point read this book from cover to cover to draw from the big picture of all it has to offer you in your comprehension journey. This book also works well as a study resource for staff development. As the entire staff reads the text they share lessons, reflections, and understandings of each strategy. Even if just you and a colleague try the lessons and then discuss your findings, that is a great way to extend and improve your teaching and ultimately your students' learning.

Staff developers and literacy coaches may draw from this resource as they teach demonstration lessons and provide ideas for other teachers to improve comprehension. In my work as a staff developer, I use these lessons, and find that students and teachers alike respond well to the interactive, hands-on strategies.

How This Book Is Organized

The book is organized around chapters that contain lessons for teaching each of the good reader strategies in-depth to your students. Chapter 1 provides an overview of the "Super Six" strategies along with lessons you can return to throughout the school year to help students see how the strategies work flexibly and in concert with one another. Each of the remaining chapters contain lessons for the Super Six strategies. The appendix includes various tools for assessing student progress in the use of the strategies. Bibliographies for research, professional books, children's books, and for adult reading materials are included. The CD-ROM is a guide for staff development for individuals, colleagues, or entire staffs. The resources provide books, videos, articles, and other valuable ideas for studying topics related to improving comprehension.

Each chapter includes

- An overview of background on the strategy and research to support its use
- A before, during, and after reading chart that provides teachers and students with prompts for using the strategy
- Vignettes from both primary and intermediate classrooms
- Scaffolded lessons with reproducibles
- A Teachers as Readers feature where teachers reflect on their strategy use in their own reading for pleasure and information
- A bibliography of research for that strategy

Each lesson contains

- List of objectives
- Materials list
- Steps for scaffolding

- Introducing the strategy, teacher modeling
- Guiding the strategy in cooperative groups or pairs
- Practicing the strategy in different classroom structures (literature circles, guided reading, independent work, cross-age buddies, small groups of struggling readers, or English language learners
- Reflecting on the strategy
- Reproducibles to use during interactive lessons with students

Appendix

- Assessment rubric for the Super Six
- Super Six student strategy survey
- A guide for interpreting the results of the strategy survey
- A class checklist for the strategies

References

- Research and professional book references
- Children's books cited
- Adult reading materials cited

Chapter 1: Comprehending with the "Super Six"

This chapter is more than an introduction to the "Super Six" comprehension strategies. It contains engaging lessons that can be taught throughout the school year to assist students in their understanding of how comprehension strategies work as a package to help us understand what we read. Lessons include creating metaphors for each strategy, decorating anchor posters to use as a reference, and sharing a bookmark and poem about the Super Six. The focus is on seeing the entire six strategies in action in a variety of reading materials and using them as a tool kit for understanding all year long.

Chapter 2: Building Background and Making Connections

Good readers use their schema or prior knowledge to help them understand the text.

The lessons in this chapter assist students in making connections to their lives, other texts, and the world around them. Students participate in a people search, one-minute quick book look, and a connection workshop.

Chapter 3: Predicting

Predicting involves the use of text clues and the students' background knowledge as they make logical forecasts about what will occur next in the text. In this chapter, students learn to Partner Predict, Whisper Skim, and Scan in a text that has no illustrations. They also stop and draw predictions, and predict words that they think will be in the text.

Chapter 4: Inferring

Inferring is a difficult strategy that separates the good from poor readers. High-level thinking is needed when students use text clues and background information to think about new insights and read between the lines. Hunting for inferences in a picture book or studying characters' feelings provides students with guided experiences with inferring. Questioning before reading and then answering questions after reading by inferring provides students with a meaningful context. Pulling passages out of the text to infer forces students to read into the author's intended meanings. A lively dinner party role-play session provides students with a hands-on opportunity to infer characters' feelings and actions.

Chapter 5: Questioning

Good readers ask questions before, during, and after reading. The lessons in this chapter guide students as they learn to ask thoughtful questions throughout the reading process.

Students learn the value of wondering before reading a fiction or nonfiction text. Question sorting provides a prereading organizer for learning. They engage in questioning while reading with a variety of prompts, and after reading they become little teachers, asking each other questions about the text.

Chapter 6: Monitoring

Keeping track of comprehension is what monitoring is all about. In this chapter, students use a variety of helpful tools to help them repair comprehension along the way. A monitor bookmark offers ways to figure out problem spots during reading. Students use the last words they read to help them get into the next day's reading. A mark-the-spot bookmark helps students pay attention to their thoughts and engage with the text during reading. Visualizing aids students in making comprehension clear with a fun drawing idea. Word puzzles are an interesting way to study and remember favorite or important words.

Chapter 7: Summarizing and Synthesizing

Summarizing is a difficult and complex strategy for many students. They need to separate the important parts of a text from the unimportant details as they tell the text in sequence. The summary hand with finger facts or story elements lends a hand to guide students. Small summaries found in many trade books give students models of succinctly written, one-sentence summaries. Synthesis is the "taste" that a book or reading leaves in the reader's mouth. It is the big picture, author's message, and theme all rolled up into one. Discussion synthesis starters prompt students in meaningful discussions about their readings. Quick responses to literature that include drama, art, or writing allow for synthesis to evolve through free response. A strip poem makes an excellent culmination to a unit of study or synthesis after reading a text.

Chapter 8: Evaluating

Good readers are like little judges, weighing and evaluating before, during, and after reading. They evaluate whether they liked the text or not and how they did as readers.

They are critics giving a thumbs up or down to issues in the text and the author's craft. Students also evaluate characters' actions throughout the reading. All of this complex thinking is made more explicit through fun activities like "Think of Three," where students select only three main ideas from a text. Then they race to gather facts from nonfiction sources in the get the facts lesson. Students argue important and controversial issues from the text and rate the author's craft and their own performance.

Appendix

The appendix includes practical assessment tools to use all year long to chart students' progress in their strategy use. An assessment rubric provides guidance for interpreting student progress in written responses to reproducibles in the book and in observing students' during lessons. A class-scoring sheet provides a handy tool for keeping track of each student's progress in strategy use. The Super Six Strategy survey can be administered several times throughout the year to see if students are internalizing the strategies and really using them as tools when they read. A guide for interpreting the Super Six Strategy Survey is also included.

References

I have also included an extensive list of professional articles, research, and books. Professional, practical teaching strategy-type books are listed both in the main bibliography and on the staff development CD-ROM. There are also lists of children's books and adult level novels that are mentioned in the vignettes throughout the book.

Most of all, Have Fun!

Hopefully, you will make these lessons your own and, in the process, find that your students are enjoying themselves while improving their comprehension.

Our challenge is to motivate students to read a wide variety of materials and to improve their comprehension and achievement. Isn't it great that we can have a good time while engaging in the process? Happy reading!

CD-ROM: Staff Development—Comprehension Inquiries

A staff development inquiry is a collaborative way to work with one other colleague or the rest of the staff to explore a topic related to comprehension. Teachers begin with a problem students are having in comprehension and generate questions for solving that problem. The inquiry study may involve professional readings, demonstration lessons, coaching each other in new strategy lessons, watching videos, or reading adult-level novels and discussing strategy use. The inquiry topics may include comprehension in general, struggling readers, second language students, reciprocal teaching strategies, guided reading, or literature circles.

▷ # Comprehending with the Super Six

> "A large volume of work indicates that we can help students acquire the strategies and processes used by good readers and that this improves their overall comprehension of text, both the texts used to teach the strategies and texts they read on their own in the future. . . . good readers use multiple strategies constantly." **Jan Duke and P. David Pearson,** *in* What Research Has to Say About Reading Instruction, *p. 206.*

> "... in Vygotskian (1978) terms, the internalization of comprehension strategies involves long-term practice with the strategies, including opportunities to reflect on strategies used with others." **Michael Pressley,** *in* What Research Has to Say About Reading Instruction, *p. 290.*

Thoughts on the Super Six

Try asking students in various grade levels to define reading and they'll provide you with a variety of interesting responses (some in invented spelling) that may include some of the following:

"Reading is fun."

"Reading is learning."

"Reading is a way of communicating."

"Reading is a good way to get more information."

"Reading is pretending that you are that person and living in that place."

"When I read a good book, I wish it would never end!"

Even the students who say reading is figuring out the words, when probed further know that they need to somehow glean meaning from the text. Comprehension is at the heart of reading. The document, *Putting Reading First* (National Reading Panel, 2000) states that "Comprehension is the reason for reading. If readers can read the words but do not understand what they are reading, they are not really reading" (p. 48).

How can we best teach comprehension strategies to elementary age children? Fortunately, in the past 20 years, advances in comprehension research have provided us with a core list of strategies to teach and some effective methods for helping students internalize key comprehension strategies.

At the schools where I teach and consult, we implement the "Super Six" list of research-based comprehension strategies that include predict/infer, question, monitor, summarize, evaluate, and make connections as the foundation of our comprehension teaching. Our goal has been to make comprehension strategies visible and accessible to children. At Randall school in Milpitas, California, the Super Six strategies are posted in classrooms from kindergarten to sixth grade. Even though the strategy instruction varies depending upon grade level, the students in the entire school experience a common list of strategies and are exposed to language that describes those strategies.

Besides posting the Super Six strategies, it is possible to reinforce comprehension strategies throughout the day during read alouds, content area reading, literature circles, and guided reading. Teachers model using think alouds and students discuss strategies with peers and the teacher. We find ways to sneak in time for reflections as we ask the students which strategies they are using and which proved most helpful in a given text. When I ask the students in any grade level, "What do good readers do to understand what they are reading?" the students eagerly raise their hands to share their thoughts on the Super Six.

The lessons in this chapter are designed for use throughout the school year as you help students make this essential list of strategies their own!

How Do the Super Six Strategies Help Students Comprehend?

Moving beyond just testing comprehension to teaching a proven set of comprehension strategies

In 1979, Dolores Durkin concluded in her landmark study on comprehension that questions in basal readers were driving comprehension instruction in classrooms. She also reported that teachers essentially were testing comprehension by asking questions after reading rather than modeling and teaching students strategies to use to understand text.

After Durkin's study, various researchers, including Dole, Duffy, Roehler, and Pearson (1991) looked at what proficient readers do when they read. From this study they came up with a core list of strategies that good readers consistently employ to make sense of text.

These "good reader" strategies include (Pearson et al., 1991; Keene & Zimmerman, 1997; McLaughlin & Allen, 2002):

- **Predicting/inferring**—previewing materials to make initial predictions about the text, using text clues throughout the reading process to predict and infer
- **Making connections**—activating prior knowledge before reading and throughout reading; promoting connections to self, other texts, and the world (Keene & Zimmerman, 1997)
- **Questioning**—self questioning (literal and inferential) throughout the reading process
- **Monitoring**—keeping track of one's reading asking, "Do I understand this?" "What do I need to do if the text doesn't make sense?" Figuring out words and visualizing to monitor.

    - Knowing how words work—uses a variety of strategies to figure out words
    - Visualizing (Pressley, 1997)—visualizes mental images while reading
- **summarizing/synthesizing**—key points and big ideas, concepts, and a theme
- **evaluating**—issues in the text; the author's craft; enjoyment and progress as a reader

These good reader strategies from the proficient reader research can be used as the foundation for teaching comprehension. Explicit instruction of these strategies improves comprehension. (Hiebert, Pearson, Taylor, Richardson, & Paris, 1998).

Photo of Super Six Posted in a Classroom

How to teach the Super Six

What is the most effective way to teach the Super Six? Master teacher, Regie Routman, warns us to keep strategy instruction in its place and to be careful to use the strategies as tools for facilitating and extending comprehension (2003). Regie suggests that we use 20 percent of the instruction time to model/teach strategies and 80 percent of the class time to apply the strategies both guided by the teacher and independently. Students need to see how the strategies fit into the broader picture of making meaning and they need to know how to apply them in their own reading.

After introducing students to the Super Six list through brief think alouds, the strategies may be posted somewhere in the classroom. While studying individual strategies in more depth, you can return to the larger list to help students develop an understanding of how the strategies work flexibly and in concert with one another to comprehend text.

Scaffolding comprehension strategy instruction

Various researchers recommend models for scaffolding, or supporting students during comprehension instruction (Fielding & Pearson, 1991; Duke & Pearson, 2002; Duffy & Roehler, 1987; Pressley, et al., 1992; Wood, Brunner, & Ross, 1976; Vygotsky, 1978).

To provide the proper support and guidance, the teacher eventually releases responsibility for the strategy by using the steps listed in Box 1.1. Notice that attention and emphasis is given to allowing time for the students and teacher to think aloud and to discuss their thinking processes or metacognition. I have designed the lessons in this book to follow this scaffolded lesson design to ensure proper support for students as they become independent with each of the strategies. The steps move from teacher modeling to cooperative guided practice and finally independent practice. Time for reflecting on the strategy and its usefulness is critical in helping students to internalize the strategy and improve comprehension.

Box 1.1. Steps for Scaffolding Any Comprehension Strategy

1. Introduce
The teacher tells students what the strategy under study is and how it will help them understand what they read.
Example: *When you are reading it is helpful to ask questions as you read. Good readers have questions before, during, and after they read.*

2. Modeling
The teacher models how to employ the strategy using a think-aloud and reading material. The teacher may also invite a student to provide a think-aloud for the class.
Example: *Before I read this Social Studies chapter, I am going to study all of the headings and illustrations and think about questions I have about the topic. I wonder . . . I want to know . . . During reading, I will stop and ask more questions like I wonder . . . I don't understand . . . Why did . . . or How did . . . ? After reading, I will go back and think of questions a teacher may ask on a test. I will also think about what else I wonder or what else I would like to know about the topic.*
(Teacher gives specific examples using the chapter.)

3. Guide the Strategy in Cooperative Groups or Pairs
The teacher works with students in the whole class setting, small groups, or with cooperative groups to guide students and give feedback as they share their responses. Further modeling may take place during this step.
Example: *Work with a partner and stop every few pages and ask questions. Ask questions that you would like to ask the author. Ask questions about the topic that a teacher could ask on a test. Ask questions about what you wonder. We will share our questions in 20 minutes . I will circulate and listen and provide support as you ask your questions.*

continued

> **4. Independent Practice**
> Students practice the strategy on their own while reading. They are to keep track of how they use the strategy and be prepared to participate in a discussion after reading.
> **Example:** As you read your book of choice during silent sustained reading (SSR), please watch for places where you asked questions. Be prepared to share at least two of your questions with your tablemates after SSR.
>
> **5. Reflection**
> The teacher provides opportunities for students to reflect on their thinking and use of the strategy. How did the strategy help them understand the text better?
> **Example**: How does asking questions before, during, and after reading help you understand what you are reading?

Adapted from Duke & Pearson (2002); Fielding & Pearson (1991).

Reinforcing the Super Six in a Variety of Classroom Settings

In an effort to provide differentiated instruction to meet the needs of all students, you may reinforce comprehension using the Super Six Strategies in a variety of classroom groupings.

You may choose to organize students in small groups that may include literature circles, cross-age tutors, guided reading groups, struggling readers, or English language learners.

Box 1.2 includes the unique ways that each of these groupings meet the needs of your students so you can more effectively reinforce the Super Six strategies and, ultimately, comprehension. Throughout this book all of the lessons include specific suggestions for incorporating the following groupings with activities that reinforce the strategy and deepen comprehension in a small group setting.

Box 1.2. Options for Reinforcing the Super Six

Classroom Setting/Grouping	Reinforcement of the Super Six Strategies
Guided Reading A small group organized by flexible need, interest, or mixed abilities meets with the teacher to read a text. The text is at grade level or at the instructional level of the students. The teacher observes students and uses regular assessments to design instruction and to create new groups. **Refer to:** *Guided Reading.* Irene Fountas & Gay Su Pinnell (1996).	• Select one strategy to focus on at a time. Organize strategy groups or groups that meet because the students need reinforcement in a particular strategy. (Keene & Zimmerman, 1997) Use reproducibles from this book to assess student progress and to decide on groupings. • Model and then allow students to take turns as you guide their practice in a particular strategy and lesson.

continued

Literature Circles

A small group of students read and discuss texts in a student-led group. Groups may read the same or different texts and are generally organized by mixed ability and interest in a particular text. Students may take on roles such as discussion director, word wizard, summarizer, or they may visit more freely without notes. (Daniels, 1994)

Refer to:

Literature Circles. Harvey Daniels (2001).

- One group models in front of the class to serve as a model for the strategy use. Classmates comment and discuss.
- Students have the opportunity to deepen their understanding of the text as they listen to the responses of others. They also have the opportunity to deepen their understanding of the strategies in strategy discussions.

Struggling Readers

The teacher meets with a small group of struggling readers to tailor the instruction to the specific needs of the students. The group may meet on a regular basis for intervention instruction. Extra support in grade level material or leveled texts may occur. Special needs can include difficulties with fluency, vocabulary, comprehension, decoding, and motivation.

Refer to:

What Really Matters For Struggling Readers. Richard Allington (2001).

Reciprocal Teaching at Work: Strategies for Improving Comprehension. Lori Oczkus (2003).

- Provide students in the small group setting more scaffolding by modeling and guiding their use of the strategies.
- Offer support in grade level texts or use texts at the students' instructional level.
- Incorporate opportunities for students to reread for fluency and to discuss selection vocabulary and concepts.
- Alternate thinking aloud about strategy use and guiding students as they share their thinking.
- Focus on a limited number of strategies during guided reading—especially the four from reciprocal teaching—predict, summarize, clarify (monitor), and question.

English Language Learners

English language learners have unique needs. The ELL students in a given classroom may be at a variety of levels of English production from preproduction, or a silent period, to more fluent stages where they use phrases or even full sentences. ELL students have special needs with vocabulary, concepts, difficulty of the text, and fluency. The skilled teacher shelters, or carefully scaffolds lessons to meet these needs in grade level and leveled texts.

Refer to:

English Learners. Reaching the Highest Level of English Literacy. Gil Garcia (2003).

- Provide extra support for vocabulary and concepts in grade level material using gestures, illustrations, visuals, realia, graphic organizers, and read alouds and shared reading.
- Use proper response and questioning techniques for each production level.

  Preproduction—during the silent period students can point and use physical responses to demonstrate understanding.

  Early Production—students use one word responses or give them either/or choices to shelter responses.

  Speech Emergence—Begin to expect students to discuss simple open ended questions like tell me about . . . . Or what do you think about . . .

  Intermediate Fluency—Students are still not totally fluent and need extra support. Now they can easily compare/contrast and express evaluations.

continued

Comprehending

Cross-Age Tutors Often called "Buddies" this arrangement calls for two classrooms from different grade levels to partner for reading together. The older and younger child are paired for the school year to form a special bond. The two take turns reading to each other. **Refer to:** *Buddy Reading.* Katherine Samway, Gail Whang, & Mary Pippitt (1995).	• Teach both buddy classes the strategies in their own classrooms first. The buddy session is for reinforcement and practice. • Select a buddy focus strategy of the day, such as inferring, and as the pair works together they work through a lesson (such as "Get the Feeling" p. 89 or "Summary Hand" p. 178). • Have older buddies practice the lesson before meeting with the younger buddy.
Independent Work Students work independently or in centers while the teacher either circulates to work with individuals or meets with small groups. Students engage in meaningful literacy activities they can complete on their own with little teacher support. The teacher has fully modeled and guided students as they use the reproducibles. After filling one out cooperatively, students are ready to fill out forms independently. **Refer to:** *Keep the Rest of the Class Reading and Writing.* Susan Finney (2000).	• Assign lesson reproducibles in this book to students as independent work only after they have worked with the same form in a guided fashion with the teacher! • Allow students to partner read and work together to fill out reproducibles. Students share with the class. • For younger children, set up centers that can be used to reinforce various strategies. (Example—Summary Hand p. 178, Stop and Draw p. 76, Small Summaries p. 174)

Box 1.3 will help you teach the Super Six before, during, and after reading.

Box 1.3. Teaching the Super Six

Using the Super Six Before Reading	Using the Super Six During Reading	Using the Super Six After Reading
Connecting What does this remind me of? What do I know about the topic? Have I read other books like this or by the same author?	**Connecting** What else do I know about the topic? What connections am I making now to self, other texts, and the world?	**Connecting** How did my prior knowledge help me? *What connections did I make?*
Predicting/Inferring Using text and picture clues, what do I think will happen? What is this text about? What do I think I will learn? How can I use my background knowledge to help me predict/infer?	**Predicting/Inferring** What will happen next? What else will I learn? What clues am I using to infer? Do I need to adjust my original predictions? What are my new predictions?	**Predicting/Inferring** How have my predictions changed? What evidence do I have for my predictions/ inferences? How did I use clues and my knowledge to infer?
Questioning What do I want to know about the text? After previewing the text, what questions do I have before reading? What am I wondering?	**Questioning** What would I like to ask the author . . . What questions might a teacher ask on a test? What am I wondering?	**Questioning** I would like to ask the author . . . What questions might a teacher ask on a test? I am still wondering . . .
Monitoring Do I have enough information to make predictions? Is anything confusing to me so far?	**Monitoring** Do I know what's going on? Are there any confusing words or parts? Am I visualizing? How can I solve problems?	**Monitoring** Did I . . . Visualize? Summarize? Clarify ideas? Clarify words? What gave me difficulty? How can I fix my understanding?
Summarizing/Synthesizing How is the text organized?	**Summarizing/Synthesizing** What has happened so far? How is the text organized? What is the theme?	**Summarizing/Synthesizing** Can I summarize? What can I leave out? What are the main ideas? What is the theme? How have my ideas changed?
Evaluating Why did I choose this text? Do I have background on the topic? Might this text be too hard, easy, or boring for me?	**Evaluating** Do I like the text so far? How am I doing as a reader? What important ideas can I agree/disagree with? Do I agree with the characters' actions?	**Evaluating** Did I like the text? Explain. How did I do? What can I agree/disagree with? What might the author want to teach the reader?

Super Six Comprehension Strategies: 35 Lessons and More for Reading Success by Lori Oczkus

Super Six Classroom Vignettes

Intermediate Example/Introducing the Super Six Anchor Lesson

The fifth graders are spread out on the floor, at tables, and in the hall working in groups to create colorful strategy anchor posters for each of the Super Six strategies. Mrs. Ramos's class has just finished reading *Tomas and the Library Lady* (Mora, 1997) while reviewing the strategies the class has studied in-depth over the past few months. Her goal was to review all of the Super Six strategies through the use of think-alouds and guided practice with the reading selection. She worked with the class after each of her demonstrations to define each strategy and to give examples from the reading. As they continue to study each of the strategies during the school year, students add to the anchor posters and use them as classroom reference tools. Mrs. Ramos circulates to offer assistance to the groups.

Brice's group discusses connections they made while reading the book.

"Connections are what the book reminds you of, so let's write that for the definition," says Manuel. "My cousins leave to work in the field in Salinas during the summer."

A lively discussion ensues and the group lists other connections they had to the book about a migrant worker family including visits to the library, escaping in a favorite book, and visiting grandparents.

Michelle's group stalls as they try to remember what monitoring means.

"I forgot what monitor means," admits Cecilly.

Mrs. Ramos reminds the students of the think-aloud she did when she became confused about reasons why Tomas didn't have a library card. She reminds them that monitor means keeping track of your reading and stopping to reread or figure out any words or parts that are confusing. The students revisit the page where Mrs. Ramos demonstrated how to monitor comprehension and heads nod. She reminds them that she also had to reread this page to visualize what Tomas was reading when he was lost in a book.

"I get it now," says Sam. "Monitoring is checking to make sure you understand what you read."

Primary Example: Reinforcing the Super Six with Cross-Age Tutors

"What do good readers do to understand what they are reading?" Mrs. Klein asks her second grade class.

Hands wave with enthusiasm as students eagerly share their recollections of the super six comprehension strategies. Mrs. Klein has taught the super six throughout the year. Most recently she reviewed all of the strategies through a series of mini lessons and think-alouds using a the book, *Ruby the Copy Cat* (Rathmann, 1997). Today the older buddy class, Mr. Cordova's sixth graders will partner read and review the story with their buddies. Then they will decorate Super Six readers to look like the younger buddies. The older buddies guide the younger buddies to write their summaries on the shirt pattern, ideas for monitoring and questions on the arms, thoughts on connections and evaluation of the selection on the legs, and predictions and inferences on the head. Giggles abound as the buddies adapt the pattern to look just like the younger buddy. Once displayed, the paper doll super readers join hands and surround the second graders with good reader strategies.

Here is a poem that you can read with your class as a way of reinforcing the Super Six. As you read each stanza, ask students to stop and give examples from their reading. Refer to the poem often as you review each of the strategies and continue to give more examples from various texts.

❧

Super Six Strategies
A Poem
Lori Oczkus

The Super Six strategies guide me whenever I read

They arm me with tools and give me what I need.

When I predict or infer I'm a detective using
all the clues to get it right

Predicting and inferring keep me interested
and reading all night.

My reading reminds me of lots of things
that I do and see

I make connections to myself, other books,
and the world around me.

Questioning and wondering are loads of fun

I ask who, what, when, where, why,
until the reading is done.

The entire time I'm reading, I monitor away

Problem solving puts me back on track
and keeps the cobwebs at bay.

Summarizing means telling just a little bit

Choosing just the important parts make
a summary a hit.

Authors often have a lesson to share or message
to impart

Synthesis helps me to dig deeper and to feel
really smart.

Every book I read gets a thumbs up or down score

Evaluating helps me judge the author's craft, key ideas, my progress, and more.

The Super Six help me to understand

When I read, they are ready to lend a helping hand.

❧

Introducing . . . The Super Six

Objective: To briefly introduce the students to all six of the strategies with teacher think-alouds using one piece of literature or nonfiction. This lesson may take several days or a week to complete. To provide students with points of reference for the six strategies, on the wall posters and the bookmark.

Materials: Any reading material, bookmark (p. 14), posters (p. 15 or CD-ROM)

Introduce/Model the Strategies

- Ask students what strategies good readers use to understand text. Invite students to discuss at tables or in pairs first, then as a whole class. List their ideas on the board. Accept all responses.

- Tell the students that good readers use lots of strategies but that there are six very important strategies that they use to help them understand the materials they read. These strategies aren't always used in a certain order but they do work as a team to help readers understand what they are reading.

- As you demonstrate and model throughout the lesson, stop and list the six strategies on the board and refer to the bookmark and or the posters on page 2. Post the strategy posters somewhere in the room.

- Pass out the bookmarks so that students can follow along. Select reading material that all students can see and follow along. If modeling in primary grades, you may wish to use a big book. With intermediate grades, a shorter article or chapter that you can put on the overhead projector works well.

Model Connections

After reading, return to the selection to point out any connections you made to your own life, books you have read, or some knowledge you have about the broader world. Ask students to turn to partners then the whole class can share connections.

Model Predicting/Inferring

- Think aloud as you predict using clues from the title, cover, and illustrations. Preview the pictures by describing what you see and what you predict based on clues from the illustrations. Write the word "predict" on the board. Invite the students to work in pairs and briefly try their own predictions by previewing the same text. Write predictions on the board.

- During reading point out places where inferring takes place. Model how to use text clues and one's background knowledge to infer what the author doesn't come out and say directly.

Model Questioning

Think aloud as you ask questions prior to reading. Model what you are wondering about the text. Invite students to work in pairs and question. List questions on the board. Read a small portion of the text aloud. Stop and ask more questions. What are you wondering now? Invite students to do the same. Discuss responses. Model how to create a "teacher quiz question" from the text using who, what, when, where, would, or should. Encourage students to try in pairs and share.

Model Monitoring

Continue reading aloud from the text. Stop reading and think aloud about any difficult or longer words you encountered. How did you figure them out? Model any portion of text that might have been unclear and tell how you reread or read ahead to fix the problem. Talk about the visual images you are building in your head as you read. Invite students to read on and stop to discuss unclear words, ideas, and visualizing with partners first and then the whole class.

Model Summarizing/Synthesizing

After completing the reading, model for students how to summarize by giving a three to five sentence summary. Discuss steps you used. Ask students to repeat the summary to a partner. Talk about any themes or special messages in the text as you model synthesis. Lead students in a discussion.

Model Evaluating

Think aloud after reading the entire or controversial selection. Example (should that character have done that? Why or why not?). Discuss your thinking about any two-sided issues in the text. Tell whether you liked reading or not and why. Did you agree with the way the author wrote the piece or book? Why or why not? How did you do as a reader? Invite students to evaluate the text in pairs.

Guide the Strategy/Cooperative Groups or Pairs

- Refer to the bookmark throughout the modeling portion of the lesson. When you have modeled all six strategies, ask students to turn to a partner and discuss the strategies and tell what they remember about them.

- Divide students into teams. Each team is responsible for one of the six strategies. They reread the material, use the bookmark as a guide, and discuss how they used the strategy. Groups share with the class.

**Box 1.4. Model—Practice—Apply the Strategy
in Different Classroom Structures**

Cross-Age Buddies	Literature Circles
Older buddies choose a strategy to focus on each time they meet with younger buddies. Ahead of time they plan a think-aloud using a target strategy and that goes with the book they'll read to the buddy. They share with the class before trying out their lesson on younger buddies.	The discussion director (Daniels, 1992) in each literature circle passes out the bookmarks and asks the students to discuss briefly how each strategy was used in the reading material.
Guided Reading	**Independent Work Time**
Select one strategy at a time to focus on with guided reading groups. Use the bookmark every time you meet with groups.	Students reflect on each of the strategies as they read using the bookmark. They may illustrate or write about how they used one of the strategies.

Reflect on the Strategy/Assess the Strategy

- Ask students to reflect on and discuss the Super Six strategies. How does each of the strategies help readers understand text?

- Refer to the assessment options in the Appendix on page 224.

- Use the Super Six Strategy Survey on page 230 as a baseline before teaching the strategies to see what students know about each strategy.

- Use the information from the survey to fill in the class checklist for the Super Six. You can select which strategies to focus on based on student needs. Give the survey again after several months to see if students have deepened their understanding of the strategies.

- Use the information to help you decide on the strategies to focus on. Teach and model from lessons in the various chapters in this book.

- If students are having trouble discussing or using certain strategies, pull small groups to reinforce strategy use by providing further modeling.

Refer to the assessment materials in the Appendix pages 223–234 for further assessment information.

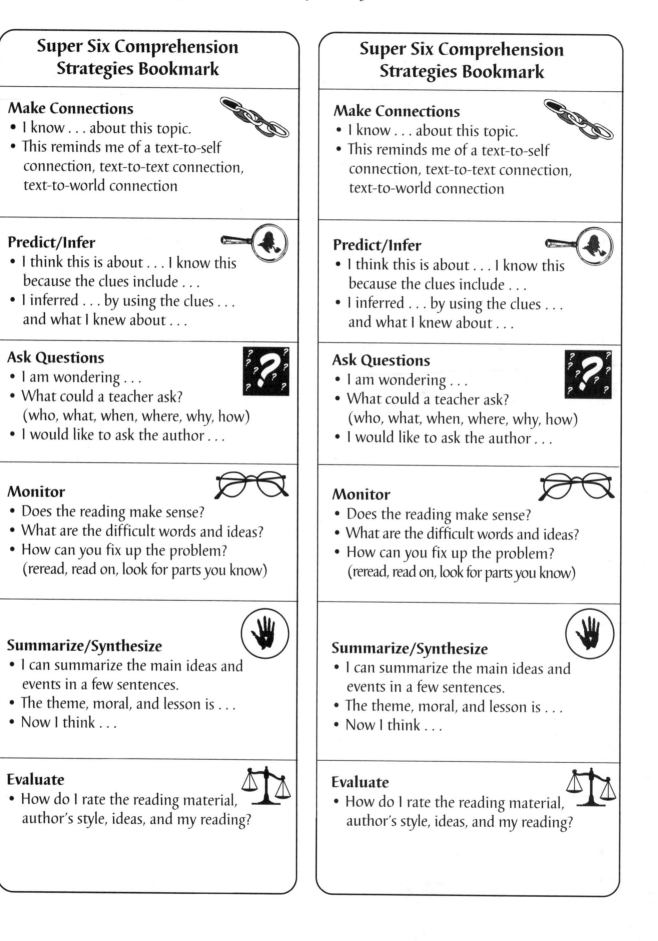

Super Six Comprehension Strategies Bookmark

Make Connections
- I know . . . about this topic.
- This reminds me of a text-to-self connection, text-to-text connection, text-to-world connection

Predict/Infer
- I think this is about . . . I know this because the clues include . . .
- I inferred . . . by using the clues . . . and what I knew about . . .

Ask Questions
- I am wondering . . .
- What could a teacher ask? (who, what, when, where, why, how)
- I would like to ask the author . . .

Monitor
- Does the reading make sense?
- What are the difficult words and ideas?
- How can you fix up the problem? (reread, read on, look for parts you know)

Summarize/Synthesize
- I can summarize the main ideas and events in a few sentences.
- The theme, moral, and lesson is . . .
- Now I think . . .

Evaluate
- How do I rate the reading material, author's style, ideas, and my reading?

Super Six Comprehension Strategies Bookmark

Make Connections
- I know . . . about this topic.
- This reminds me of a text-to-self connection, text-to-text connection, text-to-world connection

Predict/Infer
- I think this is about . . . I know this because the clues include . . .
- I inferred . . . by using the clues . . . and what I knew about . . .

Ask Questions
- I am wondering . . .
- What could a teacher ask? (who, what, when, where, why, how)
- I would like to ask the author . . .

Monitor
- Does the reading make sense?
- What are the difficult words and ideas?
- How can you fix up the problem? (reread, read on, look for parts you know)

Summarize/Synthesize
- I can summarize the main ideas and events in a few sentences.
- The theme, moral, and lesson is . . .
- Now I think . . .

Evaluate
- How do I rate the reading material, author's style, ideas, and my reading?

Student Created Super Six Anchor Posters

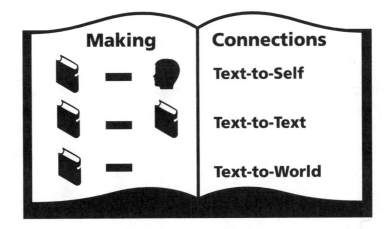

Predict/Infer

 ## Question

 ## Monitor/Clarify

 ## Summarize

 ## Evaluate

Student Created Super Six Anchor Posters

Objective: Students work in teams to synthesize their learning about the Super Six by creating posters to represent each strategy. Students make posters one at a time as each strategy is taught in-depth or all at once as a review after teaching all of the strategies. Posters include examples from reading, diagrams, sketches, and word splashes. Posters remain on the wall throughout the school year as a reference tool for students.

Materials: Large poster or butcher paper for sketching the posters with the class, markers, any reading material, the anchor poster guide form for each group.

Introduce/Model the Strategy

- Invite students to review what they know about the Super Six strategies. They may refer to their bookmarks. (see page 14) and lessons you have taught from chapters in this book.

- Tell students that they will work together to create anchor posters that will help the class remember each of the strategies and what they've learned.

- Choose reading material that you can read together as a class.

- Begin by modeling how to use text clues to predict as you preview the material. Invite students to join in and add predictions. Ask students how prediction helps them read.

- Using a large piece of butcher paper label a poster, Predict/Infer, and think aloud as you follow the anchor poster directions on page 18. Sketch a large image or two, add words that remind you of predicting and give an example from the reading selection the class is reading.

- Before reading the selection, you may wish to let students choose or assign one of the Super Six strategies to focus on. After the reading, teams will create anchor posters of that strategy.

- Continue to read the selection aloud or allow students to read in pairs. Stop periodically to model and think aloud for the students each of the Super Six strategies.

Guide the Strategy/Cooperative Groups or Pairs

- As you stop to model each of the Super Six strategies during reading, pause for students to work in pairs to also try out each strategy. Discuss.

- When the class finishes reading the selection, divide the students into six teams. Each team creates a poster for their assigned or chosen strategy.

- Encourage students to plan their poster on the anchor poster planning sheet (see page 18). Circulate around the room and guide and prompt groups to include important points and steps for each strategy poster.

- Invite groups to present their posters to the class. Post and refer to posters throughout the school year as you teach, model, and guide students to understand and use the strategies.

Box 1.5. Model—Practice—Apply the Strategy in Different Classroom Structures

Guided Reading	**Cross-Age Tutors**
During guided reading, refer to the strategy posters in mini-lessons and with teacher modeling. Select only one or two strategies and focus on those throughout the guided reading session.	All buddies read the same selection together in pairs. Then pairs of big and little buddies join other pairs to form groups of four to six. Each group selects one of the Super Six strategies and works together to create an anchor poster. Groups share with both buddy classes. Display the posters in the classrooms for reference.
Struggling Students	**Independent Work**
Work with struggling students to find more examples from their reading or a group reading to add to existing posters. Review the posters the class created.	Students make their own personal mini posters on a file folder, or using six index cards on aring. Follow the same guidelines as the larger anchor posters. Ask students to share with the class. The posters serve as reference tools that students use in other settings, such as literature circles or guided reading groups.

Reflect on the Strategy/Assess the Strategy

- Ask students to reflect on the anchor poster experience. How did creating the posters help them remember how to use the strategies?

- Continue to use the assessment materials found in the Appendix on page 223–234 to periodically assess each student's strategy use and understanding.

- Discuss with students ways they can use the strategy posters throughout the school year as a point of reference to continue using the strategies as they read.

- If students are experiencing difficulty using the posters for example they give broad statements like "Predicting helps me understand what I read" without specific examples from the text, then work with students in small groups. Read selections together and refer to the posters as you and students share your thoughts on the selection and the strategies.

**Karen Thompson's fourth-grade class made posters
for the Super Six Strategies**

Creating Anchor Posters

Super Six Comprehension Strategies

- Get a large sheet of butcher paper or construction paper and some markers.
- Use this sheet to brainstorm and plan your poster.
- After filling out this sheet, work as a team to complete a colorful and interesting poster.
- Share your poster with the class.

The strategy for our poster is_____.

(predict/infer, connections, question, monitor, summarize/synthesize, evaluate)

Describe what good readers do when they use this strategy.

1. _____

2. _____

3. _____

Here are some images/drawings we could draw to represent how a reader uses the strategy.

_____   _____

_____   _____

_____   _____

_____   _____

These are some words we think are important to remember for using this strategy.

_____ _____ _____

Here is an example of how we used this strategy in our reading.

Book Title _____   Author_____

_____

_____

_____

What's it Like?

Objective: The teacher guides the class in sharing examples of the Super Six strategies from their reading. Then for each strategy the class thinks of what using that strategy is like and sketches the analogy. This lesson works best as a review of the strategies.

Materials: A large poster or butcher paper for sketching together the analogies and writing examples with the class, markers, any reading material, the What's it Like form—teacher has a copy on the overhead.

Introduce/Model the Strategy

- Ask the class to review the Super Six strategies. What do good readers do? Tell students that a helpful way to remember the strategies is to think of an analogy or comparison.

- Start with prediction. Think aloud and predict from a text that all students can see or have copies of. Ask students to predict with partners. Write predictions on the What's it Like form. As a group, review the bookmark or posters and a definition of prediction.

- Tell the students that to remember how to predict and infer, you are going to make a comparison to a detective hunting for logical clues. Using the text, find an example and think aloud as you share the clues that you are using to make either a prediction or inference. Draw a magnifying glass or sketch a detective in the space provided on the "What's it Like" sheet.

Guide the Strategy/Cooperative Groups or Pairs

- Continue modeling by thinking aloud using the text for each of the other five strategies. Invite pairs to try the strategy and as a class discuss examples. Guide students as they define and discuss each strategy.

- Pairs work together to sketch their analogy drawings. Students share.

- Encourage students to give examples of how they used each strategy when they read on their own. Students should give specific examples from the text and give the page number. Students share their findings.

Box 1.7. Model—Practice—Apply the Strategy in Different Classroom Structures

English Language Learners	Literature Circles
Meet with second language students to give extra support and examples of each strategy. Act out the analogies giving examples from the reading (detective hunting for logical clues, a game show talk host, etc.).	The group needs each of the strategies on cards so students can draw one to talk about giving examples from the reading. The discussion director allows members to draw a strategy card and then give examples from the reading. Each student contributes to a group poster incorporating the "What's it Like" sketches and their examples.
Cross-Age Tutors	**Independent Work**
Buddy classes create quick dramas or plays about each of the Super Six analogies (game show host, news reporter, etc.) and perform them for each other.	Students give examples in their reading for each strategy from the Super Six or assign focus strategies. Students give page numbers and examples. Students sketch analogies.

Reflect on the Strategy/Assess the Strategy

- Ask students to reflect on how the analogies help them remember to use the Super Six to understand what they read. (see Super Six Strategy Survey on page 230)

- Save in portfolios and assign again periodically. Compare saved samples. Are students growing in their use of strategies and the ability to reflect on those strategies? (see Assessment Rubric for the Super Six on page 225)

- Save student samples from the various forms in this book and use observations of students in guided reading groups and literature circles to measure growth. (see student check list on page 228)

- Are students able to give examples from the reading that explain how they used the strategy to help them comprehend? If not, model examples from books the class is reading.

Comprehending

- If they are having difficulty, group students who are having trouble with the same strategy together and work with a small group to model and guide them in the use of that strategy (Keene & Zimmerman, 1997) by selecting lessons from the chapter on that strategy.

- Refer to the assessment materials in the Appendix (page 223–234) for further assessment information and tips.

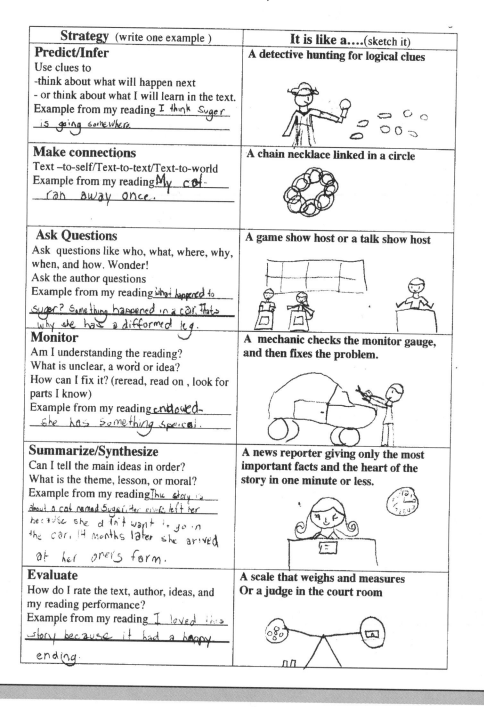

Strategy (write one example)	It is like a....(sketch it)
Predict/Infer Use clues to -think about what will happen next - or think about what I will learn in the text. Example from my reading I think Suger is going somewhere	**A detective hunting for logical clues**
Make connections Text –to-self/Text-to-text/Text-to-world Example from my reading My cat ran away once.	**A chain necklace linked in a circle**
Ask Questions Ask questions like who, what, where, why, when, and how. Wonder! Ask the author questions Example from my reading What happened to Suger? Something happened in a car. Thats why she has a difformed leg.	**A game show host or a talk show host**
Monitor Am I understanding the reading? What is unclear, a word or idea? How can I fix it? (reread, read on, look for parts I know) Example from my reading endowed- She has something speical.	**A mechanic checks the monitor gauge, and then fixes the problem.**
Summarize/Synthesize Can I tell the main ideas in order? What is the theme, lesson, or moral? Example from my reading This story is about a cat named Suger. Her owners left her because she didn't want to go in the car. 14 months later she arived at her oner's farm.	**A news reporter giving only the most important facts and the heart of the story in one minute or less.**
Evaluate How do I rate the text, author, ideas, and my reading performance? Example from my reading I loved this story because it had a happy ending.	**A scale that weighs and measures Or a judge in the court room**

What's It Like

Strategy (write one example) **Predict/Infer** Use clues to - think about what will happen next - or think about what I will learn in the text. Example from my reading_____ _____	**It is like . . .** (sketch it) **A detective hunting for logical clues**
Make connections Text–to-self/Text-to-text/Text-to-world Example from my reading_____ _____	**A chain necklace linked in a circle**
Ask Questions Ask questions like who, what, where, why, when, and how. Wonder! Ask the author questions Example from my reading_____ _____	**A game show or a talk show host**
Monitor Am I understanding the reading? What is unclear, a word or idea? How can I fix it? (reread, read on, look for parts I know) Example from my reading_____ _____	**A mechanic checks the monitor gauge, and then fixes the problem.**
Summarize/Synthesize Can I tell the main ideas in order? What is the theme, lesson, or moral? Example from my reading_____ _____	**A news reporter giving only the most important facts and the heart of the story in one minute or less.**
Evaluate How do I rate the text, author, ideas, and my reading performance? Example from my reading_____ _____	**A scale that weighs and measures Or a judge in the court room**

Super Six Artful Expressions

adapted from Mario Penman

Objective: Students work with cross-age buddies, in teams, or alone to create art forms to use to display their use of the Super Six. In doing this, students make the strategies their own and strengthen the likelihood they will remember and use the strategies

Materials: Any art materials you desire to make the forms, construction paper, markers, crayons, yarn, Glue, the artful planner form (page 27).

Introduce/Model the Strategy

- Tell students that when they will create an art project related to their reading, as a way of displaying examples of the Super Six in their reading.

- Model how to create an artful expression to display your thinking using the Super Six. Select a piece of literature or nonfiction that the class has already read to model from.

- Inform the class of the shape you will use for your Super Six display. Explain why you have selected that particular shape. (Examples: For any selection, the Super Six reader (see pages), a frog for *Frog and Toad* (Lobel, 1970) a dog sled for *Stone Fox* (Gardner, 1980), or a candy bar for *Charlie and the Chocolate Factory* (Dahl, 1964), Spider after reading a nonfiction title on spiders.

- Elicit responses from the class. Ask students to review the Super Six strategies briefly.

- Think aloud as you write your responses for each of the Super Six strategies and fill out the planning sheet on page 27. Then rewrite your responses and post on your Artful Expression form. Explain how you will complete and decorate the shape later. (To save time, you could fill in the planning sheet in front of students and make the art form later to show to students.)

Guide the Strategy/Cooperative Groups or Pairs

- Guide the entire class in creating a planning sheet and Artful Expression form together. Make one giant form that the class will share.

- After reading another selection, divide students into teams and have them complete one of the strategies to put on the Artful Expression form.

- Students work in teams to create forms for all six strategies and then share with the class. Students can use the same Artful Expression form to incorporate all the strategies. They may want to select an art form from the reading selection, such as a character to sketch or a setting and write their predictions, questions, inferences, summaries, monitoring ideas, evaluations, and connections on the form.

Artful expressions provide students with the opportunity to think creatively while writing about their strategy use and reflecting on the reading. I like to brainstorm the possibilities with the class and have the students create their own drawings or cut out their own forms.

Examples of Artful Expressions:

Primary students

Miss Nelson is Missing by Harry Allard (Houghton Mifflin, 1977).
Students create and cut out large drawing of Miss Viola Swamp and on her dress and shoes they write their predictions, questions, inferences, summaries, points to monitor/clarify, connections, and evaluations.

Intermediate

After reading *Because of Winn Dixie* by Kate DiCamillo (Scholastic, 2000) students create a large model of the main character in the book and on her arms, legs, trunk, and head they write their responses for predictions, questions, inferences, summaries, points to monitor/clarify, connections, and evaluations.

Comprehending

After reading *Harry Potter and the Prisoner of Azkaban* by J. K. Rowling (Scholastic, 1999) students create a large paper model of Harry's glasses, or any other prop of interest from the story, and write about their strategy use and responses in and around their drawings.

Box 1.9. Model—Practice—Apply the Strategy in Different Classroom Structures

Struggling Students	Cross-Age Tutors
After reading a selection with students in small groups, work together to complete an artful expression shape. Guide students in filling in the shape with their responses to the reading and the strategies.	This is an idea activity for cross-age tutors to create together! Try the Super Six Reader and encourage the buddies to make the reader look like the younger buddy. The older buddies should practice responses for the strategies before meeting with the younger buddy. Post the completed Super Six Readers in the younger buddy room.
English Language Learners Start in a small group using the Super Six Reader for several selections. Then guide students in creating together other shapes for selections they read.	**Independent Work** Students create their own individual artful expression forms incorporating the Super Six. They can do this for anthology selections, nonfiction, textbooks, or their independent reading. Allow students to share.

Reflect on the Strategy/Assess the Strategy

- Ask students to reflect on the activity. How does creating an artful expression help deepen understanding of the reading and strategy use? How do the strategies work together to help students make sense out of the text and build deeper meanings?

- What problems did students encounter with the activity? Some students may have difficulty coming up with examples from the text for every strategy. You may wish to select one strategy per day and work on a guided Artful Expression form together as a class. Then provide time for students to work on their own Artful Expression forms and fill them in with examples from their own reading. Were their responses thoughtful? If not, try discussing each strategy as a class before writing.

- If students have difficulty, meet with them in small groups or build an artful expression as a class. Which strategies are giving students the most trouble? Use assessment materials in the Appendix on page 223–234 to assist you in monitoring student progress in strategy use and in organizing flexible groups around the strategies that students need to work on.

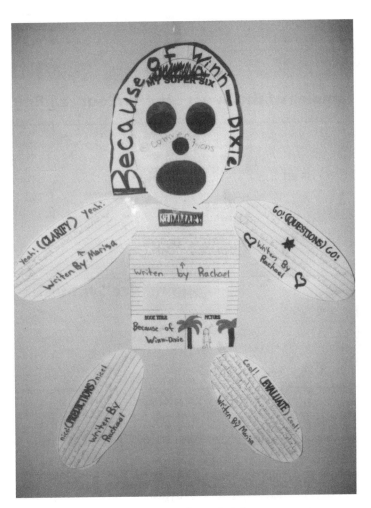

Student created artful forms

Planning Your Super Six Artful Expression

Name of artist or artists _____

My (our) expression will be in the shape of _____

I (we) choose this shape because_____

Here is how I (we) plan to include each of the strategies as part of the artful expression.

Predict /Infer _____   Summarize/Synthesize_____

Question_____   Evaluate_____

Monitor_____

Here is a draft of examples of the Super Six from our reading.

Connections	Monitor
(the reading reminded us of . . .) Example:	Example:
Predictions Example:	**Summarize/Synthesize** Example:
Questions Example:	**Evaluate** Example:

Show this draft to the teacher to check over and approve.
Now you are ready to create an artful expression of the Super Six!

Teachers As Readers

Reflecting on Our Experiences as Adult Readers

Now that I teach the Super Six I am very aware of my own use of strategies as I read. I look for ways the Super Six helps me in my own reading and then try to share examples from my reading with students during my think-alouds in class. Students enjoy hearing about our lives at home and usually perk up when we share what we do in our free time, including reading.

My Reflections on the Super Six

There is something inviting about discovering a stash of novels in a vacation rental. On one of our family getaways to Lake Tahoe, the condo we rented was loaded with just the kind of award-winning books I love to devour. At least seven of the titles on the shelf, were ones my book club buddies had raved about. I couldn't wait to get started!

The first one that caught my eye was Girl in Hyacinth Blue *(Vreeland, 1999) a well-crafted story about a fictitious Vermeer painting and the history of it's owners.*

The novel begins with the current owner of the cherished work, a university professor, and unravels backward in reverse chronology. Each chapter tells how the previous owner obtained the masterpiece until the final chapter describes the girl Vermeer painted. While reading this award-winning little gem, I was aware of how my use of the Super Six comprehension strategies enhanced my understanding and kept me engaged!

***Predicting/Inferring**—From the moment I studied the front cover, reviews, and back cover I anticipated that I might learn something about Vermeer's craft and the fate of the girl on the cover. Throughout the book I guessed based on clues who the next chapter would chronicle and I constantly worked at inferring whether the painting was a real Vermeer.*

***Questioning**—I brimmed with questions about the characters, their lives, and their experience with the painting. I often wondered the worth of the painting, then and now.*

***Making Connections**—The connections I made while reading forced me to reminisce about my own visits to art museums and feelings of awe when viewing famous masterpieces. Since I had just finished another book about a real Vermeer painting,* Girl With the Pearl Earring *(Chevalier, 1999) I made natural connections between the two books and their characters.*

***Monitoring**—Although the story is captivating, the organizational structure causes the reader to really concentrate as the puzzle pieces unveil. I found myself rereading entire chapters to keep the characters straight. I enjoyed visualizing each owner's unique interpretation of the painting.*

***Summarizing/Synthesizing**—Summarizing was an important strategy to call upon while putting together the puzzle pieces of this little novel. The theme, or synthesis developed as I read the effect the painting had on each character's lives. The author conveyed strong messages about the purpose of artful expression in our lives.*

***Evaluating**—I couldn't help but evaluate Vermeer's life calling as an artist and what he says was the "cost" to his family. This driven genius missed important moments with his eleven children. He died in debt. Was it worth it? Should the final owner of the painting relinquish it to a museum? Was the unique organization of the book, working backward in time effective? My conclusion, I loved it! How did I do as a reader? I had to work at it, but that was the cost of reading such a different and thought-provoking novel!*

Your Reflections on the Super Six

As you read, keep journal entries, or sticky notes on the ways you use the Super Six when you read. Share appropriate examples with your students. Let them know you use these important strategies when you read too! How do you use the Super Six to enhance your understanding and enjoyment of various kinds of text? Now that you know about the strategies are you more aware of them when you read? Do certain strategies move to the forefront when you read various kinds of texts? Give examples. Discuss your strategy use with another teacher.

Examples of using the super six in your reading that you can share with students.

- *Making Connections*—What connections are you making to your self, other books, and the world?

- *Predicting/Inferring*—What predictions are you making as you read? Are you changing or confirming them? How do you use your own knowledge plus the text clues to infer or read between the lines? Give an example.

- **Questioning**—What kinds of questions are you wondering about before, during, and after reading? If you could ask the author questions, what would you ask?

- *Monitoring*—Do you notice when you don't understand a word or idea? Give examples. What do you do to fix the problem?

- **Summarizing/Synthesis**—How did summarizing help you as you read? When did you begin forming a synthesis? Did it change as you read? How? Give examples. What will stick with you after you read.

- **Evaluating**—Did you like the text? How did you do as a reader? What would you have done differently?

References

Block, C. & Pressley, M. (2000). *Comprehension instruction: Research-based best practices.* New York: Guilford.

Dole, J.A., Duffy, G. G., Roehler, L.R., & Pearson, P.D. (1991). Moving from the old to the new: Research on reading comprehension instruction. *Review of Educational Research, 61* (2), 239–264.

Duffy, G.G., Roehler, L.R., Sivan, E., Rackliffe, G., Book, C., & Meloth, M. (1987). Effects of explaining the reasoning associated with using reading strategies. *Reading Research Quarterly, 22,* 347–348.

Pearson, P., & Fielding, L. (1991). Comprehension instruction. In R.Barr, M.Kamil, P. Mosenthal, and P.D. Pearson. (Eds.), *Handbook of Reading Research* (Vol. 2, pp. 815–860). New York: Longman.

Polselli-Sweet, A., & Snow, C. (2003). *Rethinking reading comprehension.* New York: Guilford.

Pressley, M., Block, C., & Gambrell, L. (2003) *Improving comprehension instruction: Rethinking research, theory, and classroom practice.* Newark, DE: International Reading Association.

Building Background and Making Connections

> "As we focus on the strategy of making connections, we can't forget that increasing understanding, not a plethora of tangential or inconsequential connections, is the goal of activating background knowledge and prior experience to make connections." **Stephanie Harvey and Ann Goudvis,** *in* Strategies that Work, *p. 80.*

Thoughts on Building Background/Making Connections

Tis the reader that makes the book good.

—Ralph Waldo Emerson

Emerson's famous quote illustrates of the role of background knowledge and the reading process. A good reader isn't passive, but rather the reader who comprehends well is interacting and bringing his or her experiences to the text.

Try asking yourself two important questions before reading a book with students: What background and experiences, or connections do my students bring to the text? What background and experiences do I need to discuss or provide before reading so students can comprehend the content of the selection?

Sometimes a simple discussion is enough to activate our students' experiences and knowledge. Other times we may need to build background in the form of a read-aloud from other texts, a hands-on experience, a video, or internet research. For example, when

reading about a talent show in Gary Soto's *La Bamba* (1990) with fifth graders I activate their prior experiences by encouraging students to discuss times when they have felt embarrassed or nervous about a performance. Before reading *From the Mixed Up Files Of Mrs. Basil E. Frankweiler* (Konigsburg, 1967), a mystery that takes place in the Metropolitan Art Museum, we build background for the paintings and work of Michelangelo. In addition to looking at art prints, we also try painting Sistine Chapel style. The students lie flat on their backs on the floor under their desks as they paint onto butcher paper taped underneath their desks or classroom tables. What a messy, but memorable, way to build background for the novel and learn about a famous artist!

Building Prior Knowledge and Valuing Students' Backgrounds

Often teachers express concern that their students do not have the experiences or vocabulary to match the selections found in publisher anthologies or other core texts. One urban fifth grade teacher informed me that, although her struggling readers didn't know what echolocation was before reading about bats, her students do know how to get around the city on four different bus lines. Since the students need background about bats, she skillfully uses discussion, picture books, read-alouds, and a model of a bat to build some necessary background for the reading.

This same urban teacher constantly takes into consideration the background students bring to texts. One afternoon while reading, *Owlbert* by Nicholas Harris (1999), a sweet story about an abandoned owl and the boy who adopts him, the students were especially concerned about the orphaned owl. Later she explained to me that two of the students in the class had parents in jail and were living with friends and extended family.

By acknowledging their backgrounds and allowing the students to talk about what the story reminds them of, she is helping her students to connect in a very deep way to the reading. It is the reader who makes the book good and it is the skillful teacher who can make it happen!

How Do Prior Knowledge and Connections Help Students Comprehend?

Readers construct meaning by using their background knowledge and experiences to integrate with the new information they read and gain from the text. Schema, background knowledge, and prior knowledge are all terms that are used interchangeably (Cooper, 1997) to describe the information and experiences students bring to reading.

For over thirty years, researchers have consistently found that prior knowledge and experiences have an enormous impact on comprehension. (Lipson, 1982) When readers know something about a topic or are able to relate their experiences to the reading, they can better understand the reading material. I tell students to visualize inside their heads either colorful file folders and a cabinet where their prior knowledge is stored or computer files for each subject. They are constantly adding and deleting information from their files and then using that information when they read to aid in comprehension.

Researchers have also found that there is a strong connection between prior knowledge and vocabulary development (Snow, Burns, & Griffin, 1998). Many of the activities I use to develop background before read-

ing also allow me to introduce vocabulary necessary for understanding the text. It is simply impossible to introduce all of the vocabulary students need to understand a text. But by familiarizing them with the larger concepts from the reading, students will have anchors for figuring out unknown words. Researchers agree that the most effective way for students to acquire massive amounts of vocabulary is incidentally through independent reading in a wide variety of materials.

Activating and Building Background Knowledge: Spicing Up a KWL Chart

One of the most effective and popular ways to activate and build background knowledge and vocabulary is with the technique known as KWL (Ogle, 1986). What I **Know**, What I **Want to Know**, and What I **Learned** is a three-column chart, used in discussing student background knowledge. This effective graphic organizer technique is "an oldie but a goodie." I can't think of a more effective way to chart student experiences when reading.

I have discovered several ways to enhance the KWL experience as I activate students' prior knowledge. Sometimes when asking, "What do you know about...?" I get either very little information from students, misinformation, or the same students raise their hands to offer ideas. The "One Minute Book Look" (p.42) has strengthened my KWL lessons by helping students remember what they know. After the initial charting in the K (What I Know) column, students flip through the book for one minute to preview illustrations and headings that remind them of prior knowledge to add to the KWL chart. This time more hands go up as students recall additional information about a topic. Then I guide students as we slowly preview the illustrations, headings, and concepts for a second time to consider what they want to know about the topic. When I ask for ideas for the W (What We Want To Know) column, students are ready to respond. I enjoy enhancing and strengthening the KWL experience with these interactive ideas that help students activate their background knowledge and build support for unfamiliar concepts and vocabulary.

Making Connections Text-to-Self, Text-to-Text, and Text-to-World

Ellin Keene and Susan Zimmerman have revolutionized the way thousands of teachers and students discuss background knowledge. The terms they introduce in their landmark book on comprehension, *Mosaic of Thought* (1997) text-to-self, text-to-text, and text-to-world are being used in classrooms everywhere. I too have adopted these terms and have used them in a variety of ways to enhance discussions throughout the reading process. We make class charts with three columns and stop periodically to discuss and record our connections. We carefully mark our connections with the abbreviations TS, TT, or TW. Some students even come up with their own clever connection abbreviations. William, a third grader, invented a new abbreviation, a TFP, text to famous person connection!

A Few Warnings and Suggestions About the Connection Craze

Some of the teachers I know have encountered a few problems with all of this connecting. Ms. Keel posted a connections chart and her fourth graders were connecting like crazy. Unfortunately, many of her students were making tangential connections (Harvey & Goudvis, 2000) or connections that only related to some detail in the text. I suggested that she continue modeling her connections so students would see the type of connections that are most effective in comprehending the text. Primary teacher, Debbie Miller in her book *Reading With Meaning* (2002) models for students how to go back to connections after reading to identify the ones that helped the students the most in making sense of the text. Regie Routman (2003) acknowledges that many teachers love teaching students to make connections. She cautions us, however, to make students aware that they are also participating simultaneously in a variety of strategies while making connections. When we focus on connections as they come up naturally during reading and discuss how they help us comprehend, connections become tools to strengthen our students' comprehension.

Connections Class Chart from Krista Koch's Fourth-Grade Classroom

Box 2.1. Using Prior Knowledge

Using Prior Knowledge Before Reading	Using Prior Knowledge After Reading	Using Prior Knowledge After Reading

For nonfiction
 	
• What do I know about the topic?
  - Look at the cover
 	
• What do I remember about the topic now?
  - Look at illustrations, headings, and captions.
 	
For fiction
 	
• Have I ever . . . ?
  - Look at the title, cover, and back of the book.
 	
• What connections am I making?
  - Preview text, chapter titles, illustrations, and captions.
 	
• I think I know . . .
 	
• My connections are . . .
	For nonfiction
	
	• What else do I know about the topic?
	
	• How did my prior knowledge help me understand the part about . . . ?
	
	• This is just like . . .
	
	For fiction
	
	• What connections am I making now?
	  - Text to self, other texts, and world.
	
	• This is just like . . .
	
	• I already knew . . . because
		For nonfiction
		
		• How did my prior knowledge help me learn about . . . ?
		
		• What prior knowledge was most helpful?
		
		I used what I knew about . . . to help me understand . . .
		
		For fiction
		
		• What connections am I making now?
		  - Text to self, text to text, and text to world
		
		• Which connections helped me understand the text the most?

Connections

Super Six Comprehension Strategies: 35 Lessons and More for Reading Success by Lori Oczkus

Building Background and Making Connections Classroom Vignettes

Intermediate Vignette/ A Whole Class Connection Chart

Fourth grade teacher, Krista Yeh is modeling how to make a connection when reading *The Mixed-Up Files of Mrs. Basil E. Frankweiler* (1968) using a class connection chart. She has hung a large butcher paper sheet with three categories neatly drawn in marker and labeled, Text to Self, Text to Text, and Text to World at the front of the room.

"This book reminds me of how I used to contemplate running away as a child, only I never actually did it. I did daydream about walking several miles to my grandmother's house to stay with her. I imagined spending my allowance on food at fast-food restaurants. It helps me connect with the characters in this book when I remember my own desire to run away as a child," says Ms. Yeh. "Also," adds Ms. Yeh, "I am reminded of my own visit to the Metropolitan Art Museum in New York. The main characters in this book hide there."

Students share connections with those at their tables and then with the class.

"My brother can act just like Jaime sometimes. He can be such a pain!"

"My teacher last year taught us about Michelangelo and I made a connection to what I knew about that since this takes place in a museum."

As they add connections to the chart for each novel or district adopted selection, Ms. Yeh directs their thinking by asking them to explain how each connection helped them to understand what they read. Over the next few weeks as she continues modeling and guiding the class in their connecting, she notices that the quality and importance of the connections improves. Students don't just give loosely related connections, but they move into sharing connections that relate to the big ideas and themes in the literature. The students are colossal connectors and that means that their comprehension will reflect deeper levels of thinking, and recall will be enhanced as a result of their connections.

Primary Vignette: Using a KWL Chart in Guided Reading

Mr. Fergus opens a small bottle and lets about ten ants loose on the overhead projector. They scurry everywhere and look like black giants on the screen as they race to escape the bright white light. The second graders squeal with delight!

Once the ants have made a run for it, Mr. Fergus asks the class, "What do you know about ants?" Hands wave wildly to be called on.

"Ants are insects."

"They live in anthills."

"Ants walk around all the time."

The ant experts abound in this room. Students eagerly get busy at their desks with their independent work that is to read alone, read with a partner, and to read and illustrate a poem the class has read.

Mr. Fergus calls up the first guided reading group to read *Ant* by Rebecca Stefoff (1998). The six students quickly gather around the table as Mr. Fergus passes out self-stick notes. "Please write one thing you know about ants on this note," he directs.

When the students are done, he places the notes on a KWL chart (Ogle, 1986) in the column labeled *What We Know*. Then he asks the students to help him categorize their notes. The information the children have offered seems to fit into several categories. So, Mr. Fergus labels the categories *What Ants Do, Where Ants Live,* and *What Ants Look Like.*

Mr. Fergus continues the lesson by asking students to preview illustrations and to help him fill in the *What We Want To Know* column of the chart with their questions about ants. After reading they will complete the *What I Learned* column as the students reflect on new understandings.

Mr. Fergus prefers using the KWL chart in a small group setting where all students can interact with it using self-stick notes for their responses. And the kids? They end up feeling like super ant experts! Plus their comprehension is strengthened because they spent time thinking about their prior knowledge and used that knowledge to help them understand the new content.

Connections

Find Someone Who...

A people search adapted from Whisler and Williams

Objective: Students will relate their background knowledge and experiences to a people search activity. The activity can be used to activate or build background knowledge necessary to understand the reading mateerial.

Materials : Any reading material, Find Someone Who... form for students to interview each other.

Introduce/Model the Strategy

- Choose a text that the class will read. Prior to the lesson, create "Find Someone Who" statements that relate to the content of the reading and the experiences of your students.

- Tell students that it is helpful to think about their experiences or knowledge about a topic before they read. The Find Someone Who people search activity will assist students in connecting their personal experiences and prior knowledge with their reading.

- Interview several students in front of the class. Get their signatures and model how to ask questions and write details for future reference.

- Students should try to interview different classmates for each Find Someone Who statement.

- Read aloud a portion of the text and tell how the Find Someone Who activity helped you understand what you read.

Guide the Strategy/Cooperative Groups or Pairs

- Pass out the Find Someone Who... sheets. Students circulate around the room asking for signatures and then interviewing each other briefly.

- As you observe pairs doing a nice job, stop the class to observe and comment.

Connections

- When finished, lead a class discussion about each Find Someone Who statement. Students share and explain the responses to help build background for the text.

- Or instead of a whole class discussion, students may share their findings in small groups.

- As students read, have them look for connections between the Find Someone Who responses and the text.

- What kinds of text-to-self, text-to-text, and text-to-world connections are they making?

Box 2.2. Model—Practice—Apply the Strategy in Different Classroom Structures

Cross-Age Buddies	**Literature Circles**
Older buddies travel around the room with younger buddies to fill out a Find Someone Who sheet together prior to reading a selection.	Literature circles can make up a Find Someone Who sheet for a title they have just finished. Then, the next group to read the selection can use the Find Someone Who as one of their prereading activities.
Special Needs	**Independent Work**
You may wish to work with English Language Learners or other special needs students using this technique in a small teacher-led group format first, then they are better prepared to work with peers in pairs or cooperative groups.	Students can illustrate or write about their interviews using their Find Someone Who sheet as a guide. After reading, they can choose the Find Someone Who statement that helped them most with their comprehension. Students create Find Someone Who sheets for books they have read as a book report project.

Connections

Reflect on the Strategy/Assess the Strategy

- Students shouldn't just race to obtain signatures, but check to see if they are indeed interviewing each other and recording their thoughts.

- Ask students to choose one Find Someone Who statement that helped them better understand the selection and explain.

- If students can't explain how the statements relate to the text, model further. Example: Before reading, I asked you to tell if you recycled newspapers at your house, and when you read you found out that the main character recycled newspapers too. Recycling was an important part of understanding the story and your experience with recycling can help you understand the reading.

- After reading, have students create Find Someone Who sheets for other classes or groups to fill out. How well do students draw on their backgrounds and the text to create statements? Do they only create Find Someone Who statements for trivial points or details in the reading, or do they make an effort to build background connections to deeper meanings, main ideas, character feelings, and themes in the reading?

- Refer to the assessment materials in the Appendix page 246 for further assessment information and tips.

Interviewer's Name _____

Find Someone Who . . .

Adapted from Whisler and Williams

- Use this sheet to circulate around the room while you collect signatures and interview classmates. Try to get a different signature for each box. Be sure to get details from each person.
- After sharing with the class, read the selection. Tell how these ideas help you make better connections to the reading.

1. Find someone who _____ _____ _____ _____ Details/ My Questions _____ _____ _____ _____ _____	2. Find someone who _____ _____ _____ _____ Details/ My Questions _____ _____ _____ _____ _____
3. Find someone who _____ _____ _____ _____ Details/ My Questions _____ _____ _____ _____ _____	4. Find someone who _____ _____ _____ _____ Details/ My Questions _____ _____ _____ _____ _____

Super Six Comprehension Strategies: 35 Lessons and More for Reading Success by Lori Oczkus

Examples for Find Someone Who Form
Grade 3

Book: The Big Nap by Bruce Hale (Harcourt, 2001)

This humorously written mystery is about a detective who happens to be a gecko named Chet. He wants to find out why all of the other creatures at school are turning into zombies. Before reading I had students interview each other using the following statements.

1. Find someone who has read a mystery.

2. Find someone who can tell what geckos eat.

3. Find someone who can give a comparison of two things such as, she was as lovely as a rose.

4. Find someone who can tell three things a "goodie goodie" does at school.

5. Find someone who can tell what skills make a good detective.

6. Find someone who can define the word "zombie." How does a zombie act?

Grades 5 and 6

Book: A Long Way From Chicago by Richard Peck (Puffin, 1998)

The book is about big city kids, Joey and his sister Mary Alice and the adventurous summer vacations they spend with Grandma in her little town. As it turns out, the town is anything but boring and Grandma is quite a kick! Before reading we interviewed each other using the following points.

1. Find someone who has visited a grandparent in the summer or over a vacation.

2. Find someone who can tell something about the Great Depression.

3. Find someone who likes to go fishing and knows how to clean a fish.

4. Find someone who has been to a county fair. Ask for three details.

5. Find someone who has traveled by train.

6. Find someone who has a relative who is considered a "character." Describe him or her and what this person does.

Connections

One-Minute Book Look
Classroom Vignettes

Intermediate Example/Whole Class

Before passing out copies of Gail Gibbons book, *Sunken Treasure* (Gibbons, 1998), to the fifth graders in Miss Chang's class, I ask the students to discuss with partners what they know about ship wrecks. As I circulate and eavesdrop, I hear most pairs commenting on the Titanic. I tell them that I'll bet they know a lot more about ship wrecks besides just some facts about the Titanic. After passing out a book and One-Minute Book Look sheet per pair, I ask the students to study the cover and write two additional things they think they know about shipwrecks.

More information is starting to surface as students offer comments that include, "Scientists and divers use maps, and other clues to find sunken ships." "They examine the artifacts and can tell how old the ships are."

I tell them that they will have one minute to quickly page through the book, looking for clues that will jog their memories and prior knowledge. I model using only the first four pages. "Oh, now I remember that strong waves and reefs can cause a ship to sink. I also know that searches for sunken boats often come up empty."

Then I signal partners to begin as I time one minute on the clock. When it is time to stop, pairs begin discussing what else they know about shipwrecks that they were reminded of in the book look. We discuss as a whole class their prior knowledge and they add to their One-Minute Book Look sheets. The book look has helped the students to be more aware of the role their background knowledge plays in helping them to comprehend.

Primary Example/Guided Reading

"I know that Octopus have 8 legs," offers Jasmine very proudly.

"And I know that they live in the ocean," adds Rebecca.

I ask the second grade students to first discuss and then write one thing they know about octopus before we read *Meet the Octopus* (James, 1996) in our guided reading group. I pass out self-stick notes and most of the students write that the octopus has eight legs. Each student places his/her note on the *What I Know About the Octopus* column of the KWL (Ogle, 1986) chart we have started.

To further jog their memories and prior knowledge bank, I invite them to participate in a One-Minute Book Look. Since I have already modeled the technique, the students eagerly jump to page through their books when I start the timer and signal, READ! By the time I say, stop reading, hands are already up and waving.

Bryan offers first "I knew already that the octopus has ink to shoot and protect himself from predators." Each student adds his or her newly remembered fact on a self-stick note and places it on the chart in the What We Know Column. I invite the students to assist me in categorizing the words we have so far. We come up with where the octopus lives, what he eats, and how he protects himself. The book look has encouraged the students to dig deeper into what they know about the octopus. They feel smart!

One-Minute Book Look

Objective: Students quickly page through reading material for one minute to jog their memories about what they already know about a topic so they can discuss prior knowledge before reading. Students use their book look information to make predictions.

Materials: Any nonfiction reading material, a timer or clock, and One-Minute Book Look form

Introduce/Model the Strategy

- Explain to students that the One-Minute Book Look is a quick way they can use text clues to activate prior knowledge before reading a nonfiction book.

- Tell students that sometimes when they are thinking about what they know about a topic before reading, they may need a few reminders to help them remember what they already know.

- Choose a nonfiction book or article to use in modeling. Look at the clock or use an egg timer and tell the students that for one minute you are going to think about what you know as you preview the headings, illustrations, diagrams, and maps in the book.

- Talk and think aloud as you demonstrate how to quickly page through the book. Make comments such as "Oh, yeah . . . I remember . . .", "I know that . . .", or "Some examples of . . . are . . ."

- After one minute, stop and write down three things you already knew but needed the text to spark your memory to remember.

- Next, make an initial prediction based on the One-Minute Book Look. "I think this book is about . . ." or "I think I will learn"

Guide the Strategy/Cooperative Groups or Pairs

- Students work in pairs to practice One-Minute Book Looks.

- Circulate to see if students are discussing prior knowledge.

Connections

- Encourage students to cover the entire book or article very briefly and to list what they already knew. Then ask them to take a slower preview of the text as they begin predicting what they will learn.

- Encourage students to use the One-Minute Book Look strategy before reading the next portion of content area reading in class.

Box 2.3. Model—Practice—Apply the Strategy in Different Classroom Structures

Guided Reading	Literature Circles
Model a One-Minute Book Look in a guided reading setting using appropriate nonfiction reading material. Use either white boards or self stick notes to record the students' What I Know statements and add to a KWL chart (Ogle, 1986).	Nonfiction literature circles can incorporate a One-Minute Book Look as part of their prereading routine. Each member can contribute their prior knowledge to a KWL chart (Ogle, 1986).
Cross Age Buddies	**Independent Work**
Older buddies can lead younger buddies in One-Minute Book Looks using non-fiction picture books. The buddies can work together to draw pictures of what they know about a topic before reading.	Students can work independently or with partners. Before reading, students can list what they know about a topic. Then after the One-Minute Book Look, they list more information they know about the topic.

Reflect on the Strategy/Assess the Strategy

- Do students list information they know before the One-Minute Book Look?

- Are students using what they know to link to predictions?

- After reading, do students return to their lists of prior knowledge to confirm ideas and discuss any misconceptions or discovered facts?

- Ask students to reflect on the One-Minute Book Look technique. How does it help them in remembering what they know about a topic and in using prior knowledge to comprehend text?

Connections

Give more examples in a small group setting using One-Minute Book Looks for students who are having difficulty with the strategy. After previewing the text, some students may not be able to discuss prior knowledge connected to the text. Model how to look for what you know by thinking aloud as you preview headings, illustrations, and chapter headings. Guide students to do the same with you. Ask them to think about what the text reminds them of as they quickly preview. Use statements from the One-Minute Book Look form such as "Oh, yeah, I already knew . . ."

Other students may have difficulty making logical predictions using text clues. Model and guide students to do so by thinking aloud with comments like, "I predict . . . because I see in the illustrations, or I see in the headings . . . so I think . . . ."

Refer to the assessment materials in the Appendix page 223–234 for further assessment information and tips.

Partners Names_____   Title/Author of the Book_____

One-Minute Book Look

Look at the title and cover of the book only!
Think about the topic. Write at least two things you already know.

What I Already Know About _____

I know _____

I know _____

Take 1 minute to quickly turn pages (carefully!) and try to remember what else you already know about the topic.

Oh, Yeah! I Also Already Know_____

I also know _____

I also know _____

I also know _____

Now, make a prediction based on what you have seen so far.
What do you think you will learn?

I think I will learn _____

because _____

I think I will learn _____

because _____

After reading, think about how the One-Minute Book Look helped you remember what you knew about the topic? How did your prior knowledge help you better understand the reading?

The One-Minute Book Look helped me because _____

_____

Super Six Comprehension Strategies: 35 Lessons and More for Reading Success by Lori Oczkus

Partners Names
Title/Author of the Book Social STudies/unit 2

One Minute Book Look

Look at the title and cover of the book only!
Think about the topic. Write at least two things you already know.

What I Already Know About First amerians
1. I know Miwok ate acorns.

2. I know the Kwakiutl made big canoes for fishing.

Take 1 minute to quickly turn pages (carefully!) and try to remember what else you already know about the topic.

Oh, Yeah! I Also Already Know
1. I also know. They made boxes for sitting and storing.

2. I also know That They lived with otter families in long houses.

3. I also know

Now, make a prediction based on what you have seen so far. What do you think you will learn?

What do you think you will learn about First american?
1. I think I will learn about the Kwakiutl
Because the pictures show stuff I know.

1. I think I will learn about the art of Totem Poles
~~because~~ and how they ~~to~~ used them.

After reading, think about how the one minute book look helped you remember what you knew about the topic? How did your prior knowledge help you better understand the reading?

The One Minute Book Look helped me because I learned more things about the Kwakiutl tribe.

Connection Workshop

Objective: Students will learn how to make connections as they read in their self-selected materials. The teacher models during read-aloud and students apply during silent sustained reading time. They discuss with peers and the teacher.

Materials: Any reading materials, self-stick notes, and My Connection Collection Chart.

Introduce/Model the Strategy

- Remind students that good readers constantly make connections to their lives, other books, and the world around them. It is helpful to be aware of connections one is making when reading.

- Today you will model for them how to be aware of a connection while reading and to mark it to share after reading. Tell students that making connections can help them understand what they read.

- If you already have a read-aloud time established, the connection workshop works well at that time. Be sure to just read aloud and do not interrupt the flow of the story to make connections.

- After reading aloud for a solid 15 to 20 minutes, select one type of strategy to model for students. Tell them about a connection you made (text to self, text to text, or text to world) while you were reading. Explain your connection.

- Write either TS, TT, or TW, (initials for text-to-self, text-to-text or text-to-world) on a self-stick note and place it on the page where you made your connection.

- Write the connection on your sample "Connection Collection Chart."

Guide the Strategy/Cooperative Groups or Pairs

- Immediately following your connection for the read aloud, invite students to turn to a partner and make one quick connection to the read aloud. Students share TS, TT, or TW.

Connections

- Invite students to begin Sustained Silent Reading (SSR) period. Pass out self-stick notes and invite students to mark one spot where they make a connection during their reading.

- Choose one focus strategy for the day. For example, if you modeled text to self after the read aloud, then ask the students to try to make a text to self in their own reading. Students use the initials only to mark TS, TT, or TW on the notes. Students might want to make more than one connection.

- After SSR, partners or cooperative groups turn to each other and share their one connection.

- Later, students may add to their "Connection Collection" sheet.

Box 2.4. Model—Practice—Apply the Strategy in Different Classroom Structures

Guided Reading	Literature Circles
Students can keep a Connection Collection at the guided reading table. As part of the post-reading discussion, they can each tell, write, or draw one connection.	The connector in the literature circle invites each student to share one connection. Students may use the initials TS, TT, or TW instead of writing out full connections on self-stick notes to mark discussion points in their reading.
Cross Age Buddies	**Independent Work**
Older buddies stop periodically during reading and ask the younger buddies to make connections. The two may draw one of the connections.	When reading the district-adopted anthology, students may fill in their connection collection sheets.

Reflect on the Strategy/Assess the Strategy

- Are students making logical connections that relate to the central theme and character motives or are they connecting to tiny details of the selection only?

- Are students progressing in the sophistication level of their connections?

- Are they making a variety of connections that cover text to self, text to text, and text to world?

- Ask students to reflect on the connections they are making and tell how making connections helps them understand what they read.

- During sustained silent reading, conference with students who are having difficulty coming up with meaningful connections as they read and guide them in making a variety using their self-selected reading material.

- Refer to the assessment materials in the Appendix page 223–234 for further assessment information and tips.

Connections

My Connection Collection Chart

1. As you read, use sticky notes to mark at least two connections you make to your own life, other books, and the world. Mark the connections with the initials TS, TT, or TW.

2. After reading, go back to your sticky notes and reread the part where you made a connection. Write a brief note or two on your connection collection to use in a discussion with a partner or team.

3. Discuss with your partner or group how connections help you understand what you read.

Your Name:

Date: My Connection (TS, TT, TW) title of reading	Date: My Connection (TS, TT, TW) title of reading	Date: My Connection (TS, TT, TW) title of reading	Date: My Connection (TS, TT, TW) title of reading	Date: My Connection (TS, TT, TW) title of reading
Date: My Connection (TS, TT, TW) title of reading	Date: My Connection (TS, TT, TW) title of reading	Date: My Connection (TS, TT, TW) title of reading	Date: My Connection (TS, TT, TW) title of reading	Date: My Connection (TS, TT, TW) title of reading
Date: My Connection (TS, TT, TW) title of reading	Date: My Connection (TS, TT, TW) title of reading	Date: My Connection (TS, TT, TW) title of reading	Date: My Connection (TS, TT, TW) title of reading	Date: My Connection (TS, TT, TW) title of reading

This Text Reminds Me Of...

Journaling Connections (adapted from Jodi Queenan)

Objective: Students learn to make connections in their personal reading. Students read at home in their self-selected books and the next morning in class, write one brief connection they remember from the home reading. The teacher may allow discussion or respond in writing.

Materials: Any reading materials that students are reading on their own, journals, or paper for recording connections, and This Text Reminds Me Of form

Introduce/Model the Strategy

- Remind students that when they read they constantly make connections to their lives, other books, and the world around them. Today they will learn to make connections in their nightly reading and be prepared to share that every morning at school. Tell students that making connections can help them understand what they read.

- Bring in some of your reading material from your home (a novel, non-fiction book, how-to manual, newspaper, news magazine, or other magazine). Tell the students that in your reading the night before you made connections as you read. Give several examples of text-to-self, text-to-text, or text-to-world connections.

- Write on a chart or overhead a quick response that begins with "This (book, article) reminds me of . . ." and elaborate on one of the connections you made. Write a few sentences and sketch a drawing. In the weeks to come, continue modeling your connections and share with students how these connections helped you to comprehend the reading material.

Guide the Strategy/Cooperative Groups or Pairs

- Invite volunteers to verbally share connections they made in their nightly reading. Allow the volunteers to write their responses on the overhead projector or chart. Invite other students to respond.

Connections

- Tell students as you dismiss them from school for the day that they should be aware of the connections they are making in their nightly reading and be prepared to share tomorrow first thing in the morning.

- When you greet students in the morning invite them to immediately pull out their journals and begin writing about the connections they made in their nightly reading. You may wish to begin some sessions by modeling using connections to your reading.

Box 2.4. Model—Practice—Apply the Strategy in Different Classroom Structures

Guided Reading	Literature Circles
Continue modeling how to make connections using guided reading material. Encourage each student to respond on a self-stick note and post on a chart in columns for TS, TT, or TW.	After writing about their connections from nightly reading, ask students to form discussion circles and to briefly take turns sharing. Or form three big groups based on students who made text-to-self, text-to-text, or text-to-world connections.
English Language Learners	Independent Work
Ask students to bring the text they are reading at home to the group and assist students in making connections. Model as necessary.	Students can use independent work times to fill in their connections from nightly reading.

Reflect on the Strategy/Assess the Strategy

- Are students making logical connections that relate to the central theme and character motives or are they connecting to tiny details of the selection only?

- Are students progressing in the sophistication level of their connections?

- Caution! Do *not* assign letter grades or scores to this activity! It will stifle and hinder personal response and reading. However, to improve quality of responses, do model, ask students to share, and list on a class-created rubric what makes a "good" response.

- Are they making a variety of connections that cover text to self, text to text, and text to world?

- Ask students to reflect on the connections they are making. How do connections help them understand what they read?

- Work in a small group with students who are having trouble making connections. Read a text together and model. Work with individual students who are having difficulty making connections. Model using the text the student is reading.

- Some students may have difficulty remembering what they read the night before or may not be reading at night. Praise and encourage all students to partake in nightly reading.

- Refer to the assessment materials in the appendix page 223–234 for further assessment information and tips.

This Text Reminds Me Of...

1. As you read at night at home, watch for connections you make to your own life, other books, or the world around you. Remember one connection so you can write about it in your journal first thing in the morning at school.

2. Write two or three sentences about your reading last night. What did it remind you of? Why? Explain. Draw or sketch something from your reading or from your connection.

Date Book or Magazine Title_____ This text reminds me of...	Date Book or Magazine Title_____ This text reminds me of...
Date Book or Magazine Title_____ This text reminds me of...	Date Book or Magazine Title_____ This text reminds me of...

Thanks to Jodi Queenan.

Teachers As Readers

Reflecting on Our Experiences as Adult Readers

Just as we ask students to make connections between what they're reading and their own lives, making text-to-self connections enriches and enhances our own comprehension as we read and enjoy a variety of texts.

My Reflection on Building Background

I don't think that I would have enjoyed Ann Lamott's book, Operating Instructions, A Journal of My Son's First Year (1993), before I had children. Lamott's brilliantly humorous writing is meant to draw in anyone who has ever survived the odd collection of experiences that constitute that shocking first year of parenting. I found myself laughing as I read her chronicles while remembering pregnancy, crying when the baby went for a round of shots, dealing with projectile vomiting, and pacing all night with a screaming child.

The book is a daily journal that Lamott kept during the first year of her son, Sam's life. The constant text-to-self connections that I made throughout every page of the book kept me both spellbound and laughing at her experiences and the memories of mine. In some ways reading her book was a bit like having two channels running simultaneously with her story on the big screen and mine the little square "picture in picture" in the corner. I found myself shaking my head agreeing with her as she explained, "I just can't get over how much babies cry. I really had no idea what I was getting into. To tell you the truth, I thought it would be more like getting a cat" (p. 66). My ba-bies were powerful criers too and I wasn't prepared for the ride either.

Lamott uses self-deprecating humor as she discovers having a new baby is an all-consuming job that can make even the most competent woman feel insufficient. She admits, "I can't even get my teeth brushed some days." (p. 67). I could picture Lamott in her little apartment and me in my little cozy first house still clad in my robe and slippers at three in the afternoon with a sink full of dirty dishes.

I could relate to the irreverent parts where Lamott sarcastically describes her baby's sort of "old man" phases. For example she refers to the one where the baby looses his hair but in a rung around his head like "Saturn," or a "Buddhist monk." We used to say that my son looked like Winston Churchhill or grandpa!

It is my own baggage that allows me to enjoy Lamott's knack for taking ordinary days and turning them into brilliantly funny commentaries on parenting a baby. In the midst of all the self-deprecating humor, Lamott shares her overwhelming feelings of love and joy that outweigh the hard parts of parenting a thousand times over. I say, touché, when she writes, "I don't remember who said this, but there really are places in the heart you don't even know exist until you love a child."(p. 214)

As we read, we continually make natural connections to our lives, thus creating a richer reading experience. Our goal is for students to also learn to make meaningful connections to help them engage with the text and ultimately end up with stronger comprehension.

Connections

Your Reflections on Background /Connections

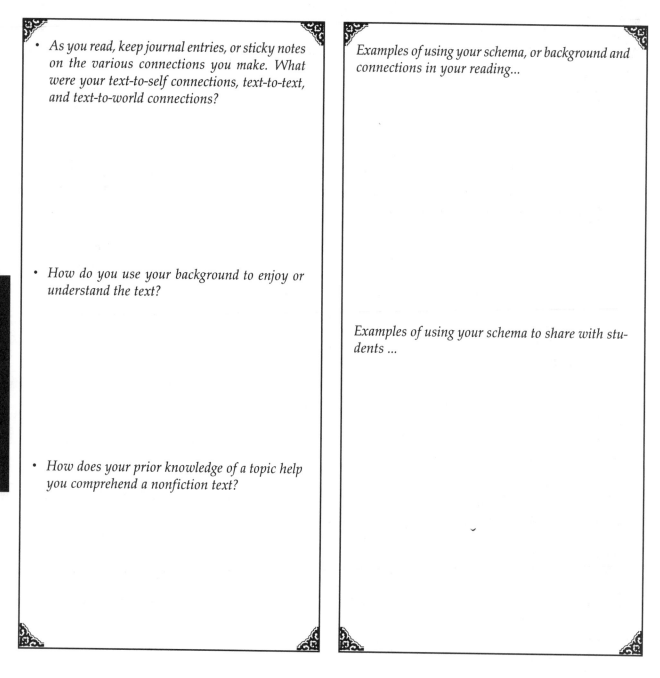

- As you read, keep journal entries, or sticky notes on the various connections you make. What were your text-to-self connections, text-to-text, and text-to-world connections?

- How do you use your background to enjoy or understand the text?

- How does your prior knowledge of a topic help you comprehend a nonfiction text?

Examples of using your schema, or background and connections in your reading...

Examples of using your schema to share with students ...

Connections

References

Anderson, R. C., & Pearson, P. D. (1984). A schema-theoretic view of basic processes in reading comprehension. In P. D. Pearson, R. Barr, M. L. Kamil, & P. Mosenthal (Eds.), *Handbook of reading research* (pp. 255–291). New York: Longman.

Cunningham, J. (1982). Generating interactions between schemata and text. In J. A. Niles & L. A. Harris (Eds.), *New inquiries in reading research and instruction* (pp. 42–47). Rochester, NY: National Reading Conference.

Rumelhart, D. E. (1982). Schemata: The building blocks of cognition. In J. Guthrie (Ed.), *Comprehension and teaching: Research reviews* (pp. 3–26). Newark, DE: International Reading Association.

Whisler, N., & Williams, J. (1990). *Literature and Cooperative Learning: Pathway to Literacy.* Sacramento, CA: Literature Coop.

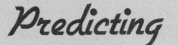

3 ▷ Predicting

> *"Research suggests that when students make predictions they understand better and are more interested in the reading material."*
> **Marge Lipson**, *in* Developing Skills and Strategies in an Integrated Literature-Based Reading Program, *p. 3.*

Thoughts on Predicting

When someone mentions prediction, perhaps the image that first comes to mind is a fortune teller adorned with a shimmery purple veil and lots of dangling beads looking into her crystal ball making predictions for the future. While predicting when reading does require some intuition, it is also based on using one's experiences, solid clues from the text, and the ability to anticipate what could logically happen next.

Predicting can also be just plain fun! Kids are naturally good at it. One evening when I was reading aloud to my four year old, Rebecca, we were previewing the cover and illustrations of a picture book, when she so aptly commented, "Mommy, I discover that the mouse will finally go to bed." I was delighted at her interpretation of the word prediction that I'd been trying out on her during our reading sessions. She inferred that prediction involves discovery or uncovering some truth. I often use Rebecca's wisdom when explaining the prediction strategy to my students.

Teachers and students are predicting like crazy in classrooms everywhere. It is a strategy that many teachers value and teach. In this chapter I have included some motivating lessons that will help you further engage your students as they grow in making even more sophisticated predictions. The lessons I have shared will also assist students in their vocabulary development and ability to monitor, or keep track of their comprehension throughout the reading process. Predicting helps students enhance their comprehension and reading enjoyment. As one third grade student put it, "Prediction keeps me interested in the reading!"

How Does Predicting Help Students Comprehend?

Defining Prediction

The American Heritage Dictionary (1985) defines the word predict to mean *"to state, tell about, or make known in advance, . . . to do so on the basis of special knowledge, foretell . . . predict the weather."* I like the part about the "special knowledge." Isn't that what we want students to do when they predict? We want them to use a combination of special knowledge to predict, and to some extent to infer what will happen next in a text. Just as a series of clues from the environment may help predict the weather, a string of hints from a reading may assist the reader in making logical predictions about upcoming events in the text.

When students use their own background or knowledge plus information from the text that might include illustration clues or bits of information from the headings or story line, they make predictions. As students actively engage in anticipating events, or characters' feelings or actions from the text they naturally become more interested in the reading (Palincsar & Brown, 1984). They also improve in their understandings of the content (Fielding & Pearson, 1991).

Finding clues to predict

Teaching students to use experiences and background to predict

Try modeling to teach students to watch for all kinds of clues to help them predict. Sometimes the strongest and most helpful clues they use to predict may come from their own backgrounds. When reading about a topic or experience that they have first-hand information about, students can incorporate that knowledge to assist them in making logical predictions. When we were reading *Harvey Moon Clean Your Room* by Patricia Cummings (1991) one of the second graders, Ben, predicted that Harvey would clean his room very slowly because that is what he does when his mom asks him to clean his room. He added that he can't seem to throw anything away because he has so many treasures like snake skins, old candy, and rocks. He also thought that Harvey might take his time going through his treasures. As we discussed, read, and continued to predict throughout the text, indeed we found out that Harvey was a pokey picker upper as he inspected each junky find. Confirming or adjusting predictions helps students to monitor their comprehension as they read.

I enjoy using realistic fiction and biographies with students to emphasize the importance of using one's own experiences to aid in making predictions. Some of my favorites at the primary level include the Ramona books by Beverly Cleary, Eve Bunting books, and anything written by Cynthia Rylant. For intermediate I use the same picture books I use in primary along with books and short stories by Gary Soto and Mildred Pitts Walter. The Gary Soto short story collection, *Baseball in April* (1990), is one of my favorite books to use in mini lessons with the entire class or small groups, because the selections are short and every student can find a way to use his or her experiences to relate to the story. One story students particularly enjoy is *"La*

Bamba," the story about a boy whose mess up in a school talent show turns out to be a good thing. The students enjoy using their experiences to predict throughout the story what the main character Faustio will do next.

Teaching students to use text features, illustrations, and text structure

Besides modeling how to use one's own background to predict, I also encourage students to look for text and illustration clues to assist them in making sensible predictions. Make students aware of the importance of text structure in forming predictions. If you are reading fiction, discuss the traditional story map structure that aids students in predicting characters, setting, problem, and resolution. If the fictional piece is a mystery, encourage students to chart and discuss text clues that help them to predict outcomes.

Students can be taught to notice nonfiction text features and structures to assist them in making better predictions. When I was reading a nonfiction book about bats with struggling fourth grade students, I modeled for them how to use the main headings in the book to make their prereading predictions. From there they eagerly contributed comments like, "I think I will learn how bats use echolocation to find their food" and "On these pages I think we will learn how bats help people." By modeling how to use headings and other nonfiction text features, the students learn to predict using these clues.

Predicting when the text doesn't have visual clues

Many times we teach from materials such as chapter books that do not have illustrations or other visual supports for making predictions. When that is the case, in addition to building on clues from the reading and their knowledge of text structure, show students how to quickly skim and scan the eyes over the pages in a chapter to glean clues for making predictions. This chapter has a lesson, Whisper Skimming and Scanning, that offers a helpful prediction technique for when the text has few or no illustrations.

Struggling Readers and Predictions

Often struggling readers make predictions that don't quite make sense and that are either not based on text clues or based on a mismatch of background knowledge. Collect students' predictions from time to time so you can monitor student thinking when making predictions.

Karen, a second grader, predicted that the rainforest in the book *The Great Kapok Tree* (Cherry, 1990) would catch on fire. There is of course, not a sign of fire in any of the selection illustrations. Karen had obviously used her background knowledge of forest fires to help her make this prediction. I discussed her prediction with her briefly and we previewed all of the selection pictures to discover that indeed a fire was not likely in this story. As the year went on, Karen grew in her ability to predict and her comprehension.

By collecting student samples of predictions, you can monitor student progress in this important strat-

egy. You might want to pull several students who are having trouble making logical predictions to work with them in a temporary prediction strategy group.

Box 3.1 can be used as you teach prediction to your students. Make sure that students are aware of the predicting they are doing throughout the reading process not just at the beginning of a selection. After reading, return to their predictions to see how well they did and determine what kind of adjustments they made as students modified predictions throughout the reading process.

Box 3.1. Teaching Prediction

Predicting Before Reading	Predicting During Reading	Predicting After Reading
• What is this book, article, or chapter about? Why do you think that?	• Do I need to adjust my original predictions? • What are my new predictions?	• Did I change my original predictions as I read? • What evidence do I have to show that my predictions were met?
For fiction • What will happen? • What are the clues? -Use setting, characters, problem, events, resolution, or story structure -Use experiences or background -Use text and visual clues I think . . . because . . . I'll bet . . . because . . .	**For fiction** • What will happen next? • Have any of my predictions been confirmed? • What clues do I have to help me make new predictions? Now I think . . . Because . . . I changed my prediction about . . . because . . .	**For fiction** • Did my predictions change or not? • Which of my predictions were most helpful? • If the selection was longer, what else might happen or what might happen next? My original prediction was . . . and now I know . . . Because . . .
For nonfiction • What will I learn? • What are the clues? -Use nonfiction structures, features, headings, visuals, and maps -Use your knowledge of the topic I think I will learn . . . because . . .	**For nonfiction** • Have my predictions been confirmed? • Have I learned what I thought I'd learn? • What else will I learn? -Continue using text structure and clues to change original predictions and to make new ones Now I think I'll learn because...	**For nonfiction** • Did I learn what I thought I would? Why or why not? • Which text clues are evidence of my learning? I thought I'd learn . . . but instead . . .

Predicting

Predicting Classroom Vignettes

Primary Vignette/Partners Predict

Two second graders are huddled closely together on the floor of the reading corner with Eve Bunting's book, *Flower Garden* (1994) carefully balancing between them on their laps. First, they study the cover of the book, which features a girl who is about their age and a variety of colorful flowers.

Rena takes the first attempt at predicting, "I think this book is about a girl and her flower garden."

Alexandra nods her head in quiet agreement. Rena continues to take the lead and the two page through the colorful and inviting illustrations without reading the text. Next they take turns looking at each page and carefully describing what they see. "I see a girl buying flowers at the grocery store. I think she will plant them when she gets home. I know this because I buy flowers to plant in my grandmother's yard," explains Rena proudly.

On the next page Alexandra excitedly adds, "And now she is at the check-out counter."

Rena notices on the next page that the father and daughter are carting the flowers and groceries through the city streets. Alexandra points out on the next page that they are holding the plants on a bus and everyone is smiling at them!

"I wonder where the girl will plant the plants. Are they for her?" questions Rena.

The second graders in Mrs. Hanson's class have been trained to work in pairs to predict using text clues from the cover and illustrations. Their teacher has modeled prediction using many lessons including read-alouds, big books, and other shared texts. Her students know that when they share a predic-

tion they need to follow with a reason why they are making that prediction. These students know that prediction involves using the text clues plus one's own experiences and background to form logical and possible predictions.

By helping her students become super predictors, Mrs. Hanson is giving them a strategy that will strengthen their comprehension and motivate them to read on. Prediction can be taught to even the youngest of readers and it promotes interest throughout the reading process as students read on to see if their predictions came about and as they formulate new predictions along the way.

Intermediate Classroom Vignette/ Social Studies Chapter Preview

The students in Mrs. Song's fifth grade class have opened their social studies textbooks to a new lesson. Today they will read and learn about English settlement in the South she tells them. The students turn to the page she is on so they can follow along while she models and guides them through prediction strategies.

"Remember what we do when we predict with nonfiction text?" she asks to initiate a strategy discussion.

Students raise their hands and give various responses.

"We look at all of the headings and turn those into questions or wonder statements."

"I usually look at all of the illustrations and maps for clues to what the text will cover."

Predicting

"I make predictions and think about what I think the text will teach me and what I will learn."

Next, Mrs. Song reads the first heading, "English Settlement in the South," and shares her thoughts with the students," "I wonder what the early contacts were like between the Native Americans and the colonists. I think that since there is a sketch done by John White of an Algonquin prayer ceremony, the text will attempt to explain the relationship between the Native American peoples and the European settlers."

On the next page, Mrs. Song encourages the students to work in pairs to scan the headings and a map for text clues and to make predictions about what they think they will learn when reading the text. She charts some of their responses on the board.

"I think we will learn about the plans for colonies and how they traded with Native Americans."

"I predict we will learn what happened at Roanoke."

By modeling and then guiding students in making predictions with nonfiction reading material, Mrs. Song is helping her students to become better comprehenders of expository texts. By spending time with the text features, students learn how nonfiction texts are organized and they use these features to assist them in making logical predictions.

This type of lesson engages students by involving them in predicting what the material will be about and helps keep their interest as they read to find out the answers to their predictions. Ultimately, the students will preview the text on their own as a study tool that can help them comprehend and remember main points from the text.

Whisper Skim and Scan

Objective: Students learn to predict by skimming and scanning over text searching for important words that may give them clues.

Materials: Any reading materials, multiple copies, optional copy on a transparency, Whisper Skim and Scan form

Introduce/Model the Strategy

- For modeling purposes, choose a text that all the students can see, possibly a text that is on the overhead projector or at least one that they all have copies of.

- Sometimes texts do not have very many illustrations or visuals to aid students in predicting. Show the students such a text and tell them that there is a way to use the text words to make predictions prior to reading.

- Model using your index fingers and place one on the left-hand side of the page and place the other on the right-hand side of the page. Move your fingers simultaneously and quickly down the page line-by-line and read aloud the important or keywords that jump out at you.

- Tell students that skimming is like scrolling quickly down the computer screen. Scanning is when you slow down long enough to highlight or read an individual word or phrase that catches your attention.

- Stop after each page and mention again some of the words that stood out as you skimmed and scanned.

- Write some of the key words on a chart. Tell students that during reading you will watch to see if these words are indeed some of the important ones to understanding the text.

- Model how to form a prediction based on the words. Tell what you think the text may be about (fiction) or what you think you will learn (nonfiction text).

Guide the Strategy/Cooperative Groups or Pairs

- Try a whole class session of whisper skimming and scanning. Invite students to try to whisper skim and scan on the next page of the text you just used to model from.

- Circulate around the room and assist students as needed. Make sure students are looking for keywords.

- Share findings as a whole class.

- Invite students to try whisper skimming and scanning when reading on their own during SSR or while reading content area textbooks.

Box 3.2. Model—Practice—Apply the Strategy in Different Classroom Structures

Guided Reading	Literature Circles
Whisper Skim and Scan is an especially effective technique to model and practice during guided reading. Try with partners or as a whole group. Wear goofy fingers or finger nails for fun with primary children. Chart words and predictions based on those words.	Small, student-led circles can work together to skim and scan a chapter in a novel or social studies text. Try having groups chart words for the same chapters and then share their predictions with the class.
Special Needs	**Independent Work**
Struggling readers who have difficulty with main ideas benefit from working in a small, teacher-led group to model Whisper Skim and Scan. Have students reflect on the steps for the technique and how it helps them comprehend better.	Set up a center or area in the room where students may choose to Whisper Skim and Scan with a partner. For accountability purposes have the pair fill out a Whisper Skim and Scan form and turn it in.

Reflect on the Strategy/Assess the Strategy

- Have students discuss how Whisper Skimming and Scanning helps them in making better predictions. How does predicting help them understand what they read?

- Observe students as they skim and scan. Can they pull the key words out of the text? Are they making logical predictions based on text clues?

- Work with individual students or small groups who are having difficulty finding key words and making predictions as they skim and scan. Practice skimming and scanning in a small group setting guiding students in a text.

- Use the assessment information found in the Appendix to assist you in documenting student progress in predicting.

Whisper Skim and Scan

1. Run your index fingers down the left and right margins of a text.

2. As your fingers move, your eyes should quickly skim down the page. As you skim , scan, or be on the lookout for key or important words. When you see a key word, whisper it aloud.

3. If you are working with a partner you can take turns skimming, scanning, and whispering or you can both do the steps at the same time to see if you choose the same words!

4. Stop every two pages and record one or two of the words you whispered.

5. Keep skimming, scanning and adding to your list until you finish skimming and scanning the entire text.

6. When you are finished , go back to each word and write what you think the selection is about(fiction) or what you think you will learn. (nonfiction)

Our Key Words	Fiction- What we think will happen Nonfiction-What we think we will learn
mummy	How they were made!
Embalming	I think I will learn what embalming means
mummification	I will learn about the processes of how different mummies were mummified
resin	I think I will learn that resin is a type of tree sap
bacteria	I think I will learn why bacteria are important in the mummifacation process.

Mummies & their mysteries
By Charlotte Wilcox.

Whisper Skim and Scan

1. Run your index fingers down the left and right margins of a text.

2. As your fingers move, your eyes should quickly skim down the page. As you skim, scan, or be on the lookout for key or important words. When you see a key word, whisper it aloud.

3. If you are working with a partner you can take turns skimming, scanning, and whispering or you can both do the steps at the same time to see if you choose the same words!

4. Stop every two pages and record one or two of the words you whispered.

5. Keep skimming, scanning, and adding to your list until you finish skimming and scanning the entire text.

6. When you are finished, go back to each word and write what you think the selection is about (fiction) or what you think you will learn (nonfiction).

Our Key Words	Fiction—What we think will happen Nonfiction—What we think we will learn

Super Six Comprehension Strategies: 35 Lessons and More for Reading Success by Lori Oczkus

Partner Picture Prediction

Objective: Students will learn to predict using illustrations in a partner activity. Pairs take turns describing pages while the partner doesn't see the page but visualizes.

Materials: One book per pair of students, and Partner Prediction form

Introduce/Model the Strategy

- Tell students that you are going to show them a fun and important way to preview a text with a partner that will assist them in making better predictions.

- Choose a text to model with and call on a student to role play as your partner.

- Select a text that all students have a copy of so they can see what you and your student partner are working from. Texts with illustrations work well. Consider using a picture book or textbook.

- Share one book with your model partner. Look at the cover and title of the text and model how to use that information to make initial predictions.

- Take turns alternating as the roles of describer and visualizer. Model how to describe what you see on the page while the other partner looks away and visualizes. The visualizer asks questions and describes the picture he/she is building in his mind. Since partners only view the page they are describing, model how to turn the page to eliminate peeking. Looking up at the ceiling while turning the page and passing the book to the partner is a silly way to accomplish this but the kids love it (see Partner Picture Prediction Vignettes page 60).

- The model pair ultimately writes two predictions.

Guide the Strategy/Cooperative Groups or Pairs

- Invite students to work in pairs. Each pair shares one book so they can pass the book back and forth and take turns role playing as the describer or visualizer.

- Guide the class as they preview the cover and title to make initial predictions. As pairs work, circulate listening for students who are making logical predictions.

- Periodically stop the entire class to listen in on a pair that is making logical predictions.

- Conduct a whole class debriefing. Share predictions and reasons for stating those predictions.

- Discuss the need for adjusting predictions often as more information is revealed. Students should check and discuss predictions after reading.

Box 3.3. Model—Practice—Apply the Strategy in Different Classroom Structures

Guided Reading	Literature Circles
When meeting with guided reading groups, after discussing the title and cover with students, ask pairs to Partner Picture Predict as you listen in and provide assistance. Lead the group in a teacher-led text preview after they have had a chance to do so with partners. Model as needed.	Prior to reading a text, or before reading the next chapter or portion of text, students may work in pairs in their literature circles to conduct Partner Picture Predictions. Pairs share their predictions with the literature circle.
Cross-Age Buddies	**Independent Work**
Older buddies will enjoy using picture books with younger buddies as they take turns visualizing, describing, and predicting. Ask older buddies to reflect on how the younger buddy predicted.	Set up a center or area in the room where students may choose to Partner Picture Predict (PPP) with a partner. For accountability purposes have the pair fill out a PPP form and turn it in.

Reflect on the Strategy/Assess the Strategy

- Have students discuss how Partner Picture Prediction helps them in making better predictions?

- How does predicting help them understand what they read?

Predicting

- Observe students in working in their pairs. Are they making logical predictions based on text clues? Provide feedback as necessary.

- Model with a pair of students in front of the class.

- Some students may not understand the role of the visualizer. Practice reading vivid descriptions aloud to the class and encourage students to close their eyes and visualize.

- Younger children may make up a story to go with the illustrations instead of just describing what they see. Model for them how to describe what is seen in detail.

- Refer to the assessment materials in the Appendix page 223–234 for further assessment information and tips.

Partners Names _____

Partner Picture Prediction

1. Share one copy of a book or article with your partner. Look at the cover only!

   Look at and discuss:

   _____Title   _____Author   _____Artwork, Illustrations   _____Illustrator

2. Write your first predictions based on clues from the cover. For fiction, write what you think will happen in the book and for nonfiction write what you think you will learn.

   Partner #1 prediction _____

   _____

   Partner #2 prediction _____

   _____

3. Take turns holding the book so your partner can't see the book. Describe what you see. The listener should try to visualize the scene. The listener may tell what is being visualized and may ask questions. Continue to trade roles for each page.

4. After you have discussed all illustrations, reread your first predictions. Do you want to keep them, change them, or add to those original predictions?

   Partner #1 prediction _____

   _____

   Partner #2 prediction _____

   _____

5. Reflect on your strategy use. How did Partner Picture Prediction help you predict?

   _____

Super Six Comprehension Strategies: 35 Lessons and More for Reading Success by Lori Oczkus

One Word Classroom Vignettes

Primary Example/One Word and English Language Learners

Prior to reading a selection, Mrs. Choy often gathers her second language learners to meet with her to preview the upcoming selection. Then the second graders are prepared when the entire class or cooperative groups read the selection. Today she has called eight students to preview the story *Thunder Cake* by Patricia Polacco in the district-adopted anthology (Delights, Houghton Mifflin, 2001). The rest of the class is engaged in sustained silent reading.

She begins by modeling using the cover page of the selection, "I see a lady and girl dressed in clothes from long ago. They are in the country and the sky is dark with storm clouds. I think there will be a storm since the title is *Thunder Cake*. One word that may be in the story is the word rain."

Mrs. Choy quickly writes the word "rain" on an index card, sketches some rain drops, and places the card in a pocket chart. Next she invites the students to discuss the selection illustrations. Then each student chooses one word they think will be in the text writes and illustrates the word on an index card. Students share reasons for their words. With all the words in the pocket chart, Mrs. Choy leads a group sort of the words. They come up with these words, categories, and predictions.

Words for baking the cake Words for the storm Words for feelings

List, eggs, flour, milk, strawberries, lightning, rain, thunder, scared, hug

Our Prediction: They will make a cake during the storm to try not to be scared.

Tomorrow the entire class will read the story. By taking the time to preview the pictures and vocabulary in a small group setting, Mrs. Choy has provided second language students with the extra support they will need to comprehend the selection.

Intermediate Example/One Word in a Whole Class Lesson Using Nonfiction

The perfectly preserved bog mummy on the cover of *Mummies and their Mysteries* by Charlotte Wilcox (1999) is inspiring Mrs. Reed's sixth grade students to generate questions and predictions about the book.

Mrs. Reed quickly reviews how to predict words from "This guy doesn't look like the Egyptian mummies we have been studying, but he is preserved. The word I choose for the cover is "preserved." Students work in pairs to preview the illustrations and write five words they think will be in the book. Using colorful markers each pair writes one word in large letters on the back of their One Word sheet.

Mrs. Reed calls the class to attention and asks pairs to hold up one word they have generated. She calls on Marcia to read the words that are held up around the room. The words the students wave in the air include mummy, dead, preserve, natural, and mummification. As she reads each word she scans the room for repeats of the word or for synonyms. This prereading vocabulary discussion motivates students to think about their predictions and prepares them for new concepts that they may encounter in the text.

One Word

Adapted from Susan Page

Objective: Students predict words that may appear in the text based on text clues. As they read they watch for their words and synonyms. During the activity they hold up their word, compare with peers, and sort words into logical categories.

Materials: Scrap paper, optional word sort sheet, and One Word form

Introduce/Model the Strategy

- Inform students that as they preview the illustrations in a text, they can begin thinking about words that may be in the text to prepare for reading and understanding the text.

- Choose a text that has illustrations and model by thinking aloud. Thumb through several pages, describe what you see and offer words you think may appear in the text.

- Close the book and write some words that you predict may be in the text on index cards and place in a pocket chart.

- Tell the students that as you read you will watch for these words or words that mean the same thing.

Guide the Strategy/Cooperative Groups or Pairs

- Students work in pairs to discuss illustrations and their word predictions.

- Students close their books and think of at least one important word that may appear in the text based on the visuals. They write the word in large bold letters, on a sheet of paper.

- Cue the pairs to all hold up their "one word." Call on students to stand up and share their words and the reasons they choose them.

- Students who also chose the same word stand. Invite students who have synonyms for various words to stand up as well.

Predicting

- After reading, return to the words for discussion. Which words actually appeared in the text?

- Display the words at the front of the room, in a chalk tray, or on a pocket chart. Misspellings can be dealt with on the spot or at a later time.

- As an optional step, students sort the words according to length, beginning or vowel sounds, meaning, or any other category they come up with. Students watch for the words as they read.

Box 3.4. Model—Practice—Apply the Strategy in Different Classroom Structures

Guided Reading	Literature Circles
A guided reading group can preview the text and each student write one word on a self-stick note or slate a word he/she thinks may be in the selection. After reading discuss whether the word or a synonym was used.	Students preview a text as a group and individuals or pairs write one word on an index card. They share words. After reading, students spread the words they selected out on the floor and as they act out or draw words, group members guess which word. (Hoyt, 2002)
Special Needs	**Independent Work**
You may wish to work with English as a Second Language students or other special needs students using this technique in a small teacher-led group format first, then they are better prepared to work with peers in pairs or cooperative groups.	Provide students with the One Word sheet at their desks or a station. Students may preview a chapter in a social studies book or a book with illustrations prior to a whole class lesson. They come to the lesson with one word to contribute.

Reflect on the Strategy/Assess the Strategy

- Ask students to reflect on the one word strategy. How does it help you predict what the reading is going to be about?

- Ask students to turn in their words for you to analyze.

- Are students offering words that make sense for the text?

- Are some students moving beyond "borrowing" words from the text by selecting words based on text clues or personal experiences?

- Are students becoming more sophisticated in their word choices?

- How are they connecting or sorting words?

• Ask students, how does the one word technique help them understand the text?

• Refer to the assessment materials in the Appendix page 223–234 for further assessment information and tips.

Partners Names_____

One Word

1. Preview the text with a partner.

Look at all illustrations, headings, photos, graphs, and drawings. Discuss what you see, your predictions, and what you think you will learn. Close the book. Write 5 words that you both think will be found in the reading.

Our words

_____	because	_____
_____	because	_____
_____	because	_____
_____	because	_____
_____	because	_____

2. On a separate sheet of paper write one of your words in big, bold letters.

Be prepared to tell why you think your word will be found in the reading. Share your word with the class or a group.

3. As the class holds up their words, look for the following
- words that mean the same as your word.
- words that are related to your word.
- words that have the same base, or root word.
- words that you have seen in other books.
- words that remind you of an experience in your own life.
- words students think sound interesting.

4. Sort the words.

Write the words on the sort sheet. Cut them out and sort them in different ways.

Sort by
- beginning sounds, ending sounds, word parts
- syllables
- meaning
- your own sorting method!

5. Word watch!

As you read, watch for the words you predicted would be in the text.

Do you find your words, or words that mean the same?

One Word
Word Sorting Sheet

- Choose words from your partner "One Word" sheet or words from the combined class list to fill in the boxes below. Make sure the words are spelled correctly.
- Cut out the words.
- Find at least three or more ways to sort them, such as by letter, by length, by meaning, syllables, or base words.

Stop and Draw

Objective: Students monitor their comprehension throughout reading by summarizing what has happened so far and predicting what will happen next in the reading.

Materials: Any reading materials, optional adding machine tape, or strips of paper, Stop and Draw form

Introduce/Model the Strategy

- As you introduce Stop and Draw tell the students that they are going to learn a technique for showing what their minds are thinking about as they read.

- Stop and Draw will help them to become better at predicting and summarizing as they read. These are two important strategies that all good readers use to make sure they are understanding what they are reading.

- Using an overhead projector or large chart and a text, read aloud to an exciting stopping point, and pause to think aloud as you draw a quick, scribbly-type sketch of what has happened so far in the text and another sketch of what you think will happen next.

- Label the sketches: summary and prediction.

- Read on in the text and stop and draw at least two more times.

- Point out to students that this is not an art project but rather a quick drawing to demonstrate comprehension and thinking.

- You may wish to use a one-minute timer when students participate in the activity.

- Nonfiction hint—When using stop and draw with nonfiction, students may have trouble predicting. They can draw their summary first, then peek at the next page or portion of text and sketch a prediction that shows "What I think I will learn . . . ."

Guide the Strategy/Cooperative Groups or Pairs

- Continue reading and stopping to draw a summary and prediction, but this time allow students to stop and draw with white boards or scrap paper and partners. One partner can draw the summary and the other the prediction.

- Discuss as a group summaries and predictions and sketch one on the overhead or sample chart.

- Encourage partners to continue with Stop and Draw as they finish the text.

- Provide stop and draw materials for individual students to use as they read. Students share their predictions.

Box 3.5. Model—Practice—Apply the Strategy in Different Classroom Structures

Guided Reading	Literature Circles
• Model how to do stop and draw in a guided reading setting using appropriate reading material for the group. Use either white boards, self-stick notes, or adding machine tape for students to record their drawings. Discuss the importance of predicting and summarizing.	A group illustrator can record the agreed upon stop and draw pictures after each chapter or assigned pages. The groups may also use stop and draw for reading textbook material.
Cross-Age Buddies	**Independent Work**
As the older buddy reads aloud to the younger buddy, he/she stops several times during a book and allows the younger buddy to participate by demonstrating comprehension in a stop and draw activity.	Set up a center or area in the room where students participate in Stop and Draw with a partner. Partners may stop and draw after every page taking turns as reader and artist. Adding machine tape strips work well for this activity. For more advanced readers, partners read an entire chapter or designated number of pages before stopping to draw.

Reflect on the Strategy/Assess the Strategy

- Have students discuss how Stop and Draw assists them in making summaries and predictions. How do predicting and summarizing help them understand what they read?

- Collect and analyze Stop and Draw samples. Are students making logical predictions and are they summarizing portions of the text?

- Ask students to record some of their answers in writing and use that to evaluate their progress.

- Use stop and draw in a small group setting to guide students who need extra assistance. Some students may experience difficulty in formulating a brief summary and in using text clues to predict what will happen next. Model and guide in a small group setting.

- Refer to the assessment materials in the Appendix page 223–234 for further assessment information and tips.

Partners Names_____

Stop and Draw

Title of book or article_____

Author_____

Stop and Draw three times during your reading.

1. Read to page_____. Stop and draw a summary of what has happened so far. Also, draw a prediction of what you think will happen next.

Summary	Prediction

2. Read to page _____. Stop and draw again.

Summary	Prediction

3. Read to page _____. Stop and draw again.

Summary	Prediction

Summarizing helps me read because _____

_____

Predicting helps me read because _____

_____

Super Six Comprehension Strategies: 35 Lessons and More for Reading Success by Lori Oczkus

Teachers As Readers

Reflecting on Our Experiences as Adult Readers

From the moment we select a text to read, we begin using clues to predict. Throughout the reading process, we constantly confirm, change, or add to our predictions. Our students need to be aware that predicting happens not just at the beginning of the reading but throughout. Tell students that you also predict as you read and provide examples of your predicting.

My Reflection on Predicting

During the December break, I enjoy choosing a holiday novel that I can knock off in a few hours or days as I desperately try to find some respite from all of the hustle and bustle of the season. One year I treated myself to Skipping Christmas *(Grisham, 2001). This small gem written by popular best-selling author, John Grisham, is about a family that decides to skip Christmas for just one season. The tale is meant to be a humorous take on the frenzy that accompanies the holiday season.*

My predicting began when the title grabbed me. I immediately began to wonder, what does this mean, skipping Christmas? The main characters must skip Christmas. But why? While standing in the grocery store aisle feeling quite indulgent to steal a moment to select a new book, I open the front cover to see if the inside jacket helps me predict some more. The blurb describes what happens when Luther and Nora Krank (cute name) decide to skip Christmas to go on a Caribbean cruise. They discover that there are ugly consequences to foregoing this major holiday. I am wondering, what are those consequences? I predict that I will find out just how other town folks treat the Kranks when they find out they are skipping Christmas. I imagine that the reactions will range from "Good for you" to "How could you!"

As I read the book, I constantly predict what will happen next as the Kranks give up bits and pieces of their ingrained Christmas traditions. Grisham has that gift for stringing the reader along and as I read each humorous encounter with the neighbors, I enjoy predicting reactions to the Kranks bold moves. I won't spoil the ending of this charming tale, but my predictions were definitely out of whack as this saga rushes to a hurried close that is full of surprises. I was in prediction limbo the entire time. Consequently, I couldn't put it down and for an entire day during the holiday craziness. I joined the Kranks and imagined what it would be like to skip Christmas!!

By sharing how predicting helps us, as adult readers, to understand and enjoy text, we encourage students to predict when they read.

Preicting

📖 *Your Reflections on Predicting*

- *As you read keep journal entries, or sticky notes, on the various predictions you make.*

- *What are some examples of how you used your own background and experiences to help you predict? How did clues from the text influence your predictions?*

- *Did you notice that you constantly adjusted or confirmed your predictions? Give an example.*

- *How did you adjust or change your predictions as you read?*

- *What other strategies worked in concert with predicting as you read? Were you aware of connections or questions you had as you predicted as well?*

- *How have you used prediction strategies with nonfiction in your reading recently?*

Examples of prediction in your reading

Examples of predicting in your reading to share with students

References

Hiebert, E. H., & Taylor, B. (Eds). (1994*). Getting reading right from the start: Effective early literacy interventions.* Needham Heights, MA: Allyn and Bacon.

Neuman, S. (1998). Enhancing children's comprehension through previewing. In J. Readence & R. S. Baldwin (Eds.), *Dialogues in literacy research* (37th Yearbook of the National Reading Conference, pp. 219-224). Chicago: National Reading Conference.

Palincsar, A.S., & Brown, A.L. (1984). Reciprocal teaching of comprehension-fostering and monitoring acitivies. *Cognition and Instruction, 1,* 117-175.

Predicting

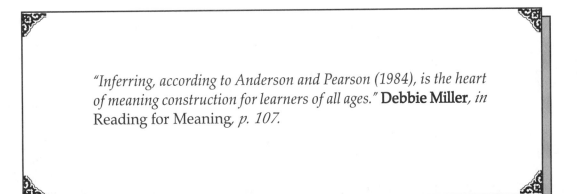

> "Inferring, according to Anderson and Pearson (1984), is the heart of meaning construction for learners of all ages." **Debbie Miller**, *in* Reading for Meaning, *p. 107.*

Thoughts on Inferring

Many of the teachers I work with complain that students can comprehend text on a literal level but have difficulty when asked to think at a higher level or to infer meaning. The National Assessment of Educational Progress (NAEP) shows that many students lack the ability to infer and require instruction and modeling in making inferences (Routman, 2000). Inferring is the defining strategy that separates good readers from struggling readers.

It is no wonder that our students have so much trouble with inferring: Inferring involves complex thinking. When readers make inferences they are a bit like detectives gathering logical clues to piece together the solution to some mystery. Picture students in "Sherlock Holmes" plaid herringbone overcoats, as they combine evidence from the text and their own experiences to come up with inferences about characters, events, and themes in literature. When reading nonfiction, they work on making sense of cause and effect relationships and answering their own wonderings about the topic. Inferring is a way to combine information from various sources to draw conclusions about the meaning of the text. When you take the time to

teach students to infer, you assist students in comprehending at a deeper level.

Besides the image of a detective scouting around with her magnifying glass, the other metaphor often used with inferring is the idea of "reading between the lines" or using clues to understand what the author meant but didn't explicitly say in the text. If writers wrote out every detail, we'd become bored rather quickly. Instead, a skilled author leads the reader to discover along the way. The author might not come out and say, "She was mad." But rather, he may write, "She stomped her foot as she scowled at him." The reader has inferred that the character is mad based on the actions of the character and his own experiences with anger. The author "shows rather than tells" (R. Caplan) the emotions of the character. Reading between the lines helps readers discover the author's meaning.

How Does Inferring Help Students Comprehend?

Inferring is at the heart of meaning construction and comprehension for readers of all ages (Anderson &

Inferring

Pearson, 1984). Good readers combine their own prior knowledge with clues from the text to infer meanings of unknown words, answers to the reader's questions, and the theme of the selection (Miller, 2002). Research suggests that inferring is necessary to comprehend well, and that students can be taught to improve their comprehension with inferences (Hansen, 1981).

So, how does inferring work? Inferring is a whopper of a strategy that requires the orchestrated use of several other strategies. When students infer they use connections, questioning, predictions, and even visualizing (Miller, 2002) to assist them as they incorporate their own knowledge along with text evidence to infer deeper meanings about the text. By thinking aloud and modeling for students the process of making inferences as they come up in the reading, you strengthen their ability to eventually infer on their own.

The Role of Inferring and Predicting

Inferring is often confused with predicting. Predictions are a form of inferring (Keene & Zimmerman, 1997) because predictions also require the use of one's background knowledge combined with text clues to draw some logical conclusion. The difference with a prediction is that as the reader reads on he will either confirm or dismiss the prediction with information from the text. When a reader infers, there isn't always a definite answer. An inference is often more open-ended. For example when I read *The Great Kapok Tree* (Cherry, 1990) with students, they like to infer why the man came into the rainforest to cut down a tree. Since the author hasn't told us why, the students make various inferences about who has sent him and why he has come. By pointing out the difference between their predictions and inferences, students become aware of their use of inferring as they read.

The Role of Self-Questioning and Inferring

One of the most natural ways to transition into a discussion of inferring is to ask students to generate questions they have about the text before reading. As they read the text they will either answer the questions directly in the text or they will need to employ the craft of inferring. You can incorporate the opportunity for students to ask questions and wonder prior to reading fiction or nonfiction. Then, use those questions after reading to talk about how students can find

answers to their questions. When an answer can't be found in the text, model inferring. By categorizing our questions into two basic columns, Questions Answered in the Text and Questions We Inferred, students begin to conclude that the more open-ended questions require inferring. The Predict, Question, Infer lesson on page 100 shows how to help readers combine all three strategies to lead to inferring.

The Evidence—Text Clues

What do you think? and How do you know? are two effective probing questions to help your students understand inferring. Tell the students that you want proof that includes evidence from their own connections and from the text. Mysteries are particularly effective for encouraging students to use text clues to infer answers as they solve a mystery. When reading a "Chet Gecko" mystery, third graders built a chart of text clues with their teacher, Mrs. Jimenez. As they gathered clues to see who was turning the students in the story into zombies. The two-column inference chart was labeled What do we think? How do we know? The activity served as an anchor lesson that Mrs. Jimenez referred to throughout the rest of the school year to encourage students to use text clues not just in mysteries but to make inferences in all texts.

Using Picture Books to Teach Students to Infer

Besides focusing on the themes in literature and students' questions, another way to teach inferring is to encourage students to study illustrations. Many picture books are loaded with opportunities for teaching and reinforcing inferences. Often, the authors of picture books give readers additional information in the illustrations that are not found in the text. When you read with younger children, pause and ask students how a particular character is feeling and ask them to answer the questions, How did you know? What is the proof from the picture and what is the proof from the text?

When reading *DW the Picky Eater* (Browne, 1995) to a group of first graders I ask them what they are thinking. They comment that they think that DW doesn't like spinach. I asked them how they know and to give me proof. They tell me that she made a funny face after finding out that spinach was in the dinner she just gobbled down. Also, DW said, "Yuck."

Many of the students make text-to-self connections as part of their inferring.

"Once my mom gave me a fish taco and I thought it was chicken. When she told me it was fish, I spit it out and made a face just like DW," shared Rachael. Other students nodded and hands went up as students shared similar eating events. I point out to the class that our own experiences can help us make inferences as we read. The How Did You Know? question reminds students to consider their experiences to aid them in making inferences to deepen their comprehension of the text.

Even some of the phonetic or decodable readers in first grade have illustrations that weave a richer story than the words. By stopping to discuss inferring and these illustrations, you provide more opportunities to deepen comprehension, even with such simple reading material. The steady stream of picture books in primary provide us with dozens of natural opportunities to model and teach inferring using illustrations.

Using picture books to infer with intermediate students

Younger children aren't the only ones who benefit from making explicit inferences using picture books. Older students often need the experience of making an inference with illustrations. There are several sources of materials that contain illustrations to use with older kids. Chris Van Allsburg books are some of my favorite books to use with intermediate students to teach inferring. Ask students to study the illustrations and then tell me what they think the characters are thinking or feeling when reading. When reading *Jumanji* (Van Allsburg, 1981), I ask students to think how the characters are feeling as the various jungle animals appear while playing the Jumanji game. For every feeling, the students also provide one piece of evidence from the text. Besides picture books, the district-adopted anthology is a ready source of illustrated grade level reading material. I often use this type of anthology and its visuals to reinforce inferring. Social studies and science texts provide natural opportunities to discuss with illustrations and to make logical inferences.

Also, older students enjoy pointing out and discussing inferences while working with a cross-age buddy in a picture book or easy reader. This is a wonderful opportunity for them to become metacognitive, or aware of their own thinking, as they "teach" the buddies to gather clues for inferring. Picture books are excellent and accessible tools for making inferring more visible for intermediate students. Try using the sources available to you, including picture books, grade level anthologies, content area text books, and books the students can read to younger students.

Inferring

Box 4.1. Teaching Inferring

Using Inferring Before Reading	Using Inferring During Reading	Using Inferring After Reading
What can I infer from the cover of the book? How do I know? (Use your prior knowledge and the clues from the book) I think . . . I know . . . because . . . What questions do I have before reading? (Watch to see if you infer answers.) Can I infer what the theme might be? What clues do I have so far from the cover, back, first page, and illustrations?	What can I infer or figure out so far? What have I inferred using the text and illustrations? My questions that needed inferring are . . . . **Fiction** I think that the main character is thinking or feeling . . . I know this because of My experiences . . . The text clues . . . I infer the character_____ because_____ . My experiences Text clues I also infer that the theme is . . . Because . . . My Experience Text Clues **Nonfiction** What have I inferred so far? What clues from the text and my experiences helped me? What kinds of comparisons can I make as I infer? _____ is like_____ because. What are the causes and effects of . . .	What have I inferred using the text and illustrations and my own knowledge? My questions that needed inferring to answer are . . . . Here's how I figured out the answers using clues from the text and my head . . . The author didn't say _____ but I knew_____ because_____ . **Fiction** I think the main character is a _____ person because_____ My experiences . . . The text clues . . . I infer that the theme is. _____ because _____ My experiences . . . Text Clues . . . **Nonfiction** What kinds of comparisons did I infer? _____ is like_____. The main causes of_____ are _____ **Self-Assessment** What helped me infer? Which text clues were the most helpful for inferring? Which of my connections to my knowledge helped me most?

Super Six Comprehension Strategies: 35 Lessons and More for Reading Success by Lori Oczkus

Inferring Classroom Vignettes

Intermediate or Primary Example/ Inferrring during a Class Read Aloud

Many hands shoot up after Mr. Ford reads Chris Van Allsburg's *Just a Dream* (1990), a story about a boy who begins to care about the environment after he has a dream about the future. As the students listened to the book for a second time, they watched for evidence of inferences.

As the students share examples of inferences, Mr. Ford begins to construct a chart that lists examples of inferences and evidence collected from the text and the students' experiences.

"I inferred Walter didn't care much about the environment when he saw the neighbor's tree she got for her birthday and he thought it was dumb!" began Simon.

"I always sort the recycles from the trash when I empty it because I want to help the environment. Walter dumped everything into one can because he was in such a hurry to watch TV," added Cecil.

Mr. Ford asked the students what inference they could make about the recycling and Walter. No one responded so he modeled and told them that he inferred that Walter didn't think his part mattered in recycling. He was careless about it. The evidence of the inference came from our experiences recycling at home and from the text that said Walter was too busy to sort the recycles. Mr. Ford invites the students to find other examples of inferring with evidence from their backgrounds and from the text.

Pairs of students share copies of the text and dive in on their inference hunt.

Sara and Jessie tell Mr. Ford as he circulates that they don't see any more inferences, so he turns to a page where Walter's bed flies over his street. The houses are half-buried and the workmen tell him that people don't live here anymore.

"What do you think happened to the houses? Does the author tell us?" prompts Mr. Ford.

The girls nod, no. He continues by asking them to guess what might have happened by using the text clues "bulging trash bags," "half-buried" houses, and the fact that people don't live there anymore. The girls sit.

Then Sara suggests, "I know there was so much trash it covered the street and the people had to move out." Mr. Ford praises and reinforces her use of text clues to infer.

The class and students share more examples of inferences from the book including that sometimes we think the things we need are more important than nature, and that Walter changed his thinking by recycling and caring for the environment.

Mr. Ford enjoys using Van Allsburg books to reinforce inferring because these entertaining, award-winning, picture books are designed to make students think and read between the lines!

Get The Feeling: Intermediate Vignette/ Whole Class Lesson/ Inferring Character Feelings

Toda la familia vino de El Salvador cuando yo era un bebe, Gonzalo informs the other fourth graders in Spanish that his family came from El Salvador when he was just an infant . He adds that sometimes his parents and grandparents feel like

Inferring

the grandfather in *Grandfather's Journey* (Say, 1993) because they miss their country.

Pairs of students are crouched over their copies of the immigrant saga about a man who comes from Japan to America when he is a young adult. Then throughout his life he misses America when he moves back to Japan. The classroom of second language students is busy rereading the selection searching for examples of inferences. Several students are eagerly pouring over their Spanish copies of the story.

Their bilingual teacher, Miss Thomas, has found that one of the most concrete ways to help her students internalize the meaning of inferring is to ask students to think about character feelings. She has modeled "Get the Feeling" many times and the students are anxious to find their own examples. She gathers the class to share their inferences.

"The man wore European clothes for the first time," shared Rita.

Miss Thomas prompts Rita to expand her thinking to infer what the grandfather might have been thinking and feeling when he wore those clothes. Rita looks at the picture and adds that he looks like he felt "proud" and "different" boarding the steamship.

"At first he only thought of America," reflects Sammy.

"How do you know? What is your evidence?" probes Miss Thomas.

"Because he wanted to visit many different places in America," Sammy adds.

The students continue sharing their feelings that stem from their first-hand experiences as immigrants themselves. Miss Thomas plans on referring to Grandfather's Journey as her "anchor" book for inferencing because her students have such strong emotional connections to the story and character feelings. Looking for clues to char-

acter feelings is an effective way to teach and practice inferring.

Primary Example/Guided Reading Inferring Characters' Feelings

Since the Valentine's Day Party around the corner, Mrs. Ray has introduced the picture book, *Roses are Pink, Your Feet Really Stink* (deGroat, 1996) to each of the second grade guided reading groups. She calls each guided reading group to explore inferences about character feelings. She asks the students to help find examples of how the characters were feeling in the story. "How did Gilbert feel when he wrote the not so nice Valentines to Lewis and Margaret? How do you know? Have you ever felt like that before?

The discussion continues as the students explore the feelings of the story characters who received the nasty valentines and their reactions. Mrs. Ray shares a personal story as she remembers when she was a child, every box of valentines came with a "skunk" card to give to a person you didn't like very much. The children are appalled and conclude that mean-spirited cards don't really make anyone feel good, including the sender or the receiver! By asking students "How do you know?" they are forced to find evidence for character feelings in the text, illustrations, and in their own experiences.

Get the Feeling

Objective: Students infer character feelings as they read by focusing on text and illustration clues.

Materials: Fiction texts, or nonfiction texts where characters may express feelings, and Get the Feeling form.

Introduce/Model the Strategy

- Often, a characters' feelings are not told, instead the author carefully shows the reader the characters' emotions by describing their behaviors. Rather than writing, "He was mad." the author may write "He stomped out of the room and slammed the door." Tell students that they naturally use inferring to use the text clues and their own experiences to figure out or infer how a character is feeling.

- Read aloud from a text the class is familiar with. Choose a spot where a character's feelings are displayed through actions. Think aloud and describe the character's actions, your own knowledge or experiences, and the inference you made about the character's feelings.

- Write an inference statement "We inferred that the character felt_____ because the text _____ and we know from experience that _____."

- Continue with several more examples of text that show character feelings.

Guide the Strategy/Cooperative Groups or Pairs

- Invite students to work in pairs or cooperative groups to find another example of the character's feelings that requires readers to infer.

- Pairs write their inference statement on a plain white paper using markers. Students write, "We inferred that the character felt _____ because the text _____ and we know from experience that _____."

- Groups display the page they used to make the inference marked with a sticky note, and their written inference. Students stand up and circulate around the room studying other pairs displayed texts, and sticky notes with inference statements.

Inferring

Box 4.2. Model—Practice—Apply the Strategy in Different Classroom Structures

Struggling Readers	Literature Circles
Keep a group chart over several stories for recording inferences the group makes about character feelings. Act out feelings.	Ask literature circles to give at least one example of using inferences for character feelings or thoughts every time they meet.
English Language Learners	Independent Work
Model in a small group setting how to make an inference about characters feelings. Use a book that the class has read or a picture book. Ask students to draw illustrations showing the character's feelings. Talk about feelings and ask volunteers to show happy, sad, angry, curious, etc. Bring a mirror for students to look. Ask group members, how does ___ feel ? How did you know?	Students illustrate one example of a character's feelings from the text. Students look for examples of inferred character's feelings using picture books. Students write a few sentences that describe a character's feelings without telling the feeling. Other students read and try to infer the feeling. Students could make two cards, one with the sentences from the text that describe the feeling and one with the feeling. Students play concentration or match the cards. Use the cards as an assessment.

Reflect on the Strategy/Assess the Strategy

- Ask students to reflect on making inferences about character's feelings. Which clues were most helpful, the text clues or your experiences? What is hard about making inferences about character feelings?

- Read students' inferences to see if they are using both text and experienced-based clues to make logical inferences.

- Meet with students who are having difficulty and use picture books, drama, and modeling to provide more opportunities to discuss and infer character feelings.

- Some English Language Learners may have difficulty identifying vocabulary to describe character feelings in English. Before working your way through the lesson, review words for feelings and ask students to dramatize facial expressions and actions for feelings.

- Refer to the appendix on page 223–234 for further suggestions on assessing inferring.

Get the Feeling

Title of book or article_____

Author_____

1. Choose a character from the story or text.
2. Reread parts of the text to look for examples of the character's behavior.
   How was the character feeling?
   How did you know?
   What clues from the text helped you figure out how the character felt?
   What clues from your own experiences help you?
3. Write your inferences in the chart and discuss.
4. Discuss how inferring a character's feelings helps you understand the text.

Character's Name_____

Inference	Character's Action	My Own Experiences
How did the character feel?	How do you know the character felt that way? What did he/she do?	Have you ever (or any-you've known or read about or seen on TV) felt that way? What did you or they do?
The character _____ felt_____ (Draw a tiny sketch of the character feeling this way.)	I know this character felt that way because in the book_____ _____ _____ _____ _____ _____ My clues came from page(s)_____ _____ _____ _____	I (or someone I have known or read about or seen on TV) felt _____ when_____ _____ _____ _____ _____ So, I (they) _____ _____ _____ _____

How does inferring character feelings help you understand the text?

_____

Super Six Comprehension Strategies: 35 Lessons and More for Reading Success by Lori Oczkus

Picture Book Detectives

Objective: Students use picture books or the illustrations in textbooks to make inferences.

Materials: Any picture book or textbook, Picture Book Detectives form

Introduce/Model the Strategy

• The illustrations in picture books are loaded with opportunities for making inferences.

• Tell students that good readers use illustration clues along with their prior knowledge and experiences to make inferences during reading. Picture book illustrations often tell as much or more about the story or text than the words. Inferring is an important strategy that can help us gather important clues.

• Choose a picture book that you think will interest students. You can use the district-adopted anthology, picture books for your grade level, or even science or social studies textbooks.

• Guide the students to predict before reading. As you read the selection aloud, stop periodically to model inferring by looking at the illustrations. Describe what you see in the illustration. Think aloud as you model an inference using your prior knowledge, or experiences and the illustration clues.

• Throughout the book, show how to be a "detective" hunting for clues about character feelings and actions. Be on the lookout for picture clues that were NOT included in the text that tell you more about the setting, characters, problem, solutions, or events.

• List inferences and clues on a chart or a transparency of page 96.

Guide the Strategy/Cooperative Groups or Pairs

• Continue reading the book while showing illustrations and modeling how to make inferences using picture clues.

- After a few examples, invite students to work in either pairs or cooperative groups to study an illustration and then tell what clues they used to make an inference. Each table shares their inference.

- After reading an entire picture book as a class, assign different illustrations to each group. The groups find examples of at least one inference they made by looking at the illustration.

- Groups share inferences.

- Encourage students to find examples of inferences in pictures as they read on their own.

Box 4.3. Model—Practice—Apply the Strategy in Different Classroom Structures

Guided Reading	Literature Circles
Model how to infer using illustrations in a small group setting. Students work in pairs to write their inferences on white boards and share. Ask how inferring helps students comprehend.	Literature circles each take different novels with illustrations or picture books. Each group member shares and explains one inference he/she made. The group makes an inference poster.
Cross-Age Tutors	**Independent Work**
Older buddies study picture books ahead of time and mark with self-stick notes inferences found in illustrations. They share in think-aloud examples and invite the younger buddy to come up with his/her own inferences.	Keep a center in the classroom stocked with picture books for students to choose. Students select a book, preview the book, read, and then return to illustrations to make inferences. They use the sheet on page 96.

Reflect on the Strategy/Assess the Strategy

- Ask students to discuss how making picture inferences helps them to understand the text.

- Are students using clues from the text, illustrations, and or their experiences and prior knowledge to come up with inferences that are logical?

- Some students may have difficulty giving clues from the text to make inferences. Try sketching the following to help students visualize inferring. Try sketching a head to represent the reader's prior knowledge, a book for the text, and then a light bulb to represent the inference that is the conclusion. Guide students in a small group format as they look for clues and think about prior knowledge to make inferences using picture books.

- For some meaningful practice encourage students to find examples of inferences in picture books that they will read aloud to cross-age buddies in a younger class.

- For more suggestions on assessing students progress in making inferences, turn to the appendix on page 223–234.

Picture Book Detectives

The book + your experiences, knowledge= an inference

1. After reading a picture book with a partner, study all of the illustrations again. Which illustrations show examples of inferences? Watch for clues that are in the illustrations but were NOT in the words.
Some examples might include:
•Character feelings
• Action clues
•Clues about the problem in the story

2. Use the chart below to record the page number, what you see, the clues from the book or your experience, and your inference.

3. Choose your favorite illustration from the selection that shows an inference. Turn this paper over and sketch the illustration. Act out the inference with a partner for the class.

Picture Detective Inference Chart

Page 23	Describe the picture. This Picture Shows calvin and hobbes waking up.	Clues from the picture he jump out of bed our experiences In the morning I jump up of the bed	Inference I think they'll have a great day
Page 23	Describe the picture. They're playing with water guns.	Clues from the picture They have water guns in their hand our experiences I play with water guns in my vacation.	Inference they'll play war maybe
Page 23	Describe the picture. They're climing a tree.	Clues from the picture they're on the tree. our experiences I like to climb trees.	Inference I think they want to climb it to the top.

Picture Book Detectives

The book + your experiences, knowledge = an inference

1. After reading a picture book with a partner, study all of the illustrations again. Which illustrations show examples of inferences? Watch for clues that are in the illustrations but were NOT in the words.

   Some examples might include:
   - Character feelings
   - Action clues
   - Clues about the problem in the story

2. Use the chart below to record the page number, what you see, the clues from the book or your experience, and your inference.

3. Choose your favorite illustration from the selection that shows an inference. On a separate sheet of paper sketch the illustration. Act out the inference with a partner for the class.

Picture Detective Inference Chart

Page ___	Describe the picture.	Clues from the picture Our experiences	Inference
Page ___	Describe the picture.	Clues from the picture Our experiences	Inference
Page ___	Describe the picture.	Clues from the picture Our experiences	Inference

Pull a Passage

Adapted from Candy Cease

Objective: Students read a text and afterward "pull a passage" from the text and discuss inferences they made when reading the passage.

Materials: The Pull a Passage form, any text

Introduce/Model the Strategy

- Explain to students that when good readers read they often use inferences to help them understand what they are reading. An inference is when a reader uses clues from the book and from his/her experiences or background knowledge to fill in gaps that the author hasn't fully explained. Explain that you'll model how to pull a passage or sentence out of the text and tell how you made inferences that helped you understand the reading.

- Model by reading a new or familiar text to students. Stop and "pull a passage" or sentence and write it on a chart or the overhead.

- Give two or three inferences that you made when you read the text. Tell what you visualized, remembered, and inferred.

- Say something like "The author didn't say this, but I know that _____ because the clues from the text were _____ and my experience is _____."

Guide the Strategy/Cooperative Groups or Pairs

- Guide the class by reading a text together and stopping when the author expects the reader to make an inference.

- Then they think about what the author meant but didn't come out and actually say. What did the author expect us to infer? The author didn't say this, but I know that _____ because the clues from the text were _____ and my experience is _____.

- Students share their inferences. Model further to assist those students who were unable to discuss their inferences. Ask, "How did you know?" to encourage use of evidence from text and experiences.

- Practice riddle descriptions for further practice. Give a description of a person or place complete with clues that show and not tell the answer. Students guess and tell which clues helped them infer the answer. (Example: describe a desert—hot, dry, cactus, but don't say the word desert or the name of a desert).

Box 4.4. Model—Practice—Apply the Strategy in Different Classroom Structures

Guided Reading	Literature Circles
Keep a chart for recording inferences as they come up in the reading. Discuss clues from the text and students' backgrounds that helped them. Look for inferences in fiction and nonfiction texts.	The student who has the passage picker (Daniels, 1994) role identifies one passage where the author doesn't saying everything but expects us to infer.
Struggling Readers	**Independent Work**
Use the frame "The author didn't say this, but I know that _____ because the clues from the text were _____ and my experience is _____." To model and guide students as they hunt through reading materials for examples of inferring.	Students write riddle descriptions of people or places and other students use the clues to answer. Students work with partners or alone as they search for examples of inferring. They can illustrate their inferences.

Reflect on the Strategy/Assess the Strategy

- Ask students to reflect on the strategy of inferring.

- How does inferring help them understand what they read?

- How does inferring make reading enjoyable?

- Are students using clues from both the text and their experiences?

- Model by pulling passages and thinking aloud about the inferences you made.

- Guide students as you pull passages together and make inferences.

- Refer to the assessment materials in the appendix on page 223–234 for further suggestions.

Pull a Passage

Adapted from Candy Cease

1. As you reread a text, watch out for sentences or passages that force you to make inferences. Watch for character feelings.
2. Work with a partner or team and copy a passage directly from the text and write at least two inferences you made with that passage. Tell which clues helped you.
3. Share your passage with the class. Ask the other students if they have an additional inference that they are making with the text.

Sentence or passage is from (title)_____

Author_____ Page number_____

Sentence or passage from the reading is _____

_____

_____

Inference #1	Inference #2
The author didn't say _____	The author didn't say _____
But I know that _____	But I know that _____
_____	_____
_____	_____
because the clues from the text were	because the clues from the text were
_____	_____
_____	_____
_____	_____
_____	_____
My own experiences that helped me infer	My own experiences that helped me infer
_____	_____
_____	_____
_____	_____
_____	_____

Explain how inferring by using clues from the reading and your experiences helps you to read. Write a description riddle on a separate sheet of paper. Write clues but show and don't tell what you are describing (describe an animal, person, place, event).

Predict/Question/Infer Classroom Vignette

The Great Kapok Tree by Lynne Cherry (1990) is one of Mr. Ford's favorite children's books to read with children. He shares his passion for the rainforest with his fourth graders as he builds background for the story by reading aloud various nonfiction articles and books. The picture book is a wonderful selection to use for inferring because students usually have many unanswered questions after reading it. The story is about a man who enters the rainforest to chop down a kapok tree and falls asleep at the foot of the tree. Animals take turns approaching him and while he rests, they share their persuasive arguments for keeping the tree alive. The ambiguous nature of the story is perfect for inferring.

Prior to reading the selection the students are busy previewing the illustrations with a partner and drawing their predictions. Then they will write five questions about the selection prior to reading it and use the form on page 104 as a guide.

Mari writes, " I predict the man will not cut down the tree because the animals talk to him in a dream." Belinda adds, " I predict he got tired and couldn't chop down the tree."

The pairs also ask questions using the question word guides who, what, where, when, and why as they preview the illustrations once again. They copy their questions on colorful strips of paper using bold markers. Mr. Ford reminds the students to pay attention as they read to see if their questions are answered in the text or if they have to infer.

Once the pairs have completed their five questions and predictions, Mr. Ford encourages the pairs to read the selection together. After reading, the students will answer their questions on the back of their question strips and share their find-ings. Two posters cover the white board in the front of the room. One says, "Questions that are Answered in the Story" and the other reads, "Questions that We Inferred by Using Text Clues and Our Knowledge." Mr. Ford glances over Jeffrey's shoulder, and reads his question, " What are the animals doing?" Mr. Ford asks the class to answer the question and decide which poster Jeffrey should tape his question on. Hands go up and Mark says that the animals are trying to tell the man to not cut down the tree. Heads nod in agreement as Jeffrey adds that the question should go on the "Questions that are Answered in the Story" chart.

Volunteers share one question at a time and place questions on the appropriate charts.

Belinda reads her question (the one Mr. Ford has been waiting for!) "Why does the man want to cut down the tree?" Mr. Ford directs all the pairs to discuss a logical answer.

Belinda and Mari offer their idea. "We think that the man came to cut down the tree to make into paper. He works for a paper company," shares Mari. Mr. Ford asks if there are other ideas. Hands shoot up and students add that the man could have cut down the tree for lumber for houses. The class concludes that this question definitely fits on the "Questions that We Inferred by Using Text Clues and Our Knowledge" chart.

"We know that trees can be used for paper or lumber, so we inferred that the man might want to cut down the tree for some company," adds Michael. The lesson is a hit and students have applied inferring as they answered their own questions. Michael concludes, "Some of the most interesting questions are the ones that aren't answered in the text!"

Predict/Question/Infer

Objective: Students preview a text and write predictions and questions before reading. After reading they answer questions and categorize questions as either questions answered in the text or questions that required inferring.

Materials: chart paper for recording class questions, self stick notes for writing questions to go on chart, the predict, question, infer form

Introduce/Model the Strategy

- Ask students to tell you what good readers do before they read. Build on student comments and remind them that before reading good readers predict and ask questions.

- Tell students that when we read we look for the answers to our questions. Some of their questions may be answered directly in the text, while others are answered by inferring. Inferring is when our brains use information from the text and our background knowledge to create a sensible answer to a high-level question. Inferring means using background information plus the text or "Me plus the text" to read between the lines.

- Select a text to model from. Preview illustrations, headings, captions, and make predictions.

- Model how to ask questions before reading using clues from the text. Generate questions that begin with who, what, when, where, why, and how. Also, use could, would, should, and why to help students generate questions that require inferences.

- Write each question on separate self- stick note. Make a Predict, Question, Infer chart (p. 105). Place all of the questions in the *Questions I Have Before Reading* column.

- Read aloud from the text.

- After reading, refer to your column of questions. Read each question, answer it, and determine which column to move the question to either *Questions with Answers in the Text* or *Inference Questions*. Students may assist you in categorizing questions.

Guide the Strategy/Cooperative Groups or Pairs

- During your modeling session, encourage pairs of students to work together to generate additional questions for the chart. Students write questions on strips or sticky notes and post them on the chart.

- After reading, answer and categorize questions and place in either the *Questions with Answers in the Text* column or *Inference Questions* column. Write answers on the back of the questions.

- Pairs of students can work together to generate questions, read the text, and answer and categorize questions. If they use the form on page 105 they can either cut apart their question strips to place on the Predict, Question, Infer chart or copy onto self-stick notes.

Box 4.5. Model—Practice—Apply the Strategy in Different Classroom Structures

Struggling Readers	Gifted Students
Work in a strategy group with students who have trouble inferring. Create the chart and guide students as they infer answers to their questions. Encourage students to use why, how, could, would, or should as question beginnings because these words lead to inferences.	Gifted students create as many inferential questions that they can ask a partner, literature circle, or the class. Make a game show or board game with all inferential questions and answers.
Guided Reading Work with small groups to build Predict, Question, Infer charts with guided reading material.	**Literature Circles** Each student brings two questions for the group chart. After reading, the discussion director leads the group in answering and categorizing the questions.

Reflecting on the Strategy/ Assessing the Strategy

- Ask students to discuss how the three strategies, predict, question, and infer work together to help them understand what they read. Which kind of question is harder to answer?

- If students are only asking simple in the text questions, model and guide them toward inferential questioning. Do students infer as they answer their own questions?

- Provide additional modeling as necessary with small groups.

- English language learners may have difficulty inferring because of the language demands of the task. Use a drawing of a head for prior knowledge plus a book to show which clues contributed to the inference. Another idea is to work with students to fill in a three-column chart labeled My Clues+Book Clues= Inference Made.

- Use the assessment suggestions from the appendix on page 223-234.

Sample Predict/Question/Infer Chart

Predict/Question/Infer, Part I

Preview pictures with a partner or alone.
Write two predictions you have about the text. What you predict or think you will learn?

1. I predict (fiction)
   I think I will learn (fiction) _____
   _____

2. I predict (fiction)
   I think I will learn (nonfiction) _____
   _____

Draw your first prediction.	Draw your second prediction.

Questions: Write questions you have about the text before you read.

Why
Who
What
Where
How

Predict/Question/Infer, Part II

- **Before reading,** look at all the pictures and headings. Think of questions you have. Use question words, such as Who, What, Where, When, How, and Why to start questions. Write each question on a separate sticky note or paper and place questions in the ***Questions I Have Before Reading*** column.

- **After reading**, reread each question and answer it. Write answers on the back of the notes. Move the questions to either the *Questions Answers in the Text* column or the *Inference Questions* column. Discuss with classmates.

Questions I have Before Reading	Questions with Answers in the Text (example and page number)	Inference Questions (my information+text clues)

Super Six Comprehension Strategies: 35 Lessons and More for Reading Success by Lori Oczkus

Inferring

Questions for a Dinner Party

Adapted from MaryEllen Vogt and Maureen McLaughlin

Objective: Students keep a log of questions they would ask a character from a text if they could meet. Then, students role play as characters from the reading(s) who might be at a dinner party and ask each other questions
Materials: Any fiction or nonfiction text, optional costumes and dinner party dishes, and Question for a Dinner Party sheet.

Introduce/Model the Strategy

- Explain to students that when good readers infer information about story or nonfiction characters, they use text information combined with their experiences. Tell them that when they role play as a character they are inferring how they think the character would act and answer questions.

- Ask students to imagine what it would be like to meet one of the characters from a book the class has read or a person from history.

- Guide the class to brainstorm a list of questions they would like to ask that character if they could meet that character in person.

- Role play as a character from the reading. Call on students to ask questions.

- Model and think aloud as you answer a few of the questions by inferring, "I think I will answer like this . . . because I know from the story that the character usually . . . and I know from my experiences that . . . "

Guide the Strategy/Cooperative Groups or Pairs

- Invite a group of students to model in front of the class a dinner party of characters from different time periods or pieces of literature (Vogt & McLaughlin, 2000).

- What if these various fictional and real characters from different books could meet and have dinner together? What would they talk about? Use name tags so students can remember who they are talking to. An option is to role play as various characters from different time periods in history. What would these folks say if they met? What can you infer about what they might say to each other?

- Each dinner party character takes a turn to ask a question of fellow pretend guests.

- Encourage the class to give the group feedback regarding content of the conversations.

- These questions can be used with the class as a rubric to assess their performance.

    - What was the quality of the conversations?

    - Did the students role play and answer with logical responses that are based on what that character would most likely do and say?

- What kinds of questions encouraged the characters to give more interesting responses?

Box 4.6. Model—Practice—Apply the Strategy in Different Classroom Structures

Guided Reading	Literature Circles
While students read a selection, ask them to keep track of questions they will will ask characters from the piece you are reading together. Role play during guided reading. Observe how students infer answers and the quality of their questions.	Vary the routine in literature circles by including a dinner party. Students prepare questions ahead of time and role play. The discussion director in each group leads. If circles read different titles titles, try mixing up students to have dinner parties with students who have read different titles.
Struggling Readers	**Independent Work**
Meet with struggling readers before the class or literature circles play dinner party to rehearse and write questions and answers for selection characters.	Students write questions to ask during a dinner party. They write at least three questions per character. Collect and evaluate the quality of the questions. Are the questions answered from the text or do they require inferring?

Reflect on the Strategy/Assess the Strategy

- Invite students to tell how Dinner Party Questions and the role playing helps them to infer.

- Collect written questions. Are students asking relevant questions that require inferring?

- Observe during dinner parties. Do students use what they know about a character to infer his or her answers and behaviors?

- Model in a small guided reading group for students who are having trouble with asking questions or inferring answers. ELL students may have difficulty with the dinner party concept. Explain.

- Ask the class to vote on the questions they think are the "best" and tell why.

  Generate a class rubric to define what "best" questions look like.

  - they generate lots of responses

  - they require background knowledge plus text clues

  - they are likely based on text clues

- Refer to the appendix on page223–234 for further suggestions on assessing students.

Questions for a Dinner Party

As you read, think of questions you would ask the main characters and the author (Beck, McKeown, Worthy, Sandora, & Kucan, 1996) if you could meet them. Write at least three questions to ask each character. Use the questions and role play a dinner party (Vogt & McLaughlin, 2000). Take turns asking questions as you role play as a character. Some possibilities to start questions are included in the following chart.

What if . . .	How could you . . .	Why did you . . .	What do you think . . .
If you could have . . .	How did you feel when . . .	When did you realize . .	What would you have done differently instead . . .

Character's Name _____
I would like to ask _____(character's name) these questions.
1.

2.

3.

Character's Name _____
I would like to ask _____(character's name) these questions.
1.

2.

3.

Character's Name _____
I would like to ask _____(character's name) these questions.
1.

2.

3.

Author's Name _____
I would like to ask _____(author's name) these questions.
1.

2.

3.

Teachers As Readers

Reflecting on Our Experiences as Adult Readers

Inferring is a high-level strategy that good readers employ when a text calls for reading between the lines. When we are required to infer, we fully engage with the text to combine our prior knowledge with text clues to create the author's intended meanings. By being aware of our own constant use of inferring, we can also point out to students the importance of this critical reading strategy.

My Reflection on Inferring

I absolutely love children's literature. I can't go into a big chain book store, you know the kind with cappuccino that stay open well past my bedtime, without making a journey to the children's section to take a peek. I am a kid's book addict. So, I was especially delighted when the staff at Randall School surprised me with a lovely gift book, Dear Genius *(the letters of Ursula Nordstrom collected and edited by Leonard S. Marcus, 1998). Ursula Nordstrom was director of Harper's Children's Books from 1940–1973. This brilliant woman is considered by some to be the single most important editor in children's book publishing this century! She nurtured the author's of many classic favorites such as* Goodnight Moon *(1947),* Charlotte's Web *(1952),* Where the Wild Things Are *(1963), and* The Giving Tree *(1964).*

So, why did I select Dear Genius *as a book for inferring? I noticed that as I read the collection of letters she wrote to these favorite authors, I gathered clues about this woman and constantly inferred what she must have been like. Letter reading is an interesting experience where one has to piece the clues together to figure out the story.*

I inferred that Ursula was funny because she displayed such wry humor in many of her letters. In a note to Maurice Sendak she says that now that he had written Where the Wild Things Are *he no longer needed her comments of "dopiness" like "beautiful job." Ursula used her humor to spur her authors on. She wrote a simple four word letter to Crosby Bonsall, "Where is the book?" and then proceeded to send one letter at a time over a week with the same request translated into five languages.*

Ursula's most enduring quality was her unique ability to relate to children. After reading the letters and dozens of examples of her child-like wonder, I inferred that she was truly talented at spotting what delights children. Every once in a while she willingly published a book other publishers rejected and it would become a hit. She wrote " It is always the adults we have to contend with—most children under ten will react creatively to the best work of a truly creative person" (Marcus, p. 168). She believed in kids: " . . . how hard we look for creative talent to present to children—most of whom are creative themselves" (p. 265).

Reading these letters took some work. Often I had to infer what happened between letters, or who the author was, or if the author was being wooed, encouraged, or scolded. But most of all I enjoyed piecing together clues about this amazingly talented woman.

I learned she was humorous, a good friend, and that her genius will live on in her books.

I also reflected on the way inferring forces students to read between the lines to comprehend and the importance of teaching them to infer as they read.

📖 *Your Reflections on Inferring*

- *Over the course of a week, notice how you use inferring to comprehend what you are reading? How do you use inferring when reading fiction, or nonfiction? What happens when you know a great deal about a topic or you know very little? How does inferring help you then?*

- *What kinds of clues help you infer? How do you use the text to infer? How do you use your own prior knowledge to infer?*

- *Do you ever read and NOT infer? When? Or is it impossible to read without inferring?*

- *How does inferring work in conjunction with other reading strategies like questioning and predicting?*

- *What does it mean to "read between the lines"?*

- *How does inferring make reading more interesting? Give an example from a book you are reading.*

- *Make note of a few examples of inferring from your own reading to share with your students.*

Examples of inferring in your reading . . .

Examples of inferring from your reading to share with students . . .

References

Hansen, J. (1981). The effects of inference training and practice on young children's reading comprehension. *Reading Research Quarterly 16,* 391–417.

Hansen, J., & Pearson, P. D. (1983). An instructional study: Improving the inferential comprehension of good and poor fourth grade readers. *Journal of Educational Pschology, 75,* 821–829.

McKoon, G., & Ratcliff, R. (1992). Inference during reading. *Psychological Review, 99,* 440–466.

Questioning

> "Good readers engage in self-questioning before, during, and after reading to monitor their own comprehension and to integrate readings with prior knowledge (Cooper, 1993)." **Linda Hoyt**, *in* Snapshots, *p. 16.*
>
> "Proficient readers understand how asking questions deepens their comprehension; proficient readers are aware that as they hear others' questions, new ones are inspired in their own minds." **Ellin Keene**, *in* Mosaic of Thought, *p. 119.*

Thoughts on Questioning

"Can we ask each other questions first, Mrs. Oczkus?"

That is the request I often hear as I work with students to improve their questioning techniques. Children enjoy and welcome the opportunity to ask questions. This shouldn't be so surprising to us since they are naturally curious. Each of my own children went through that super inquisitive phase of toddlerhood when they asked a constant string of "Why" questions to the point of driving me crazy.

Students enter our school doors full of questions and instead of encouraging and deepening those questions, schools require answers and the teacher is the one doing most of the asking. Like those question-filled toddlers, good readers constantly and very naturally ask questions throughout the reading process. Our job is to encourage and build on student's innate sense of wonder.

Think of the questioning classroom as a laboratory of inquiry or a place where students' questions are valued, treasured, and explored. One sixth-grade teacher I know puts inquiry into action. She posts and fills a gigantic bulletin board with colorful sentence strips loaded with student-generated questions about Egypt. Each day as the students learn more, they add more questions and discuss answers to the multitude of inquiries. Another friend of mine, a second grade teacher, uses a wall-sized "Our Questions" chart to display and keep track of students' questions about insects during their spring science unit. The small scientists add their wonders, confusions, and understandings to the kid-accessible chart. The result? Their questions drive the unit and deepen their understanding!

How Does Questioning Help Students Comprehend?

Proficient readers ask a variety of questions before, during, and after reading (Cooper, 1993). When students pose their own questions they show more improvement in comprehension than students who simply answer the teacher's questions (Singer & Donlan, 1982). Self-questioning before reading peaks the reader's interest and sets the purpose for reading. During reading the reader may ask a variety of clarifying and predicting questions that propel the reading forward like *What will happen next? What is he doing? I don't understand why . . . Why is the main character feeling that way?* After reading, the reader may wonder what would happen if there were another chapter or sequel. He may question the theme or important or controversial issues brought out in the reading. Throughout the reading, the reader may wonder about the author's craft, style, and choice of content (Keene & Zimmerman, 1997).

Questioning Works in Concert With Other Strategies

Questioning works in conjunction with other good reader comprehension strategies. When students predict, they naturally transition to asking questions about the material. As they work their way through the reading, questioning goes hand-in-hand with monitoring comprehension as the reader seeks clarification. After reading, the reader naturally asks questions as he evaluates how he did as a reader or an important issue or theme brought out in the book.

For example before reading the book *The Great Kapok Tree* (Cherry, 1990), the students may ask after a preview of the illustrations, "*What is the man doing in the rainforest? Why does he want to cut down the tree? How did he get there? What are the animals saying to him?*" As the students formulate their predictions about what the man will do in the rainforest, they are also asking a multitude of questions about the story line. During reading, they continue to ask whether the man will cut down the tree or not and they formulate questions about each of the animals that come to whisper in his ear. They may wonder if he is dreaming. After reading as they summarize and reflect on the reading, they develop new questions, such as "*Why did the man leave the rainforest? What will happen to the tree?*" They may even evaluate issues surrounding saving the rainforest. They may even discover that there are not clear-cut correct answers to all of their questions. Questioning is the thread that pulls readers through the text by keeping them interested, while working in concert with all of the other reading strategies to deepen comprehension.

Teaching Questioning

Students can be taught to ask good questions as they read with the goal of improving their compre-

hension (Palincsar & Brown, 1984). When you model wonder questions, different types of questions, and how to answer our questions, you are scaffolding the "how tos" of good reading. By going beyond the list of questions in the teacher's guide and allowing students to ask the questions, comprehension is enhanced and students are taught to learn.

The Magic of Wonder

In the past few years I started using the word "wonder" to facilitate questioning in my classroom teaching. For some reason when we ask students to record what they are wondering rather than what "questions" they have, we get more. They seem to jump into the task easier and with less intimidation. When they don't have to worry about starting with a certain "question word" or whether it is a "good question" or not, they are freed to wonder with joy and curiosity.

Many teachers are recognizing the magic of the word wonder (Hoyt, 1998 ; McLaughlin & Allen, 2002) and are also finding that students often generate more questions when they begin with "I wonder . . .". When I asked third grade students in Mrs. Jimenez's class to give me their wonders before reading *Whales* (DuTemple, 1999) they generated quite a list. They wondered how whales take care of their young and why they migrated. They wondered how whales communicated with each other and what they feed on. The" I wonder" frame prompted many interesting child-centered discussions throughout the book. The word wonder often frees student thinking and promotes the magic of learning.

Types of Questions to Model

If asking questions promotes thoughtful reading, then what types of questions do good readers ask? Box 5.1 outlines types of questions, the purpose of those questions, and some examples of the language readers may use in those questions. As you model, you can choose various types of questions to use in think-alouds and mini lessons with a variety of reading materials. Students can work with partners and cooperative groups to create various types of questions and answers. They should include both questions that can be answered in the text and those that require inferences or their use of text clues and their prior knowledge.

Box 5.1. Questioning in Your Classroom

Type of Question	Purpose	Examples of Question Words
Predicting questions	Set purpose for reading and helps spur reader on to find out what happens	What, When, Where, Why, How, Might, Who, Where
Clarifying questions	Help reader monitor comprehension and clarify points of misunderstanding	Who, What, How, When, Where, Why, Can, Does
Wonder questions	Instead of a formal question	I wonder when . . . why . . . how . . . who . . . what, where, if . . .
Author's Craft	Readers explore the author's craft, style, content, or format. (Keene & Zimmerman, 1997)	Why did the author . . . ? How did the author . . . ? What else would the author . . . ?
Teacher Questions -main idea -important details -sequence questions -cause and effect questions -literal questions	If a teacher gives a test on this material, what types of questions might he/she ask?	Who, What, When, Where, Why, How, Tell . . . Explain . . . Give . . . What if . . .
Higher Order Questions/ Inferential Evaluative	These questions require that the students use text information combined with their own synthesis of ideas to come up with a logical answer.	How come . . . Should . . . Could . . . Would . . . What if . . . Do you think . . . ? How do you know . . . ? Why . . . ?

Answering Questions

Try asking students to contribute their constant questions about the reading material to a class question chart. Choose a few questions each day to model and discuss how to answer. Models and discuss strategies for answering questions including rereading, skimming and scanning, using text and illustration clues, and inferring by using one's own background knowledge or experiences along with text clues.

Box 5.2 shows how good readers use questioning before, during, and after reading. You can use these guidelines to help you present and model mini-lessons on the role of questioning while reading.

Questioning

Box 5.2. Teaching Questioning

Using Questioning Before Reading	Using Questioning During Reading	Using Questioning After Reading
Self-questioning I wonder . . . What do I think I will learn? Who, What, When, Where, Why, How? What is this about? What do I know?	**Self-questioning** I wonder . . . How come . . . Who, What, When, Where, Why, How? I don't understand why . . . I'd like to talk about . . .	**Self-questioning** I still wonder . . . I am wondering now Who, What, When, Where, Why, How? I still don't understand why . . . . How come . . . Why did? My questions about . . . were answered.
Questions for the author What is the author trying to do? (entertain, persuade, inform)	**Questions for the author** I would like to ask the author about . . . Content—Why did the author include . . . Style—Why did he/she write this way? Theme—How did he/she want me to learn? How did the author want me to feel?	**Questions for the author** I would like to ask the author about: • Content • Style • Theme
Teacher Questions What does the teacher want me to get out of this reading? Who . . . . What . . . . When . . . . Where . . . . Why . . . . How	**Teacher Questions** What questions might my teacher expect me to answer now? The teacher might ask about • main ideas • theme, message • important details • sequence of events • cause and effect questions • compare ____ and ____ • rate ____	**Teacher Questions** The teacher might ask about: • main ideas • theme, message • important details • sequence of events • cause and effect question • compare ____ and ____ • rate ____

Questioning

Questioning Classroom Vignettes

Primary Vignette/Guided Reading and Research

The sweaty second graders file into the room after the two o'clock recess. During "late bird" time half of the class has gone home and Mrs. Osborne divides the remaining students into two guided reading groups. One group is engaged in smart work at their desks (Susan Page), which includes rereading an anthology story and filling out a story map, sorting spelling words, and reading a poem. She calls the other group to her kidney shaped guided reading table to begin a unit on whales. The day before the entire class built a "What We Already Know About Whales" chart so today she moves them to questioning and wondering about whales.

The students eagerly gather at the table ready to dive into their first whale book. "Today, you are researchers. Our topic is whales and before we begin reading several books about whales, we are going to brainstorm our questions," says Mrs. Osborne. She passes out the first whale book, *Whales* (Short & Bird, 1997) and asks the students to take a One-Minute Book Look (page 42) to assist them as they think about what they wonder about whales.

She passes out two self-stick notes to each student and invites them to record two wonderings or questions about whales. Each student shares their ideas aloud and Mrs. Osborne places their self-stick question notes on a piece of construction paper.

"What do whales eat?" asks Billy.

"How far do whales swim?" adds Belinda.

"How many fish do they eat?" wonders Sam.

As each student contributes his/her question, Mrs. Osborne asks if that question goes with or could be grouped with a similar question. After all have shared, she rearranges the questions to form three clusters of questions. She leads the group in naming a category for each set of questions. They end up with a three-column chart with headings and the student self-stick notes clustered in the appropriate columns.

What Whales Eat	What Whales Do	Whales Bodies

(self stick notes underneath each category)

Mrs. Osborne tells the group that they will use the chart and their questions to guide their research in the weeks to come. Next, they preview the cover of the book and first five pages. She asks them to think about which of the questions might be answered on these pages. The group consensus is that this section of text will give them information about whale bodies since the next headings say "Physical Features" and "Size." After reading silently, and then again as partners, the group looks to the chart and their questions about whales' bodies as they answer some of their questions. She records their answers on the chart.

"How big are whales? I read that they can be as big as 98 feet!" informs Adam.

By using student questions to guide their reading, Mrs. Osborne, will show students how to read across several texts to continue to add answers to the chart.

Questioning

The little researchers are asking big questions about whales and learning that their questions matter!

Intermediate Vignette: I Know . . . I See . . . I Wonder . . . Content Area Reading/ Whole Class/Cooperative

I am visiting the sixth graders at Epiphany School and for our first lesson together, I decide to use the fascinating nonfiction book, *Mummies and Their Mysteries* (1999) by Charlotte Wilcox. I begin by telling the students that good readers wonder before, during, and after reading. As I hold up the book, I ask the group to think about what they already know about Mummies. After allowing students to talk among themselves at their tables for a minute or two, I call on various students to share.

"Mummies are dead."

"Mummies are old."

"They are wrapped in white gauze and are in Egypt."

I tell the students that as I look through the illustrations in the book I am only going to read the captions and headings. I begin to model by thinking aloud what I see and what I am wondering.

"I see a guy on the front who has dark skin and is obviously dead, but I wonder why he is considered a mummy. I wonder what happened to him." I continue wondering my way through the first few pages of text." On pages 6 and 7, I see the heading, "What is A Mummy?" and I see a little Arctic ground squirrel that was naturally mummified when it froze long ago. I wonder how freezing causes an animal to become a mummy." I quickly jot down the page number, what I see, and what I am wondering.

Next, I ask the totally engaged sixth graders (see why I like this book so much!) to open their books and to turn to the next two pages, discuss with a partner what they see, and come up with a wonder to share. Many hands go up when I call on students to share their wonders. After asking each table to review the directions, I pass out the I Know . . . I See . . . I Wonder . . . sheets and students spend the next fifteen minutes hungrily pouring over the sometimes gory pages describing what they see and their wonders. They know to go ahead and read the book when they have completed at least ten wonders.

While the students busy themselves with wondering, recording, and reading, I call a mixed ability group of six students to read with me for ten minutes. Together we discuss our wonders for the first chapter of the book and after they read the pages silently, we return to their wonders to see if the text answered them. We also make a quick list of what we are wondering now.

Not all of the students in the class are finished reading the text, but I signal them and ask them to share some of their wonders and ideas. "How does wondering help you when you read?" I ask them to reflect on their thinking. One student responds,

"Wondering keeps me interested in the book."

By asking students to take their time studying nonfiction text features and wondering about the content, they enjoy the experience, interact with the text, and remember what they have read. After all, isn't wondering what children are so good at naturally?

I Know . . . I See . . . I Wonder . . .

Objective: Students preview illustrations in a text and describe what they know about the topic, what they see, and what they wonder based on the illustration clues.

Materials: Any text fiction or nonfiction, the I know, I see, I wonder form

Introduce/Model the Strategy

- Tell students that good readers ask questions throughout the reading process. Today you will model how to use prior knowledge and "wondering" as a way to focus on the text and ask questions before reading.

- Using the cover of a book, tell students you are going to think about what you know about the topic of the book. Let students know that by tapping into prior knowledge, a reader can understand the book better.

- Write a brief statement or two about what you know about the topic of the book.

- Turn to the first page of the text. Describe what you see in the headings and captions or illustrations and chapter title. Tell students "As I slowly study page one, I see . . . ."

- Model how to use what you see on the page to wonder something about the text. "I see . . . and I wonder if . . . I wonder how . . . I wonder why."

- Write the page number, what you see, and what you wonder on a chart, overhead transparency, or white board.

- Continue modeling by studying each page as you describe what you see and wonder.

Guide the Strategy/Cooperative Groups or Pairs

- Ask students to work cooperatively to brainstorm other information they may know about the topic you just modeled. Students can fill in their I know . . . portions of their sheets (p. 122).

- Invite students to assist you by offering *I see and I wonder* statements as you continue turning pages in your book to see and wonder.

- Stop to ask tables or pairs to write their wonders on strips and post those on the chart. Students can also record wonders on their individual sheets.

- Encourage students to work independently as they write wonders for content area reading and their self-selected books.

- Return to wonders after reading and verbally discuss which ones were answered.

Box 5.3. Model—Practice—Apply the Strategy in Different Classroom Structures

Guided Reading	Literature Circles
Make a group chart. Students quickly record one I Know and one I Wonder statement on the notes to place on the chart. After reading they see if they found out their wondering statements. Students can initial responses. Save charts and note growth.	Each member of the group writes an I know, I See, and I Wonder statement to add to a chart. They can write on self-stick notes. All members add to their individual sheets. P.122
English Language Learners	Independent Work
Meet with English language learners before reading to guide them through the illustrations using wonder statements.Discuss vocabulary and concepts. Ask students what they see and know first, then ask ELL students to wonder.	Before reading a social studies chapter or other nonfiction material, students work independently to fill in an I Know, I See, I Wonder sheet.

Reflect on the Strategy/Assess the Strategy

- Ask students to discuss and reflect on the I Know, I See, I Wonder strategy helps them to understand what they read.

- Do students use the text clues and illustrations along with other text features to create wonder statements that relate directly to the text?

If students are having trouble, or are just filling in random wonders that don't come from the text clues, pull a small strategy group to provide more modeling and practice the technique.

- Ask students to tell how wondering helped them to understand the reading.

- Refer to the assessment materials in the Appendix page 223–233 for further assessment information and tips.

Questioning

I Know… I See …. I Wonder…

Look at the cover of the book. What do you know about the topic?

I Know…..

1. I know Some spiders are ponzin.

2. I know Spiders have eight legs.

3. I know Spiders make webs.

Before reading look at all of the illustrations and headings.
What do you see ? What do you wonder?

Page	I See…	I Wonder….
4-5	I see a un tarantula and on diagram	I wonder if the tarantula is the biggest spider.
8-9	I see a wolf spider in his house.	I wonder how spiders make ther houses?
12-13	I see a spider makeing a web.	I wonder how spiders make diy web and sticky webs.
19	I see a black widow is cauching a lizard in his web.	I wonder How a black widow could eat a lizard.
22-23	I see a trap Door spider.	I wonder if a Black widow spider is a Boy or girl.

Read the text. Watch for your wonders. After reading, go back to your wonders to see if you found them out! How did wondering before reading help you as you read the material?

Spiders by Esther cullen

I Know... I See... I Wonder...

Look at the cover and a few pages of the book. What do you know about the topic?

I Know...

1. I know _____

2. I know _____

3. I know _____

Before reading look at all of the illustrations and headings.

What do you see? What do you wonder?

Page	I See...	I Wonder...
	I see	I wonder
	I see	I wonder
	I see	I wonder
	I see	I wonder
	I see	I wonder

Read the text. Watch for your wonders. After reading, go back to your wonders to see if you found them out! How did wondering before reading help you as you read the material?

Question Sort

Objective: Students generate questions before reading. Then they sort their questions into categories. After reading, they answer their questions.
Materials: Paper or cards, or the Question Sort form to write questions on, and any reading material.

Introduce/Model the Strategy

- Let students know that today you will show them how to categorize or sort their questions before reading a text.

- Categorizing questions before reading nonfiction helps students remember what they read and is a way to organize information for report writing. Before reading fiction, question sorting keeps students focused on the story.

- Students should have copies of the same text.

- Model and think aloud as you study illustrations, heading, and text features to ask questions before reading.

- Write each of your questions on self-stick notes and show how you might group the questions into logical categories. Label the categories.

- Tell students that as you read you'll watch to see if the text answers your questions.

- Read the text to or with students. Model how to refer to each question category and verbally answer each question. Students may write answers on the back.

- On another day, model how you might use the categories, questions and their respective answers to write some paragraphs for a report.

Guide the Strategy/Cooperative Groups or Pairs

- Students work individually, in pairs, or groups to preview text and write questions on cards or self-stick notes.

- Allow students to share their questions. Post questions and work together to decide on logical categories for the questions.

- Students read the text alone, in groups, or with teacher support. After reading they answer questions verbally. Groups or pairs can choose categories to focus and report on.

- If you are teaching report writing, students work in teams to write answers to each question in a given category. Then they use assigned question categories to write brief paragraphs. The text headings may provide natural categories for questions. Display all paragraphs and vote on a logical order. Guide the class and together, write transitions, beginning and concluding paragraphs.

Box 5.4. Model—Practice—Apply the Strategy in Different Classroom Structures

Guided Reading	Literature Circles
Students work in a teacher-led small group to generate, categorize, and answer questions. Assign categories of questions to pairs of students to research. Write a report as a group by combining answers to questions into paragraphs, adding transitions, an opening and a closing.	All of the literature circles participate in a jigsaw. (Kagen, 1989) Each home group of six students divides into pairs who take a third of the material. The pairs leave their home group to generate questions and read their chunk of material in an expert group. The pairs return to their home groups and share their findings.
English Language Learners	**Independent Work**
Meet with second language learners prior to conducting the lesson with the rest of the class. Introduce unfamiliar vocabulary and concepts using selection illustrations, drama, and other concrete examples including realia. Assist students in creating questions.	Students can work independently to come up with a certain number of questions and categorize those before reading a text.

Reflect on the Strategy/Assess the Strategy

- Ask students to reflect on asking and sorting questions before reading. How does this process help them understand what they read?

- Are students asking questions that use clues from the text?

- Are students creating categories that make sense?

- Are students writing questions that are easily answered from information in the text?

- Are students writing inferential questions that require text clues and the student's background knowledge to answer?

- Can students answer their questions after reading about the text?

- Meet with students who are having trouble in small groups to model further. Focus on one type of question at a time. (Who questions, what questions, how questions, etc.) Some students may have difficulty asking inferential questions and may only ask literal ones.

- Model and guide students to ask and then sort literal and inferential type questions. Encourage students to use would, should, could, and why to move to inferential questioning.

- Refer to the assessment materials in the Appendix page 223–234 for further assessment information and tips.

Question Sort

1. Before reading, look at the title and cover of the book. Write at least two questions you have about the book.

2. Preview the text before reading to write four more questions.
   Nonfiction—look at all headings and illustrations
   Fiction—look at all illustrations, table of contents, chapter titles, or skim and scan over a few pages and use key words to think of questions.

3. Cut your questions out and sort them into categories. Paste your questions in categories on another paper. Label the categories.
   My Categories for questions are (list as many as you need to)

   _____

   _____

   _____

4. Read the text. Watch for answers in your reading.

5. After reading, discuss which questions were most helpful in understanding the text. Tell how these questions helped you.

   _____

   _____

   _____

*Question Words to Use
Who, What, When, Where, Why, and How

Question:	Question:	Question:
Question:	Question:	Question:

Questioning

Question While You Read

Objective: While students are reading, they watch for portions of text that they could use to formulate questions. After reading they pose their questions to classmates.

Materials: Nonfiction text or fiction texts, self-stick notes, Question While You Read form.

Introduce/Model the Strategy

- Tell students that besides watching out for their predictions as they read, good readers often think about what kinds of questions a teacher might ask on a test. Some of those questions can be answered in the text and others require inferring.

- Ask students what words are used at the beginning of most questions. Review question words: who, what, when, where, why, and how. Using a text the class is familiar with, model a question using each of the question words. Also include could, would, and should and expect students to also tell why.

- Read a portion of text aloud. Stop and tell the students that you are deciding which question word you will use to go with the text you just read.

- Reread the portion of text and tell students that rereading is a valuable skill that will help you remember what you read so that you can formulate a question about the text. Say " This paragraph, page, sentence, was about ____ so I think I will ask a question starting with _____."

- Write questions on sentence strips or a chart.

- Continue reading, formulating questions, and answers. Model how to read a text with a certain question word in mind. Example: I am looking for a place where I can ask a how question, or a why question.

- Model how to reread and ask a main idea question (Lubliner, 2001).

Guide the Strategy/Cooperative Groups or Pairs

- Reread a text together and ask the students to help you think of a question or questions they could ask about the text. Volunteers ask their questions of the group.

- Continue guiding students through several paragraphs by reading silently, then aloud, and then asking questions together.

- Guide tables or pairs to reread portions of a text the class is reading to formulate questions. You may wish to assign question words to each group.

- Students share their questions with the class. Students must know the answers to their questions.

Box 5.5. Model—Practice—Apply the Strategy in Different Classroom Structures

Guided Reading	Literature Circles
Prior to reading pass out self-stick notes and ask students to be on the lookout for places in the text where they could ask questions as they read silently. Require that they read once looking for the question place, and a second time to formulate the question and answer. Students write their questions on self-stick notes and pose to the group. They initial their questions. Save as documentation and show growth in question formulation over time.	Each member of a literature circle asks a question of the group. Yes or no questions are not allowed! Students attempt to ask questions that illicit discussion and inferring, or questions that are not answered directly in the text. The student asking questions must know the answers with clues they used to infer the answer.
Cross-Age Tutors	English Language Learners
Buddies stop at various points in a text to ask questions. The older buddy plans his/her questions ahead of time but allows the younger buddy to also create some questions about the text.	Model for ELL students using question words. Work in pairs and use pretend microphones (their fists or paper tubes) when questioning. Act out answers when appropriate or support answers with visuals from the text.

Reflect on the Strategy/Assess the Strategy

- Ask students to reflect on question formulation.

- How does asking questions during and after reading help them comprehend and remember what they read?

- Are students only asking detail questions?

- Are they asking relevant, logical questions?

- When prompted, can students formulate main idea questions?

- Can students ask inferential level questions that require them to use text information plus their own knowledge to infer an answer?

- If students are having trouble moving beyond detail questions, provide more support and modeling in a small group setting. Read smaller chunks of text and stop, think aloud, model how to create a question using the text information.

- Refer to the assessment materials in the appendix page 223-234 for further assessment information and tips.

Question While You Read

As you read, think about what questions you can ask your group. Reread to think of more questions. Try to not write questions that can be answered with yes or no. Cut the strips apart and put into an envelope. Trade with a partner or group member. Answer each other's questions.

Who . . . ?
What . . . ?
Where . . . ?
When . . . ?
Why . . . ?
How . . . ?
What if . . . ?
Would you have . . . why or why not?
Compare two of the main characters _____ and _____. How are they alike and different?
What is the theme of the story _____? (ask another question about theme)
What if . . .
Do you agree with _____? Why or why not?

Question Match
Classroom Vignettes

Intermediate Example/Question Match with Literature Circles

Miss Anderson's fifth grade literature circles are meeting today. As the students settle in to their agreed upon meeting spots, the children begin taking turns with their respective roles of discussion director, connector, word wizard, passage picker, and artist (Daniels, 1994). Ozzie is the word wizard in his group and has created a question match game for the group to play with the novel they just read, *Dave at Night* (Levine, 1999). He asks each student to think of a question and instead of reading the question, he asks that they read the answer and the other students guess the question that goes with the answer.

Bryan begins with his answer, " Heatless House of Bloom, Hated Home for Boys, Hopeless House for Beggars, and HHB." Lisa raises her hand and replies, " What are some nicknames the boys in the orphanage had for the Hebrew Home for Boys?"

"Right," confirms Bryan, smiling.

Once students learn to generate questions and answers for a text, the possibilities for game-like activities are endless. In many intermediate classrooms teachers use students' questions and answers to play spin-offs on various television game shows. By practicing their ability to create all kinds of questions and answers, they are developing important study skills that improve comprehension. Maybe they'll become so informed they won't need to "phone a friend" for answers!

Primary Example/Question Match Center

During guided reading Mrs. Sharp builds students literacy skills and independence by providing opportunities for her second graders to read alone and with partners. She also has several centers set up where students respond to literature and participate in word work. Today the *Question Match* center is open and four students are busy rereading *The Keeping Quilt* by Patricia Polaco (1998).

"I want to ask why did Patricia Polaco talk about her great grandma wearing big boots?" says Rebecca.

"I have a question: how was life in New York different from their life in Russia?" adds Ava.

The girls continue paging throughout the book creating a variety of questions that begin with who, what, when, where, why, and how questions for their question match game.

Today they decide to make their game for the overhead projector so they write the questions on the transparency of the Question Match form page 136. Juan and Lee, who are also working at the center, decide to create a game board and use their stack of question and answer cards for other students to draw from and match as they make their way around the game board they designed.

When Mrs. Sharp's students create games in the Question Match center, the students enjoy finding meaningful ways to practice question formulation. Ultimately, all of this questioning improves their comprehension as they focus more closely on the reading material. The goal is for students to ask a variety of questions as they read on their own to enhance their understanding and engagement with the reading material.

Questioning

Question Match

Adapted from Ozzie Allenberg

Objective: Students create questions for classmates after reading. The class plays a matching game with answers and questions.

Materials: The Question Match sheet and reading material.

Introduce/Model the Strategy

- Tell students that as they read they should be thinking about several types of questions. Questioning while reading can help you understand the text better and prepare for tests. In addition to thinking about teacher questions, good readers also have their own wonder questions and inferential questions that sometimes can't be answered directly in the text. Today they will have the opportunity to ask and answer questions they create to help themselves remember and understand what they have read.

- Choose a text that the class has already read. The class can follow along using their copies of the text or you can put a page on the overhead projector to use as you model.

- Reread a few pages or paragraphs and think aloud as you come to portions of text where you might stop to create a question. Model questions that begin with who, what, when, where, why, and how.

- Write questions on one index card and write answers on another index card.

- Turn the cards face down or blank side out in a pocket chart and arrange in rows. Invite a student to play concentration with you. Each player turns over two cards, reads them aloud and if the cards are a matching question and answer, a match is made and the player keeps the cards. If the cards don't match, the player turns the cards face down and the next player takes a turn.

- The player with the most matches when the cards run out wins.

- In subsequent lessons, increase the level of sophistication of the questions by modeling different types of questions including main idea, detail, sequence questions, inferential, evaluative (what was best and worst) and wonder statements.

- A nice variation is to select an answer and put it on a card. When another student draws one of the answer cards, he makes up a question verbally to go with it. If he can't he forfeits the turn.

Guide the Strategy/Cooperative Groups or Pairs

- Provide students with a guided step by first modeling, then working in cooperative groups or pairs to formulate questions and answers. Divide up the types of questions and the pages. Tables or pairs combine their cards for Concentration games.

Box 5.6. Model–Practice–Apply the Strategy in Different Classroom Structures

Guided Reading	Literature Circles
Each student in the guided reading group creates one question and one answer. Take turns sharing questions. Use cards later in a center for Concentration.	The discussion director can create a question match game for the group to play that is based on the text that the group read.
English Language Learners Second language students illustrate their questions and answers. Model for ELL students questions that require an inference to answer. Guide them in creating questions that are inferential and that require deeper thinking. Use why and how as question starters.	**Independent Work** Students create question match cards to study for a social studies or science text. They exchange cards with a partner.

Reflect on the Strategy/Assess the Strategy

- Use student cards as assessment tools. Do students only ask detail questions? Do they include main idea, who, what, where, when, why, and how questions? Do they include inferential questions with correct answers and evaluative questions?

- What happens when a student includes a wonder question?

- Ask students to reflect on Question Match and how it helps them understand what they read.

- Do students use text language to formulate questions? Save student questions occasionally for portfolios to show growth.

- Work with students in a small group setting to guide those who are having difficulty. Formulate one type of question at a time with a group. Example: Today create a question match using only who questions.

- Refer to the assessment materials in the Appendix page 223–234 for further assessment information and tips.

Question:	Answer :
Who is Daemon?	The creature that represents a person's feelings in the Golden Compass. Tell how.
Question: Who are the Gyptians?	Answer: The Gyptians are a group of people who travel around. Tell what they do.
Question: What is a Fire Hurler?	Answer: A Fire Hurler is a dangerous weapon. Draw it.
Question: Who is Lyra?	Answer: Lyra is the main character in the story. Tell one thing Lyra did.
Question: What is a Bivouac?	Answer: A Bivouac is a temporary shelter or settlement. Describe one. Would you like to live there? Why or why not?
Question: Who is Farder Coam?	Answer: Farder Coam is the person who takes care of Lyra when they are on the expedition. Tell how Farder Coam takes care of Lyra.

Question Match Example

Ozzie, a fifth grader, created this question match to use with his literature circle when they read *The Golden Compass* by Phillip Pullman (1995), New York: Knopf. The game can be played as a concentration matching game or game show with points. You can also ask students to tell why, how, what if, or to draw as a way of extending their thinking.

Questioning

Question Match
Adapted from Ozzie Allenberg

1. Reread the selection, story, chapter, or article. Create questions on the question cards and answers to match. Cut apart the questions and answers.

2. Meet with a partner or group and mix cards up and place them face down in rows. Take turns turning over two cards. If you get a question–answer match, go again. If not, turn the cards over and the next player goes.

Question:	Answer:	Question:	Answer:
Question:	Answer:	Question:	Answer:
Question:	Answer:	Question:	Answer:
Question:	Answer:	Question:	Answer:

Teachers As Readers

Reflecting on Our Experiences as Adult Readers

When we question as readers, we are the ultimate super sleuths hunting for logical clues in the text. Our students need to understand that good readers ask questions throughout the reading process. The questioning strategy helps keep us engaged and motivated to finish the text.

My Reflection on Questioning

I have to admit I usually don't like to read mysteries. I'm not really sure why they don't appeal to me. But recently I saw an interesting looking new Mommy-Track Mystery book on display in a bookstore and couldn't resist especially when the bookstore owner gave it such a powerful endorsement. The sales pitch he delivered included such inviting descriptors as "light," "fun," and "page turner" (isn't that what they always say about mysteries?) and he informed me that the books by this local mommy turned author usually fly off the shelf. The big plus that put this book into my basket, was that Ayelet Waldman is a Bay Area writer from Berkeley, which is about fifteen minutes from my home. I just love reading works written by authors who are regular folks who probably see the same sunsets I do and sit in the same traffic jams. So, that is how I ended up with The Big Nap *by Ayelet Waldman (2001). It sort of chose me.*

I can't think of a better genre than mystery for focusing on questioning. Actually, mysteries are great for inferring too. It is impossible to separate our questions from the inferring we do to answer them. But as I read this mystery I tried to focus on the questions that constantly popped into my mind. As mature readers we self-question in all of our reading, but it is as though someone turns up the volume on the question dial when we read a mystery. From the moment I picked up The Big Nap *I began to question. Who is taking the nap? The mom? The kid? Why would a stay-at-home mom*

get involved in a mystery? What has happened to the babysitter? Why has she vanished?

Of course the questions continue as I read. I have a multitude of questions about the mom turned detective character. Why is this sleep-deprived mom involving herself in investigating this disappearance? Is she nuts? She must be tired of folding socks and wiping noses. Maybe she misses her old job. Why would she drag her kids with her to investigate and put them in danger too? Of course I am wondering about the mystery story line. I wonder if the boyfriend is responsible for the babysitter's disappearance I would like to know what the sister knows about the disappearance. Has the girl run off or has she been murdered? I really wish I could question the author in person. I would ask her where she gets her ideas for her mysteries. I notice the book jacket says that she really is a public defender turned stay-at-home mom and now author. Are her books composite ideas based on cases she has worked on or seen? Her funny style is so enjoyable. What inspired her to write mysteries like these with such rich humor and satire?

A multitude of questions drive us to read a mystery to the bitter end. I have to confess that this time I thoroughly enjoyed the ride!

Questioning

Your Reflections on Questioning

- *As you read, notice which genres or topics that require you to question more.*

- *What kinds of questions do you have about the content?*

- *What are you wondering about the characters?*

- *Notice how questioning sets a purpose for reading and keeps you interested in the material. When you find the reading is boring, what happens to your questioning? Do you stop?*

- *How do you use questioning with other strategies such as prediction and inferring?*

- *What kinds of questions do you have for the author? About content? About his/her style?*

- *What types of questions do you have before and during reading?*

- *After reading what are you questioning or wondering?*

Examples of questioning in your reading

Examples of questioning from your reading to share with students

References

Beck, I. L., McKeown, M. G., Worthy, J., Sandora, C. A., & Kucan, L. (1996). Question the author: A year-long classroom implementation to engage students with text. *Elementary School Journal, 96*, 385–414.

Rosenshine, B., Meister, C., & Chapman, S. (1996). Teaching students to generate questions: A review of the intervention studies. *Review of Educational Research, 66 (2)*, 181–221.

Singer, J., & Donlan, E. (1982). Active comprehension: Problem-solving schema with question generation for comprehension of complex short stories. *Reading Research Quaterly, 17*, 166–168.

> *"Students cannot read for meaning until they can monitor the things they do to make sense of text and maintain comprehension – before, during, and after reading, yes, but especially as they read."* **Regie Routman**, *in* Reading Essentials, *p. 124.*
>
> *"Readers create images to form unique interpretations, clarify thinking, draw conclusions, and enhance understanding."* **Debbie Miller**, *in* Reading with Meaning, *p. 81.*

Thoughts on Monitoring Comprehension

When I was in elementary school the various jobs we were assigned in class had the word "monitor" in the title like the chalkboard monitor, the pencil monitor, or the paper monitor. Monitor in that context meant keeping track of or being in charge of something. Monitoring comprehension is, in essence, also a form of being in charge, or keeping track of one's own comprehension and taking responsibility for keeping it in working condition.

Many students we work with read through text without interacting with it or without monitoring whether they are understanding what they read or not. I tell students that good readers constantly check their comprehension monitoring gauge as they read. Sometimes the gauge ranges anywhere from "I totally get it" to "I am lost" or "Somewhere in between." Once the reader realizes there is a problem, the reader should identify what that problem is and how to fix it.

Students need to know that it is quite natural for all readers to encounter texts that present problems

for them. I tell students that sometimes if I am reading a text, I often read the same paragraph over and over because I realize I am lost. I reread the confusing parts and try to figure out what is going on in the text. If I still don't get it, I may read on and try to make sense that way. By modeling for students using your own reading confusions as examples, you can help students feel more secure in admitting when they don't understand a text.

This chapter includes a variety of lessons that offer suggestions for helping students more effectively keep track of and repair their own comprehension. Fix up strategies may include rereading, summarizing, reading on, strategies for clarifying difficult words, or talking to a friend. I have included visualizing as a monitoring strategy for helping students monitor their comprehension. This makes sense to me as I have noticed in my own reading that when I am not able to create a visual image, my comprehension falls apart a bit and I need to reread or read on to begin building a mental picture of the text again. Other sensory images also play a role in monitoring. As we read we may also imagine smells, sounds, and even textures as the text comes alive in our minds (Keene & Zimmerman, 1997). Sensory images, along with other monitoring strategies, help readers to measure their own progress in a text.

How Does Monitoring Comprehension Help Students Comprehend?

Comprehension monitoring is a critical metacognitive strategy that involves thinking about one's own thinking. Research clearly indicates that comprehension monitoring is an important strategy that separates the good from poor readers (Paris, Wasik, & Turner, 1991). Many of the students we work with do not recognize when meaning breaks down as they read (Routman, 2003). Good readers know how they are doing as they read and they first notice problems or confusions, and then apply strategies for repairing understanding.

Monitoring involves reflecting on one's reading and asking questions like, Do I understand the author's intent here? Am I following what is happening? How am I doing as a reader? What can I do to fix this misunderstanding or confusion? Does this part fit with earlier information (Lipson, 1996)? How can I remember this information (Lipson, 1996)?

The National Reading Panel (2000) suggests that when we teach students to monitor their comprehension we teach them to be aware of what they do understand, to identify what they do not understand, and to use necessary fix-up strategies to resolve problems in comprehension. Key monitoring strategies include constant checking for understanding, identifying the portion of text that doesn't make sense, determining what is so hard or confusing about it, and finding ways to look back through the text or to read ahead to solve the break in meaning.

Checking Understanding

Throughout the reading process, before, during, and after reading a text good readers constantly ask themselves the following:
- Does this make sense?
- Do I know what is going on in the text?
- Am I getting the main ideas?
- Is there anything that I don't understand? (a word, sentence, paragraph, page, or chapter)

- Do I know this word? What does it mean? How do you pronounce it?
- Am I doing okay as a reader?
- Am I understanding what I am reading?

Teacher Regie Routman (2003) tells us that too many of the students we work with are not aware when meaning breaks down. We need to teach our students to ask themselves if they are understanding the text or not. If students experience a break in meaning, they should know how to identify the problem and how to use various strategies to fix it.

Identifying the Problem

As students read, they need to be aware of problems or confusions in their comprehension. Confusions that need clarifying may involve unfamiliar words, difficult concepts, or confusing events in the story line, or the reading may require background knowledge that doesn't match the student's experiences. Students benefit from practice in identifying the difficult portions of text or places where their comprehension is impaired (Palincsar & Brown, 1984).

When I ask students to identify which part of the text they didn't understand, they can readily come up with a word that was difficult. If I want them to begin to identify problems with understanding ideas or difficult portions of text, I usually have to model confusions first before anyone will volunteer some. I continue modeling throughout the year different types of confusions a reader may have in addition to trouble with words.

Try asking students to tell which word, sentence, paragraph, page, or even chapter is giving them the challenge. Rephrasing the difficult passage or sentence in their own words is often helpful when clarifying. (National Reading Panel, 2000) If students are having difficulty with a particular word, they tell the page number and read the sentence the word is in.

Students may use these prompts to identify problems as they read

Problems with words:
I had trouble pronouncing . . .
I don't know what . . . means.

Problems with confusing parts of text:
I didn't understand the part where . . .
I can't figure out . . .
It doesn't make sense . . .

By identifying the problem spot in the text, students can then begin to employ the strategies that help them solve the difficulty.

Fixing the Problem

Often we use more than one strategy to repair comprehension. We may summarize what has happened so far, or tap into our expertise, or tap into the background on the subject or genre we are reading. We may try a variety of useful fix-up strategies, such as reading on or rereading, which serves as an extremely useful strategy for repairing meaning. (Routman, 2003; National Reading Panel, 2000) I find that rereading can solve a good number of problems students are having with a text. Also, reading on to the next portion of text often solves the problem and provides the "Aha" or "Oh, I get it now" we are searching for. Sometimes talking within a literature circle or teacher-led discussion group is just what we need to clear up problems in understanding the text.

Here are some prompts that may help remind readers of stratgies to use in clarifying confusions while reading.

Strategies for Clarifying Words:
- *Reread the sentence.*
- Check word parts you know.
- Do I notice any prefixes, suffixes, or other word parts that carry meaning?
- Try sounding the word out.
- Is there another word that looks like this one?

Strategies for Clarifying Confusing Ideas:
- *Reread the confusing part.*
- Slow down.
- Reread the whole page and parts before the confusing part.
- Summarize what has happened so far.
- Think about the parts you do understand.
- Read on. Now do you get it?
- Think about what you know about . . .
- Talk to a friend, teacher, or other adult.

Visualizing/Sensory Images Help Monitor Comprehension

Making students aware of the visual images and other sensory images they are forming in their heads can be very helpful in comprehension monitoring. When a reader realizes that he isn't forming a mental image and he is losing meaning, he can slow down and reread or read on to clear up the confusion. Discussion may also help the reader finally clarify enough to begin to visualize again.

Prompts to encourage students to visualize include:
- Am I building a mental picture to go with the reading?
- What mental images can I see clearly?
- What part am I having trouble seeing?
- Are there any other sensory images that I need to imagine?
- Can I reread, read on, or talk with a friend to try to clear up the problem?

Monitoring Helps Build Comprehension

Comprehension monitoring is a strategy that involves metacognition, or thinking about one's thinking during the reading process. Students who are good at monitoring their own comprehension, know when they understand the text and when they do not. These students also know what to do to fix problems when comprehension breaks down. Monitoring is critical for understanding text and research supports teaching students to use various strategies for comprehension monitoring.

Box 6.1 will help you as you develop mini-lessons and think-alouds for helping students monitor their comprehension.

Monitoring

Box 6.1. Teaching Monitoring

Using Monitoring Before Reading	Using Monitoring During Reading	Using Monitoring After Reading
Checking Understanding Do I have enough information to make predictions? Is anything confusing to me now? **Identifying the Problem.** I don't understand what this book is about. I'm having trouble making predictions. **Strategies for Predicting.** -Preview illustrations, titles, and headings. - Think about what I already know about the topic. - I think this might be about _____because_____ -What do I think I might learn from reading this text? How do I know? What are the clues? **Get Ready to Keep Track as You Read!** How will I fix this confusion as I read? If I am still confused, I'll try to figure it out as I read and gather clues.	**Checking Understanding** Do I know what is going on in the text? Am I getting the main idea? Can I summarize? Do I have a mental image of the reading? Is there any part I don't understand? Do I need help with a word? **Identifying the Problem With a word** I had trouble pronouncing . . . I don't know what the word means. With a confusing part I didn't understand the part where . . . I don't get . . . It doesn't make sense . . . **Strategies for Clarifying a Word** - Reread the sentence - Check parts you know. - Try sounding out the word. - Does it look like another word? **Strategies for Clarifying a Part** - Reread the confusing part. - Slow down. - Read on. - Summarize what has happened. - Think about what you know about the topic. - Try visualizing again. Use your senses - Talk to a friend or adult.	**Checking Understanding** Did I . . . ? __ visualize __ summarize/tell main ideas __ understand all the words __ understand all the ideas, sentences, pages, and parts __ make connections Can I tell what the theme of the reading is? **Identifying the Problems With words** I had trouble pronouncing . . . I don't know what . . . means **With a confusing part** I didn't get . . . I didn't understand the part where . . . I'm still confused about . . . It doesn't make sense . . . **Strategies for Clarifying A Word** - Reread, reread, reread! - Check known parts. - Try sounding out the word. - Compare it to other words. **Strategies for Clarifying a Part** - Reread the confusing part. - Reread other parts around the confusing part. - Summarize. - Think about what you know. - Visualize again. Use your senses. - Talk to a friend or adult.

Super Six Comprehension Strategies: 35 Lessons and More for Reading Success by Lori Oczkus

Monitoring Classroom Vignettes

Primary Vignette/Monitoring Comprehension During A Read Aloud

After lunch the third graders slowly file into the classroom and gladly rest their heads on their desks as they listen to Mr. Gragen read aloud from chapter 12 of *The Wanderer* (Creech, 2000), a book about a family's voyage across the Atlantic to England aboard a sailboat. The book is the account of the trip as recorded by two cousins, Cody and Sopie in their personal journals.

Mr. Gragen asks the class if they remember which character wrote in his or her journal yesterday. Peter replies that he thinks it was Cody. Several other students nod in agreement while others forget to raise their hands in disagreement.

"I think we need to try the strategy, "Famous Last Words" that we have been learning to help us find an answer to this one. Who remembers how to use "Famous Last Words" (page 147) to assist you in remembering what is going on in a book?"

Fernando raises his hand and explains that "Famous Last Words" requires simply rereading the very end of yesterday's chapter to try to remember what was happening and to visualize the action. Mr. Gragen then rereads the last paragraph of chapter 11 where the group is forewarned about an upcoming bad weather.

"Who knows now which character is writing?" asks Mr. Gragen.

Most students vote for Sopie but a few holdouts refuse to agree. So, Mr. Gragen rereads more of the last page and a part where Sopie is quoting Brian. Now all hands vote for Sopie. Mr. Gragen begins to read chapter 12 written by Cody aloud to the anxious group. You'd never know that Mr. Gragen's students are learning to monitor their comprehension, as they sink comfortably into their desks and let their minds wander off into an exciting ocean voyage. By reviewing briefly yesterday's reading, the students effectively monitor their comprehension.

Intermediate Vignette/Monitoring Comprehension with A Social Studies Book

"Today we are going to create our own bookmark to help us check our understanding as we read the next lesson in the social studies book." Mrs. Black begins as she passes out the "Mark the Spot" (page) bookmark forms to fourth graders. The students get out their colored pencils and Mrs. Black uses the overhead projector and colored pen collection to model. Mrs. Black asks the class what symbols they should use for each example on the bookmark. They decide to draw a light bulb for new information, an exclamation for surprises, a question mark for questions, a smiley face for information they knew before reading, the word "Ohhh" for realizing something now, an A+ for great writing, and a chain for a connection. The students seem pleased with their newly created code.

"As I read aloud today, I am going to stop every page and go back and mark on my bookmark what I am thinking about as I read. After previewing illustrations and predicting, Mrs. Black begins to read aloud from the chapter titled, "California's Regions" (1991). She stops after a page and thinks aloud. She shares "Wow! I was surprised" after reading that Death Valley and Mount Whitney are so different but so close together." She writes the page number and example on the bookmark. After two more pages, the students work in pairs to follow the same procedure. The students especially enjoy monitoring their comprehension by using the symbols they've created.

Famous Last Words

Adapted from Jan Karels

Objective: Students will discuss, record, and summarize the last part of the text they've read to assist them in remembering what they have read and monitoring their comprehension. When they pick up a particular text again, they will also use the same "Famous Last Words" to jog their memories before they read on.

Materials: Famous Last Words sheet, and any article, book, or text

Introduce/Model the Strategy

- Ask students if they have ever picked up a book they are reading after a day or so and realize they have forgotten what was going on in the text. Assure them this happens to all readers, even adults.

- Tell students that good readers often use the last words, paragraph, or even page they read, to help them remember the story line, or main ideas before they read on.

- Model "Famous Last Words" with a chapter book or nonfiction book the class is reading. Open the book to your place in the book. Tell students that you want to remember what is going on in the story/text, so before reading you are going to try "Famous Last Words."

- Continue thinking aloud and tell students that to help you remember the story/text, you are going to read the last paragraph or other portions of the previous chapter to see if that sparks your memory. Read the last paragraph aloud. Tell how this helps you remember what you read before going on. Reread more if necessary.

- Read aloud from the next portion of text. After a few pages, tell the students before you put your bookmark in the text, you are going to quickly summarize what has just happened and reread the last few paragraphs. This quick mental summary will help you remember the story when you pick up the book again.

Guide the Strategy/Cooperative Groups or Pairs

- Ask pairs to practice "Famous Last Words" with a book/text the class is reading. Students put a bookmark in the reading material and after a period of time—overnight, after recess, or after lunch—they resume the reading.

- Pairs should review what is happening so far in the text by rereading the last paragraph or page.

- Then after reading on to a designated stopping point, they pause to summarize and write one or two last words (or a sentence) that will help them jog their memories tomorrow when they resume reading.

Box 6.2. Model—Practice—Apply the Strategy in Different Classroom Structures

Guided Reading	Literature Circles
Try "Famous Last Words" in a text that students are reading in a guided reading group. The text should be at the students' instructional levels and take several meetings to read. Model for students the "Famous Last Words" strategy using a group chart to help them monitor their comprehension throughout the reading of a given book.	The student who has the role of summarizer refers to "Famous Last Words" twice. 1. The summarizer takes a quick turn before the group reads today's text to use the "Famous Last Words" technique to discuss the very last event from yesterday's text. 2. After reading the text, the summarizer supplies the brief "Famous Last Words." All students in the group jot down a word, sentence, phrase, or drawing to remember what happened in the very last portion of text. The students should refer to these points before reading on tomorrow.
Cross-Age Tutors	**Independent Work**
Encourage older buddies to find a stopping point in a book and briefly model how to summarize. When the buddies meet again they can model how to refer to the "Famous Last Words" to remember what they have read before going on.	Students record very brief "Famous Last Words" while reading independently or with a partner using the assigned grade level reading material (use core literature, district adopted anthology, or content area reading materials).

Monitoring

Reflect on the Strategy/Assess the Strategy

- Discuss as a class what "Famous Last Words" helped to jog their memories of the reading. Did the students visualize the setting of the text again? Did they remember what was happening?

- How much text did they need to reread to reconstruct what was going on? What did students do when they couldn't summarize what happened yesterday?

- Use the "Famous Last Words" sheet and your observations to assess if students are using the last words from a text to help them remember, summarize, and monitor their comprehension.

- If students have trouble employing "Famous Last Words" for summarizing today's reading or if they don't remember their place in yesterday's text then try:

  -skimming and scanning to review even more text or to summarize today's text;

  -talking with a friend;

  -model a quick Famous Last Words summary or draw a quick sketch to summarize; or

  -reread yesterday's "Famous Last Words" and then read on for a few paragraphs. Stop to discuss where the group is in the reading.

- If you need further suggestions for assessing students' progress in monitoring comprehension, see the Appendix on page 223-234.

Famous Last Words

Adapted from Jan Karels

1. When it is time to stop reading, jot down quickly one sentence or a few words that tell what happened last in the text.
2. The next day read the "Famous Last Words" from the day before to help you remember what was going on in the book. Discuss with a partner.
3. If you need to, reread the last paragraph or page from yesterday's reading before reading on. Remember to record today's "Famous Last Words."
4. How does remembering the "last words" help you to remember what you read yesterday?

Date Book Page Last Words	Date Book Page Last Words	Date Book Page Last Words
Date Book Page Last Words	Date Book Page Last Words	Date Book Page Last Words
Date Book Page Last Words	Date Book Page Last Words	Date Book Page Last Words
Date Book Page Last Words	Date Book Page Last Words	Date Book Page Last Words

Right On Track Bookmark

Objective: Students will use a bookmark in various helpful ways to assist them in monitoring their comprehension as they read. They will identify problems in understanding words, ideas, and in visualizing and then choose from various strategies to repair their comprehension.

Materials: The "Right On Track" bookmark, and fiction or nonfiction texts to share passages.

Introduce/Model the Strategy

- Tell students that during reading good readers try to stay "on track" and pay attention to whether they are understanding the text or not. If they aren't "on track" they try various strategies to help them understand hard words or parts of the text.

- The "Right On Track" bookmark is a tool that students can use to periodically check their comprehension and then to employ strategies to repair any difficulties. Just like a train engineer who identifies and fixes a problem with a train that is off the track, good readers need to identify and repair their comprehension when they experience difficulties.

- Select a text to use when you model monitoring with the bookmark. Students should have copies of the text and bookmark. Preview the text by discussing illustrations and headings. Begin reading aloud. Stop reading after each page (or even every couple of paragraphs in a shorter piece) and model the bookmark checkpoints.

- At the end of each page, select one of the problems outlined on the bookmark to model how to repair (figuring out words; figuring out confusing sentences, parts, and ideas; or visualizing).

- Think aloud as you model how to state the problem and how to initially use rereading as a repair strategy. Then work your way through the various suggested strategies listed on the bookmark for the particular problem you are modeling.

Guide the Strategy/Cooperative Groups or Pairs

- Read aloud from a text and stop periodically so students can work in pairs to try the bookmark strategies. Suggest difficult words or parts so students can clarify those in pairs first and then discuss as a whole class.

- Keep laminated copies of the bookmarks at students' desks so they can practice using the strategies as they read on their own.

- Throughout the day, reinforce the strategies on the bookmark during content area reading. (Try using during math too!)

- Continue modeling examples of problems and ways to fix those problems using the strategies listed on the bookmark.

Box 6.3. Model–Practice–Apply the Strategy in Different Classroom Structures

Guided Reading	Literature Circles
Students should use the bookmark during guided reading lessons to help them monitor their comprehension. Model with small groups' specific examples using the bookmark. Make a chart of the bookmark strategies to hang where students can see during guided reading.	During literature circles, groups can use the bookmark. If you are using roles (Daniels, 1992) then, ask the Word Wizard to identify one word to clarify using the bookmark strategies. The Passage Picker identifies portions of text that are difficult and shares ways to clarify those using bookmark strategies.
Struggling Students It is especially important that struggling students understand that they need to be aware when their comprehension breaks down. They need to also know how to "fix" it. Meet as a group and model each of the strategies in separate lessons using a variety of texts both fiction and nonfiction. Coach individual students in the use of the strategies.	**Independent Work** Students should have access to the bookmark during independent reading and work times. Encourage students to refer to the bookmark often. Reward students who do so.

Monitoring

Reflect on the Strategy/Assess the Strategy

- Ask students to reflect on the strategy and to think about how identifying and fixing problems when reading is so important to understanding the reading.

  -How is keeping on track during reading like a train engineer keeping a train on track?

  -How do you know when you are stuck?

  -How do you find the difficult part and state it?

  -Which strategies can you choose to solve the problems?

- Record student's attempts at monitoring comprehension based on observations when pairs or literature circles work together and when students work with you in small groups. Keep informal dated notes on how each student employs the bookmark strategies.

  -Try to record a comment about each student at least several times a month.

- Try flexibly grouping students based on whether they are having trouble

  -identifying problem spots

  -clarifying words

  -clarifying ideas, portions of a particular text

- Many struggling readers have difficulty identifying portions of text that are difficult due to ideas not vocabulary. Model and share examples of clarifying ideas in texts.

- Let the proficient readers know that they may be automatic with their monitoring and not even aware they are encountering and solving problems as they read. Model and ask them to try to be aware of their monitoring as they read. Share examples.

- Refer to the Appendix on page 223-234 for further ideas on assessing student monitoring.

Monitoring Comprehension

Right On Track
Bookmark

1. Check Point/How are you doing?
Stop during reading to see if you are on track;
Can you . . .
__ visualize, use other senses
__ summarize/tell main ideas
__ predict what will happen next
__ understand all the words
__ understand all the ideas, sentences, pages

2. State the problem.
I am having problems with _____
(a word, part, idea, or visualizing).
I don't get _____.

3. Fix the problem and get back on track!
If you are off track, then first try to fix the problem and

REREAD, REREAD, REREAD!
Try figuring out words by
__ checking parts you know
__ sounding out the word
__ comparing it to another word
__ rereading the sentence
__ reading on
Try figuring out confusing sentences, parts, or pages by
__ rereading
__ reading on
__ thinking about what you know
__ talking to a friend
Try visualizing
__ reread
__ think about what has happened so far
__ read on
__ close your eyes and build a picture in your mind
__ use other senses
__ talk to a friend

Go Back to Reading
You're On Track!

Can You See It?
Classroom Vignettes

Primary Example Can You See It? During guided reading

The second graders gather on the rug, as Mrs. Wisner sets up the big book *Thinking About Ants* by Barbara Brenner (1997). The students have read the book several times. Today Mrs. Wisner focuses on helping students identify the author's use of comparisons to help students visualize and learn more about nonfiction topics.

She begins rereading the book and stops on page seven to ask students to listen very closely and try to visualize. The author tells the reader that the world's largest ants are as large as a person's thumb and the smallest ant can hide in an apple seed.

"Hold up your thumb. Can you imagine an ant this size?" she invites the students to participate. They giggle and talk among themselves with thumbs up.

"Who would like to draw a thumb and an ant on the chart and I'll write the sentence from the book that gives us this comparison. Who would like to draw the small ant that fits in an apple seed," she asks.

Sammy and Rebecca eagerly volunteer and quickly sketch for all to see.

After two more examples students move to their desks to continue finding places in the text where the author has used various comparisons to help the reader visualize and understand the topic.

"Look, Mrs. Wisner," calls Billy, "The ant has feelers that wave like magic wands."

The students watch for and even begin to expect such rich metaphors as they read nonfiction texts. Visualizing the nonfiction comparisons improves their comprehension.

Intermediate Example/Using Can You See It? During SSR

The sixth graders are nestled in their desks and on the couch and rocking chair in the reading center of the classroom for the daily thirty minutes of SSR (sustained silent reading) in the book of their choice. Mrs. Jimenez is also reading at her desk. The students have the charge to first enjoy what they are reading, and second be on the look out for rich descriptions that they can share with fellow classmates in a literature discussion following SSR. Each student has a self-stick note, to simply mark a descriptive passage. After twenty quiet reading minutes, Mrs. Jimenez signals students to share descriptive passages at their tables. Each student folds a paper into six boxes. When a fellow team member describes his or her scene, the listeners quickly sketch what they "see" and are allowed to ask questions for clarification. Mrs. Jimenez circulates around the room to listen in on the conversations.

One little group looks rather puzzled as Harry reads his description again from *The Lion, The Witch, and the Wardrobe* (1978). The scene he has selected describes the setting as the story characters step into the magical wardrobe that transforms from a coat closet with mothballs, to a winter woodsy wonderland.

"I don't get how he can be two places at once," asks Gina. Mrs. Jimenez suggests that Harry reread the description again and that the group close their eyes to try and visualize before drawing the scene. Harry gladly rereads the scene, a little more slowly this time, and the group members begin their quick sketches. Harry comments, "I am seeing the land of Narnia because the author does such a great job describing it." The students are now aware of the impact visualizing has on their comprehension and reading enjoyment.

Can You See It?

Objective: Students select passages from fiction or nonfiction texts that are written to help the reader build strong visual images to enhance understanding. They share passages with others and draw as they visualize.

Materials: Can You See It form and fiction or nonfiction texts to share passages

Introduce/Model the Strategy

- Explain to students that when they read, one way to improve their comprehension is to create pictures in their minds or visualize as they read.

- Select various texts to read aloud from to model visualize. Choose fiction and nonfiction. Think aloud as you read and describe what you are visualizing or picturing in your mind.

- Read aloud from a nonfiction book that uses comparisons to help students visualize. Seymor Simon books are great for this. An example from his *Whales* (1989) book is "the tongue of a blue whale is weighs as much as an elephant." Discuss visualizing such comparisons and how they help with comprehending nonfiction text.

- Sketch a quick drawing of one of the texts that you have visualized. Tell the students that they have to infer some ideas because the author may not describe everything in great detail.

- Tell students that they need to build pictures in their minds as they read to fully understand the text. If they can't visualize they can reread. Model rereading to visualize.

Guide the Strategy/Cooperative Groups or Pairs

- Read aloud from a fiction or nonfiction text. Ask students to close their eyes and try to "see" what the author is describing. Ask students to turn to a partner and describe what they visualize. They may sketch a quick drawing.

- Invite various students to come up to the white board or overhead projector to sketch after you read aloud from the next portion of text.

- Students work in pairs or groups. Each student selects a description to read aloud from a text they are reading. (Students may give examples from the same text or different texts.) While one student reads, the other students draw what they visualize.

- While reading, students stop to sketch drawings when they encounter particularly descriptive passages in fiction or nonfiction. Students share their sketches.

Box 6.4. Model—Practice—Apply the Strategy in Different Classroom Structures

Guided Reading	Literature Circles
Keep a chart titled "Can You See It?" for each title you use with your guided reading groups. The chart could include page number of passage, descriptive language excerpts, and either a quick sketch or comments on what students visualized.	Each student selects a passage to illustrate from the text. They talk about what they see. Or each student in the circle reads aloud a favorite descriptive passage and describes what they pictured.
English Language Learners	Independent Work
Find explicit examples of descriptive passages or comparisons in nonfiction texts and invite students to use gestures to act out some of the events or scenes from various texts. Also, encourage second language students to draw to help them visualize.	Students select a descriptive paragraph or portion of text and illustrate more fully to share or display on a bulletin board.

Reflect on the Strategy/Assess the Strategy

- Ask students to reflect on visualizing while reading. How does visualizing help us understand the text more deeply? How does visualizing help the reader keep track of what is going on in the text?

Monitoring

- Ask students to think about what they can do if they are having trouble visualizing for a given text. They can (1) reread the text; (2) read ahead; or (3) talk to a friend

- Model how to continue visualizing and how to reread if visualizing ceases.

- Collect student work from this lesson and observe students throughout the lessons. If students have difficulty visualizing or describing what they are visualizing, then meet with small groups and select passages to focus on and to discuss.

- For further assessment suggestions refer to the Appendix on page 223–234.

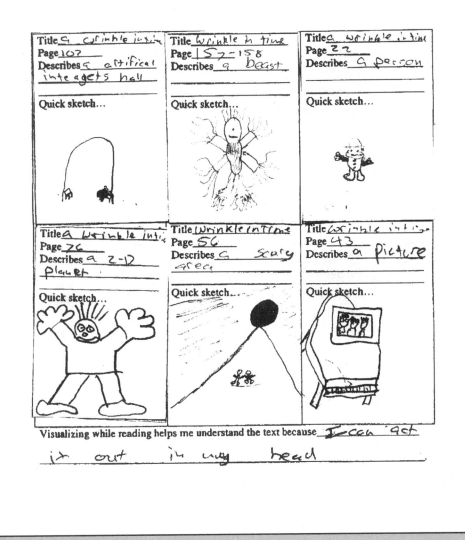

Can You See It?

1. As you read, be on the lookout for words that the author uses to help you create visual images or pictures in your mind.
2. Keep track of examples while reading. Sketch your favorite on the back of this page.
3. Share examples with a partner or group. Read from the text pages and ask the friends to sketch what they visualize. Did you pick a passage they can picture?
4. Watch for examples in fiction and nonfiction.

Fiction a description of . . .

-a setting

-a character

-an event

-a comparison

Nonfiction

-an environment

-an event

-steps for how something works

-a comparison

Title_____ Page_____ Describes_____ Quick sketch	Title_____ Page_____ Describes_____ Quick sketch	Title_____ Page_____ Describes_____ Quick sketch
Title_____ Page_____ Describes_____ Quick sketch	Title_____ Page_____ Describes_____ Quick sketch	Title_____ Page_____ Describes_____ Quick sketch

Visualizing while reading helps me understand the text because _____

_____ .

Mark the Spot

Objective: Students work with the teacher to create various agreed upon class symbols to mark their thoughts, questions, connections, confusions, and ideas while reading. A bookmark reminder provides students with the symbols and a tool to help them monitor their comprehension as they read.

Materials: Bookmark and any text, big book, or content area text book, copies of book for students, optional—overhead transparency copy of text page to mark up with symbols. Optional—laminated copies of the bookmark or copies the students can write on.

Introduce/Model the Strategy

- Explain to students that as good readers read, a variety of thoughts, questions, and ideas are passing through their minds. In this lesson they will learn how to "Mark the Spot" when a notable idea comes to mind during reading.

- Students should have a text to follow along as you read aloud from either a page from an article or book, an overhead transparency of a page, or from a big book.

- Pass out copies of the "Mark the Spot" bookmark and ask students to help you create some symbols to represent what you are thinking as you read.

- Talk about each example on the bookmark and ask students to discuss and sketch symbols to use. (For example, new information might be represented by a light bulb.)

- Read aloud from the text while students follow along. Stop throughout the reading and choose points from the bookmark to discuss. Examples: Wow! This part surprised me because . . . Or I already knew that . . .

- Using the bookmark form, record page numbers or examples for each "Mark the Spot" point. Or when using an article or overhead transparency, draw symbols directly next to the paragraphs where you thought about that symbol.

- Guide the Strategy/Cooperative Groups or Pairs

- Students add the symbols to their bookmarks. They might want to decorate the symbols with colored pencils or markers.

- Guide the class or work with small groups. Read pages of text either together or silently stopping periodically to record thoughts on the "Mark the Spot" form.

- Students discuss the spots they have marked with partners or tables and then the entire class.

Box 6.5. Model—Practice—Apply the Strategy in Different Classroom Structures

Struggling Readers	Literature Circles
Struggling readers often do not realize that they should interact with the text to monitor their comprehension. Meet with a small temporary group of struggling readers and model one or two of the "Mark the Spot" symbols the class had agreed on. Students read silently and share their markings with the group.	Students get into informal literature circles, or discussion groups of 4–6 students and take turns around the circles sharing examples from their bookmarks.
Second Language Students	**Independent Work**
Model each of the "Mark the Spot" symbols with a text that is at the instructional reading level of the students. Or you may wish to use a text with lots of visual support, such as a high-interest nonfiction text to help you as you model and practice "Mark the Spot" points with a small group of second language students. Discuss any clarifications needed especially any idioms or vocabulary that they might not be familiar with.	Students mark page numbers or spots in a text that they will discuss later. They are accountable for marking one symbol per page. They must be prepared to share in a small group or whole class format.

Reflect on the Strategy/Assess the Strategy

- Ask students to reflect on the "Mark the Spot" bookmark. How does thinking about these points and interacting with the text as one reads, help in keeping track of or monitoring one's understanding of the reading?

- Observe students in discussions in small groups and with pairs. Also, collect the bookmark forms to see where students may need assistance. If students need more support try the ideas suggested below.

  - Some students may favor discussing or marking only a few of the bookmark points and may need assistance and support to expand their thinking.

  - If students have trouble marking spots and backing their thinking with examples try calling up small groups of students to work with you. Model one or two of the spots.

  - Let students color code each of the types of markings and have them share their examples.

  - Send home an article to read with a parent or sibling (if parents don't read in English). The adult or older sibling tells which of the symbols he/she was thinking of the most while reading and explains. Students share their findings in class.

- Refer to the Appendix for further suggestions on assessing student progress in monitoring their comprehension on page 223–234.

Mark the Spot

1. Create a bookmark with the class, your partner, or a team.
2. Draw symbols to represent your thinking during reading on bookmark. Write page numbers or examples on the bookmark. Discuss with a partner or group.
3. Create your own "Mark the Spot" ideas and symbols to mark as you read.

Mark the Spot

Symbol

While I read, I am thinking about . . .

Something new I learned . . .
Page numbers:
Example:

Really? I was surprised when . . .
Page numbers:
Example:

What does this mean?
Page numbers:
Example:

I knew this before I read.
Page numbers:
Example:

I realize now that . . .
Page numbers:
Example:

This is great, A+ writing!
Page numbers:
Example:

I made a connection . . .
(to self, text, or world)
Page numbers:
Example:

Word Puzzles

Objective: Students work in teams or independently and select interesting vocabulary and analyze meanings, draw analogies, and study the word's spelling. The activity promotes interest in vocabulary and decoding strategies.

Materials: The Word Puzzles form on transparencies for each group, or the form for individuals or groups, and any text.

Introduce/Model the Strategy

- Tell students that the best way for them to increase their vocabulary is to read every day. Tell students that as they read they encounter many interesting words that they may wish to learn and remember.

- Show students an example and inform them that Word Puzzle is a fun, cooperative activity that helps students study some of the interesting or important words from a given text.

- Read through a portion of text and select a word you find interesting or that you think is important. Think aloud and share with students why you selected this particular word.

- Using the word puzzle, fill in the various puzzle pieces for your word.

Guide the Strategy/Cooperative Groups or Pairs

- Choose another word from the text and assign partners to work together to fill in the puzzle pieces. All pairs work on the same word. Partners can rotate to new pairs and share their findings. Discuss as a class.

- Cooperative teams work together to fill in puzzle pieces. In "home" teams of eight, each member takes a puzzle piece to be in charge of completing. Then the "home" groups of eight mix up and students with like puzzle pieces meet to complete their pieces in "expert groups." Once the pieces are ready, students return to their "home" puzzle group to piece together the entire puzzle and share findings (Kagan, 1989).

- Display word puzzles.

Monitoring

- Assign one word to groups of four. The teams complete the puzzle and share with the class. Each team develops a quiz question about their word. Combine questions and use as part of a quiz on the words.

Box 6.6. Model—Practice—Apply the Strategy in Different Classroom Structures

Guided Reading	Literature Circles
After reading a text with a guided reading group, students each select a word to study and create a word puzzle at their desks to bring to the next guided reading group meeting.	The student in charge of vocabulary (the Word Wizard) in each group selects a word to study. The Word Wizard passes out the pieces to each member who gives a response. (Harvey, 1992)
Cross-Age Tutors	Independent Work
Older buddies assist younger buddies in learning vocabulary from a social studies or science unit. The pairs work together to fill out a word puzzle for one word they think is important or interesting. Pairs share in front of the group.	Students work in pairs or independently to complete word puzzles.

Reflect on the Strategy/Assess the Strategy

- Ask students to reflect on creating word puzzles. How do word puzzles help them to learn interesting or important words?

- Collect word puzzles students have created. Which areas of the puzzle are the most challenging for them to complete? Offer support where needed.

- Give a quiz on the words. Have students learned selection words?

- Are students using some of the word puzzle words in their writing?

- If students are having difficulty with a particular puzzle piece, then model and guide practice for that piece in a small group format.

- Refer to the Appendix for further suggestions on how to assess student progress in monitoring comprehension on page 223–234.

Word Puzzle

1. Get into a group of 3 to 4 students.
2. One person can cut apart the puzzle pieces.
3. Pass out the pieces and each member can fill in his or her puzzle pieces.
4. Put the puzzle together.
5. Variation: Each member moves to another group and takes their pieces to form a new puzzle at another table.

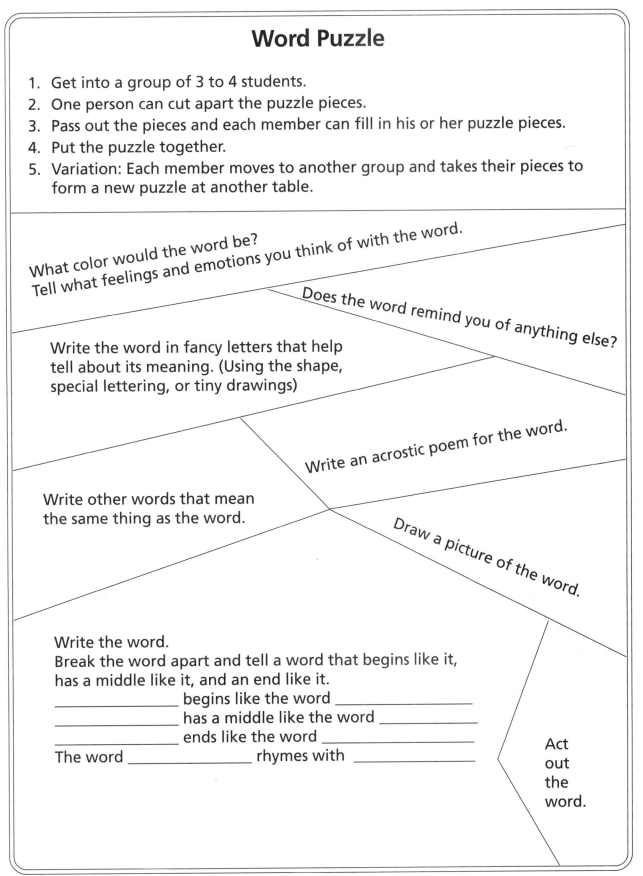

What color would the word be?
Tell what feelings and emotions you think of with the word.

Does the word remind you of anything else?

Write the word in fancy letters that help tell about its meaning. (Using the shape, special lettering, or tiny drawings)

Write an acrostic poem for the word.

Write other words that mean the same thing as the word.

Draw a picture of the word.

Write the word.
Break the word apart and tell a word that begins like it, has a middle like it, and an end like it.

_____ begins like the word _____
_____ has a middle like the word _____
_____ ends like the word _____
The word _____ rhymes with _____

Act out the word.

Super Six Comprehension Strategies: 35 Lessons and More for Reading Success by Lori Oczkus

Teachers As Readers

Reflecting on Our Experiences as Adult Readers

As adult readers we automatically monitor whether our reading is making sense and then shift into fix it mode when a break in meaning occurs. We might try out rereading, figuring out a word, reading on, or even talking to a friend. When we become aware of our monitoring habits, we can begin to reflect on examples to share with students.

My Reflections on Monitoring Comprehension

When I am dead tired after a long day of teaching I love to curl up with a great book. Sometimes I do okay and can read for an hour or so without a hitch. Other evenings, I am so beat that I read the same paragraph over and over only to find that I can't remember what I've read. Or I find I can't recall what was happening with the story line or that I don't have a clue who a character is much less his relationship to other characters in the book. Perhaps I find that I am not visualizing or building the story in my head.

As a mature adult reader, I am essentially monitoring my comprehension, only to find that sometimes I am off track. When I recognize that I'm not "getting it" I have a variety of fix-up strategies that I can employ, including trying again when I'm not so tired, rereading, reading on, summarizing for a moment, or talking with a friend.

Besides making time to read for enjoyment, I also read professional books and journals to stay abreast of the very latest research-based, proven teaching methods. To truly comprehend this type of reading material, I must turn into a "super monitor" as I search for the most important ideas to improve my work with students and teachers.

One helpful resource that I found on the age-old problem of helping children deal with bullies and peer pressure, is the little book Sticks and Stones by Scott Cooper (2000). The author, a coach, former teacher, and school board member, offers a unique approach that includes a wide variety of verbal tools for sticky situations.

Each chapter is creatively organized around the characteristics of a particular bird such as "The Way of the Blue Jay" to resist peer pressure, or the "Way of the Hummingbird" to shut down bullies. The bird analogies provide children with a clever way of remembering the strategies they can use. The parent or teacher is provided with sample scripts, and ideas for teaching children to use the ideas presented in the book.

I began monitoring my comprehension immediately when I first picked up this book and read the back cover and table of contents. The author provided me with the bird framework as a way of organizing key ideas. As I read each chapter, I highlighted and constantly reread important concepts and steps to use with children. Almost every page I stopped to ask myself if the material was making sense to me and I quizzed myself as I reread, while summarizing techniques from each chapter. I found myself wanting to do more than just read and understand this important material, but I wanted to actually know it well enough to use it with my own children and students.

Keeping track of my own comprehension has greatly enhanced the way I teach reading. I often share with students my reading material and let them in on how I manage to monitor and solve problems as I read. Kids love hearing that adult readers don't always immediately understand what they read. It takes some work to comprehend fully.

Monitoring

Your Reflections on Monitoring Comprehension

- *Over the course of a week, notice strategies you use to monitor your comprehension to comprehend what you are reading.*

- *How do you monitor your progress when reading fiction and nonfiction? What support do the authors give you to help you monitor?*

- *Do you first notice there is a problem and then do you find a way to "fix" it?*

- *How do you utilize other strategies as you monitor—summarizing, questioning, predicting, and inferring?*

- *Do you often have trouble visualizing when you read? What do you do to solve this problem?*

- *How does rereading assist you in monitoring your comprehension?*

- *Keep track of how you solve difficult words as you read. How often do you reread to help you monitor your comprehension? Think about times when you have talked to a friend to help in clarifying your reading.*

- *Give a examples from a book you are reading to share with students. Include*

   - times when you realized you were stuck or having problems understanding the text;

   - words or concepts you needed to clarify; and

   - times when you weren't visualizing and what you did to correct that problem.

Examples of monitoring comprehension in your reading

Examples of monitoring from my reading to share with students

Monitoring

References

Palincsar, A. S., & Brown, A. L. (1984). Reciprocal teaching of comprehension fostering and monitoring activities. *Cognition and Instruction, 1,* 117–175.

Pressley, M. (1997). Imagery and children's learning: Putting the picture in developmental perspective. *Review of Educational Research, 47,* 586–622.

Schwanenflugel, P. J., Stahl, S. A., & McFals, E. L. (1997). Partial word knowledge and vocabulary growth during reading comprehension. *Journal of Literacy Research, 29,* 531–553.

Monitoring

7 ▷ Summarizing and Synthesizing

> *"Teaching students to summarize what they read is another way to improve their overall comprehension of text."* **Nell Duke and P. David Pearson**, *in* What Research Has to Say About Reading Instruction, *p. 220.*
>
> *"Comprehension cannot be fostered by transmitting information from the page into the children's heads. Learning occurs when one creates a personal interpretation."* **Linda Hoyt**, *in* Revisit, Reflect, Retell, *p. 165.*

Thoughts on Summarizing and Synthesizing

If you ask a group of students to summarize, watch out for a sudden release of sighs or groans! Students and teachers alike often complain that summarizing is a difficult task. After all, summarizing involves remembering what one has read, selecting only the most important points to share, and ordering those in a logical manner. Summarizing seems like it might be a rather literal skill but it is indeed complex. It is no wonder students grumble when we ask them to summarize.

When younger primary students try to summarize we often hear a long string of "and thens" that really constitute a retelling rather than a succinct summary. Freddie, a preschooler registering for kindergarten, gave me a long, elaborate retelling of "The Three Billy Goats Gruff" that included the sound effects, "Trip Trap" and character voices. Although he wasn't "reading" just yet, I knew that he would become an excellent reader because of his keen ability to retell. Eventually, the long retellings become shorter summaries in later grades. Even primary children can begin to learn ways to shorten their retellings into summaries.

Synthesis goes way beyond retelling. During reading, good readers naturally form a big picture of the reading material that may include an evolving theme, moral, or point of view. Harvey and Goudivis (2000) refer to synthesis as an insight, new line of thinking, or light bulb "aha" experience in response to the text. Some teachers compare synthesis to baking a cake or putting a jigsaw puzzle together because the pieces or ingredients form a bigger product (Harvey & Goudivis, 2000). P. David Pearson, in a speech, defines synthesis as a summary plus the reader's own opinion or thinking.

I think of synthesis as the "taste in your mouth" that a good book or article often leaves you with. Three years after reading a favorite book, you may not be capable of giving an accurate summary, but you probably do remember your synthesis, which may include the lesson or moral of the book, visual images from the reading, or a feeling or "aura" that has stuck with you. You have been changed or your viewpoint has been altered in some way.

I like to categorize all of those good "response to literature" type activities under synthesis. Sometimes we ask students to write in journals during and after reading and express their thoughts, responses, and feelings in response to the literature. Other times we ask them to dramatize, write, draw, or even sing to share their synthesis and ideas about what they have read. Focusing on synthesis and creative response activities helps deepen comprehension. (Hoyt, 1992)

This chapter includes lessons that will help your students improve their ability to summarize and develop deeper meanings as they respond to text.

How Do Summarizing and Synthesizing Help Students Comprehend?

Summarizing and Retelling to Improve Comprehension

When students are taught to summarize, comprehension is enhanced and improved (Rinehart, Stahl, and Erickson, 1986; Taylor, 1982; Lipson, 1996). Summarizing is a complex strategy that involves the orchestration of a variety of skills including determining the key ideas from details, logically ordering those ideas, and paraphrasing.

Retelling is an important precursor to summarizing that is essentially a longer version of a summary that may include more scenes and details from the reading. For many students, especially younger children, retelling is easier for them. We utilize many creative ways to encourage retellings including puppets, a clothesline to hang and sequence selection pictures from, dramatizations, and story maps.

Reciprocal Teaching—More Practice in Summarizing

I use reciprocal teaching (Palincsar & Brown, 1986; Oczkus, 2003) with younger and older students alike to move them from retellings to more succinct summaries. After reading each page of a text together, we summarize that brief "chunk" of text before moving on to the next page. Often, we need to reread, a critical tool in summarizing, to review what we read and to hone in on key words we may wish to paraphrase or use in our summaries. In addition to summarizing, we predict, question, and find a point or word to clarify as part of the reciprocal teaching lesson. This frequent practice in summarizing provides students with constant modeling and success with summarizing. Also every few days, I ask partners to take turns and summarize page by page the reading in fiction and nonfiction materials.

Graphic Organizers—To Guide Summarizing

Good readers use their knowledge of text organization and structure to assist them in summarizing (Lipson, 1996). Graphic organizers, such as story maps for narrative text and Venn diagrams and charts for expository text, improve comprehension (Heimlich & Pittelman, 1986; Pehrsson & Robinson, 1985).

Although I continue to use graphic organizers during whole class lessons, I find them particularly effective when working in guided reading with small groups of students. Many of our students do not pay close attention to graphic organizers during whole class instruction. By using these same tools with small groups, you provide students more opportunities to practice summarizing.

Synthesis—Evolving Meaning

Synthesis goes further than summarizing as readers infer deeper meanings the author intended for the text while experiencing new insights of their own. Synthesis has always been with us but ever since Keene and Zimmerman revisited synthesis in their landmark book *Mosaic of Thought* (1997), more teachers are introducing synthesis as a strategy to students. Debbie Miller in her book, *Reading With Meaning* (2002) tells us that as good readers read, they monitor the overall meaning, themes, and new thinking evolves.

Louise Rosenblatt (1938) took the perspective that the as the reader reads along, he is personally responding to the literature and constructing meaning that is unique to his experiences. Besides thinking about the author's message, students may form new ideas and insights for their own lives based on the reading.

When I think about synthesis, I am reminded of the verbs from Bloom's Taxonomy that imply that we move students to higher levels of thinking. That list includes: compose, design, formulate, construct, hypothesize, show change, combine, evolve, and suppose. By explaining to students what synthesis is and making them aware of their use of it, we assist students in improving their comprehension.

Movies As Examples of Synthesis

Sometimes I use movies as examples to explain synthesis effectively to students. I tell them that while we are watching the movie unfold we keep track of what is going on as we add to our summary but we also try to answer the questions, "What is this really about?" or "What is the theme or big idea?"

When I watched the movie *About a Boy* I admit guiltily that I hadn't read the book yet. But as I watched, I summarized as the story unfolded a series of events that brought two unlikely people together, a confirmed bachelor and a twelve-year-old awkward fatherless boy. My synthesis also forged on as I pieced together insights about their feelings and need for each other. The message of love, friendship, and the theme that "no man is an island," evolved throughout the story line. I also responded to the theme by thinking about many different definitions of "family," which today may include neighbors, coworkers, and friends.

You too may find that when you enjoy a movie, it "sticks" with you into the next day as you ponder ideas and insights. That "aura" is synthesis, which happens with books as well. Students eagerly listen to and share their experiences with synthesis and movies. These movie discussions serve as hooks to invite students to do the same thing with books.

Response To Literature—A Path To Synthesis

I like to think of that category of activities often called "personal response to literature" as a bank of great ideas for guiding students to form a synthesis as they read. Personal responses may include: giving an opinion or viewpoint, reflecting on author's craft, discussing feelings, mood, or theme, sharing surprises, and thinking about changes in characters. There are many creative activities and assignments that will lead students to use personal response in meaningful ways. We can ask students to dramatize, draw, write, create, or discuss to develop their synthesis of a text and arrive at deeper meanings.

In Jill Hope's fourth grade class the students choose a time period in California history to research. Then the students create a fictional character and write a series of letters written by that character to describe events that took place in history. When my son, Bryan, was in Jill's class he wrote letters from a miner during the California Gold Rush. He came up with the idea of signing each letter in a creative way to reflect the character's feelings. Some of the salutations included: "From a future rich man"; "Shivering and cold in a strange city"; and" From a citizen of the new state." Bryan had to synthesize all that he had read about the

time period to create a believable character. Afterwards the students created dioramas of their character. What a great way to assist students in formulating a lasting synthesis of the big ideas from California history!

Journal Writing and Discussion For Synthesis

Many teachers complain that when they ask their students to write a personal response to literature, they end up writing summaries. Good readers may have the need to summarize first before taking time to reflect and take on new insights. For many students, writing a summary first facilitates their response. Harvey and Goudivis (2000) suggest having students write a brief summary followed by a response.

Often students do have difficulty understanding exactly what a personal response is supposed to look like. We can provide students with thought provoking questions to move them into synthesis. Some questions and prompts that help students to think deeply about what they have read might include (Adapted from Routman, 1991):

Discuss the main character's feelings. Why do you suppose he/she felt that way? Have you ever felt that way? When?

What does that remind you of? Explain.

What surprised you in your reading?

What is the author's message or theme?

How did the characters change? Give examples from the beginning, middle, end of the text.

What might happen if . . . ?

Compare two characters or a character to yourself. How are you alike or different? What would you have done the same or differently? Why?

A two-column journal is often a very effective format for encouraging students to take a statement from the text and then respond to it in some way to form a synthesis (Harvey & Goudivis, 2000). Students copy a phrase, quote, or sentence from the text that strikes them as interesting or significant on the left-hand side of the page and on the right-hand side next to it they respond with a thought, question, response, reflection on author's craft, or insight. By modeling how to write a personal response or synthesis and by encouraging students to share their responses with one another, students begin to deepen their responses to literature and improve their comprehension.

Box 7.1. Teaching Summarizing/Synthesizing

Before Reading Summarizing/Synthesizing	During Reading Summarizing/Synthesizing	After Reading Summarizing/Synthesizing
Summary -How is the reading material organized? -Preview cover, table of contents, and illustrations.	**Summary** -What has happened so far? -Based on what you have read, what do you think will happen next? -What have you already put into the graphic organizer? What is left?	**Summary** -Skim and reread to prepare to retell and summarize. -Retell your favorite part. -Retell the reading in order. -Shorten your retelling. -What were the most important parts? -Use the graphic organizer to help you summarize. -Summarize in 3–5 sentences. -What can you leave out?
Synthesis -What connections are you making? -What do you think the author wants to teach us? -What is the message going to be? -What are you wondering or thinking?	**Synthesis** -What are you thinking or wondering now? -What connections are you making now? -How have your opinions, ideas, feelings, and thoughts about the characters, ideas, or problems in the reading changed?	**Synthesis** -What did the author want you to learn? -What was the theme of the reading? -How have your ideas, thoughts, and feelings about the characters, ideas, or problems in the reading changed? -What visual images will you remember from the reading? -What will you remember and take with you?

Summarize/Synthesize Classroom Vignettes

Primary or IntermediateSynthesis/ Discussing the Theme

The mood in Mrs. Buscheck's classroom can be summed up in a word: somber. The third graders just finished the last chapter of *Stone Fox* by John Reynolds Gardiner (1980). The classic story is about a boy who tries to support his ailing grandfather by entering a dog sled race with just one dog who dies in the effort. She gathers the class on the rug to invite the students to reflect.

"What do you think is the author's message in *Stone Fox*? I want you to think of one word that represents the theme in *Stone Fox*," she asks.

The students sit for a moment. Then hands slowly creep into the air. Mrs. Buscheck records the students' responses on the white board. The barrage of words include: love, miracles, friendship, and trust. Students offer explanations of their words.

"I picked friendship because *Stone Fox* became a friend," remarked Billy.

"I think this story is about love," begins Rachael, "because Willie loved his grandpa, and they both loved Searchlight. Little Willie entered the race just to help his grandfather pay his taxes. That is how he showed his love."

After some more discussion of the theme words, Mrs. Buscheck asks the children to select one of the theme words, decorate it, and write a few sentences explaining what they thought the author's message was. Students write their responses on sled dog patterns for a playful display.

"I chose miracle," wrote Danya, "because even the smallest person, can make miracles happen."

Mrs. Buscheck skillfully leads a heartfelt discussion to capture the tone of the book and then invites the students to deepen their thinking through a writing activity. What word comes to mind to sum up the lesson? Synthesis!

Intermediate/Primary/Summarizing- Finding finger facts with nonfiction

"I think it is important that Greece comes in first," announces second grade Nicola to her fourth grade buddy, Belinda. Belinda diligently records the fact on the thumb of the "Summary Hand" pattern. Then she asks, "Let's search through the magazine, *Olympics* (Mondo, 2001), for the other most important facts about the opening ceremonies."

Buddies from Ms. Hope's and Mrs. Webster's classroom meet every Thursday afternoon to read together. Both teachers have focused their lessons for the past week on summarizing nonfiction texts by pulling out main ideas. Ms. Hope's intermediate students worked through the text searching for facts before they met with the buddies. As the two teachers circulate the room, they coach pairs who are stuck on details.

"The girl in this magazine is excited about the Olympics," decides Sam. His older buddy, Andrew begins to write this "fact" on the hand, when Mrs. Webster stops the pair.

"Boys, think about the five most important facts to share with someone who hasn't read the article. We are choosing facts about the opening ceremonies. Andrew, nods his head in agreement and turns back to the book to search for ideas. "I know," he shared, " I'll ask Sam how the athletes come into the stadium."

The end result is a "handful" of important ideas and the students learn to summarize just the key ideas in a text.

Summarizing

Small Summaries

Objective: Students search the copyright page of trade books for examples of small one- or two-sentence summaries. Then they analyze the summaries, possibly copy them, and on occasion rewrite them. When they write their own works, they include "small summaries."

Materials: A variety of trade books that have summaries on the copyright pages and small summaries form.

Introduce/Model the Strategy

- Inform students that summarizing is a useful strategy that helps them remember the important ideas from their reading. However, making a summary small enough and deciding which details to leave out is often difficult. By studying "small summaries" in trade books, they'll see many examples that will serve as models for writing their own summaries.

- Ask students if they have ever seen the copyright page in a book. Tell students that sometimes the copyright page is at the end of a book and other times it is at the beginning. Explain the purpose of the copyright page.

- Open a trade book to the copyright page and locate the small one- or two-sentence summary. Hold up the book to show students where the summary is and read it aloud.

- Ask students what they notice about the summary. Decide as a group if you agree or disagree with the summary the publisher has chosen. (Sometimes the small summary is more like a commercial for the book. In that case, we often rewrite it as a class!)

- Read aloud several small summaries and think aloud about what you notice about how they are constructed. Invite students to help you and chart their responses. Move to guiding the strategy in cooperative groups or pairs or continue with modeling how to write a small summary.

- After students have read and discussed lots of small summaries from trade books, you may also opt to gather the students and also model how to write a small summary.

- Before writing a small summary, ask students to review what they noticed about small summaries in books. Then select a literature anthology selection, or a chapter from a social studies or science book that the class has read and model how to write a one- or two-sentence summary. Ask students to help you chart the steps involved in writing the small summary.

  Steps to writing a small summary may include:

  -rereading the text

  -studying the visuals

  -talking with a friend first

Guide the Strategy/Cooperative Groups or Pairs

- After modeling for students how to find a small summary on a copyright page, pass out books and invite either pairs of students or cooperative groups to locate and read small summaries. When you signal, invite the groups or pairs to exchange or rotate the titles for a new example.

- When students have read several small summaries, invite the class to assist you in making a list of characteristics they notice in the summaries. How are the summaries different for fiction and nonfiction? If they have read the books, ask students to think about which summaries they disagree with and why?

- If you are instructing the class to write small summaries, ask pairs or groups to write summaries of reading material the class has read. If each group writes a summary for the same reading selection, then the class can vote on the best small summary and give reasons for their choice (Hacker & Tenent, 2002).

- When students write their own stories, reports, or other writings, invite them to write small summaries to place at the beginning or end of their work along with a copyright date.

Summarizing

Box 7.2. Model—Practice—Apply the Strategy in Different Classroom Structures

English Language Learners	Literature Circles
For the benefit of the ELL students, point out the selection visuals as a way of making the book summary more comprehensible for second language students. Make copies of illustrations or have students draw them to put in order for a retelling before constructing a summary as a group.	Ask students to read the small summaries that accompany their literature circle titles. After reading the book, the group members read the small summary and discuss if they agree or disagree with the small summary provided. They must give reasons for their opinions.
Struggling Students	**Independent Work**
Struggling readers need more practice in writing and analyzing small summaries. Guide struggling readers in a small group. Instead of summarizing the entire reading selection, practice writing or giving oral small summaries for paragraphs or pages of text. Use topic sentences from the text to guide students in summarizing.	Place a variety of trade book samples for fiction and nonfiction in a center. Students locate small summaries and copy and illustrate them to post on a bulletin board. Younger children enjoy using magnifying glasses to read the small print used for the summaries.

Reflect on the Strategy/Assess the Strategy

- Ask students to reflect on the small summaries they have read. What characteristics do they share? Invite students to tell how creating a small summary helps them comprehend

- Are students creating succinct, brief one- or two-sentence summaries that include main highlights of the reading? Are students including too many details?

- If students are having difficulty creating their own small summaries, then meet with a small group and read more books and small summaries together before writing several together.

- For further assessment suggestions refer to the Appendix on page 246.

Small Summaries

- Most books have a one- or two-sentence summary written in very small print on the copyright page.
- Find at least 5 examples of small summaries from books in your classroom, school library, or home. Copy them down. Read the books or use books you've already read. Read the summaries carefully. Do you agree with each summary? Would you have written a different one?
- Choose a book you have read. Don't look at the small summary. Write your own small summary first and then read the publisher's summary. How do they compare?

Small Summaries

1. Book Title_____ Author_____

Small Summary _____

_____

2. Book Title_____ Author_____

 Small Summary _____

_____

3. Book Title_____ Author_____

Small Summary _____

_____

4. Book Title_____ Author_____

Small Summary _____

_____

_____

5. Book Title_____ Author_____

Small Summary _____

_____

Super Six Comprehension Strategies: 35 Lessons and More for Reading Success by Lori Oczkus

Summary Hand

Adapted from various hand ideas including Linda Hoyt (1999), Dr. George Gonzales, Jon Bindloss

Objective: Students trace their own hands on the summary hand sheet to summarize key events in fiction and in nonfiction to remember important "finger" facts. The hand may also serve as an organizer for writing paragraphs.

Materials: Summary hand form, or paper for students to trace their hands.

Introduce/Model the Strategy

- Tell students that when they summarize they need to focus on the most important handful of ideas. A summary hand is a useful organizer for summarizing.

- Draw a large hand on a butcher paper or trace your hand on the overhead projector where all students can see.

- Select a text to read with the class or use a text the class has already read. Ask the students what they know about summarizing.

- Model and think aloud as you summarize using the summary hand.

- For nonfiction, write the most important facts from the text in the fingers (finger facts!). Sketch some drawings or graphics in the palm. Illustrate one of the main points, or a mini-mural of all the main points.

- For fiction (thanks to Prof. George Gonzales' workshops; in Linda Hoyt *Revisit, Reflect, Retell,* 1999), write in each finger and the thumb the story elements- setting, characters, problem, the resolution or a key event, and the ending. Model how to illustrate one of the main points or a mini-mural in the palm that combines several main ideas or a lesson learned from the reading.

- For paragraph writing (thanks to Jon Bindloss, fifth grade teacher), hold up your hand and show how the thumb and pinkie can reach out and touch. Show the students how they can write a paragraph that has a topic sentence, supporting details, and a final sentence that relates or "touches" back to the original topic sentence.

Guide the Strategy/Cooperative Groups or Pairs*

- After reading a selection of fiction or nonfiction, guide the class to work with you to complete a summary hand. Ask the group to list main ideas first, list those on the board, and as a group circle the most important ones to include in the summary hand. Write the main points on the hand.

- Review a text with the class and then break into groups or pairs to fill in a summary hand. Students share drafts of hands before writing final copy so they can make changes.

* There are many variations on using the hand idea for summarizing. I have credited several but many classroom teachers have created their own versions.

Box 7.3. Model—Practice—Apply the Strategy in Different Classroom Structures

Guided Reading	Literature Circles
As a culminating activity after reading a text together, sketch a summary hand on a poster board. Invite the group to assist you as you fill in the thumb and fingers with main ideas from the reading. Fill in a main idea hand for smaller chunks of text—not always an entire text. After reading a few pages, create a summary hand. Use the summary idea hand in a guided reading group to model how to first fill in the hand and then use the hand to write a paragraph.	The summarizer (Daniels, 1994) completes a summary hand to share with the literature circle. After literature circles meet, all students can be held accountable for the reading material, by completing their own individual summary hands.
Cross-Age Tutors	Independent Work
Older buddies read a text with younger buddies and then fill in a summary hand together. Older buddies may wish to read the text in their classroom ahead of time to work with their teacher in identifying main points to teach the younger buddies. Both students illustrate in the palm of the summary hand.	Students complete summary hands for anthology selections, social studies and science chapters, and short articles. Primary teachers may wish to provide a group summary.

Reflect on the Strategy/Assess the Strategy

- Invite students to discuss how using the summary hand helps them to remember main ideas as they summarize.

- Are students choosing main ideas or details for their summary hands?

- If students need more support for selecting main ideas try using easier to read texts to practice with the summary hand. Also, try guiding students who need extra support in a small group setting. Try summarizing smaller amounts of text such as a page or chapter, instead of an entire book.

- For further assessment suggestions refer to the Appendix on page 223–234.

Summary Hand Pattern

Fiction—Write the summary using fingers as the place where students write story elements, such as setting, characters, problem, event, solution, and story or your personal meaning. Draw in the palm.

Nonfiction—Use fingers and thumb to write most important "finger facts."

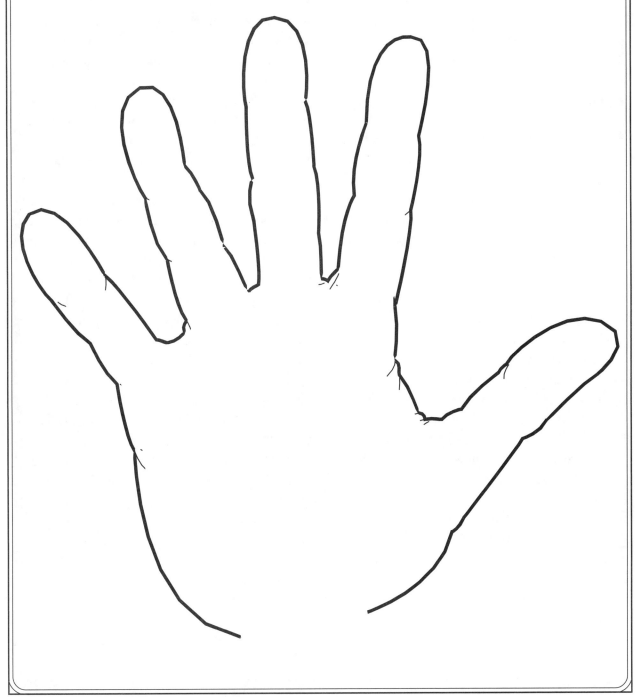

Choose A Quick One
Classroom Vignette

Primary Vignette/Choose A Quick One During Guided Reading

"Wow! That was a great story," professed Fernando, as his guided reading group just finished reading silently, Dav Pilkey's *Dogzilla* (Harcourt, 1993). The entire third grade group giggled and smiled their way through the goofy story about some mice who run Dogzilla away from their town of Mousopolis by threatening him with a bubble bath. Mr. Orner offers the students two quick choices, either to select a page and pantomime or to sketch a scene on a white board. Each student quietly studies and flips through the pages to decide on a scene to represent. Mr. Orner calls time and the students eagerly raise their hands to volunteer their dramas or drawings.

Billy stands up behind his chair at the guided reading table and pantomimes a scene where Dogzilla is run out of town as the mice try to bathe him. During his mini-drama hands go up and several students guess incorrectly, so he dramatizes again. This time they get it. When Andrea guesses the page Billy acted out, Mr. Orner asks the group to turn to that page and read it in unison. The high-interest activity continues as students take turns displaying their acting and drawing talents while the group guesses and then reads the page in unison.

As Mr. Orner dismisses the group, Alisha comments that they are now experts at doggie drama and doggie drawings! Isn't third grade humor wonderful? Through this activity the students remember and review key selection events. Afterward the students are prepared to write a written response for specific events or pull together a summary.

Intermediate Choose A Quick One After A Social Studies Unit

Every week in Mrs. King's fifth grade class the students synthesize and summarize what they have learned from the social studies and science lessons by choosing a quick one to practice and perform in cooperative groups. The students know that the purpose of this activity is to review and summarize the lesson while synthesizing the information to think critically and to remember what they've read.

Each cooperative group meets to review the lesson of seven pages and to select the page and event they'll draw, act out, or write to perform. Mrs. King circulates during the brief ten minutes the groups have to prepare their quick responses. One group starts writing a recipe for conflict using ingredients—pour in colonists, drop in two acts like the Stamp Act or Sugar Act, mix in soldiers, and stir in the Boston Tea Party. The group stalls, unable to think of what to throw in next, so Mrs. King suggests they review the lesson in the book.

Another group is busy pantomiming the Boston Tea Party while two other groups are huddled around large pieces of butcher paper sketching and putting quotes and key words from the vocabulary on quick murals.

After an additional five minutes, Mrs. King calls each group to perform while other groups respond with compliments and questions. Every Friday, her students look forward to these quick, creative ways to review content area chapters. And the weekly quiz? Most students pass with flying colors after creating and sharing quick ones!

Choose A Quick One

Objective: Students work in small groups to select a response mode to present to the class. In response to reading, they dramatize, write, draw, or combine any of these responses. Students prepare their quick ones in just a few minutes.

Materials: Student choices will dictate materials—may include paper, markers, or props for a skit, and choose a Quick One form,

Introduce/Model the Strategy

- Tell students that when they respond to their reading in a creative way through art, drama, or writing, they can deepen their comprehension.

- Select a text (fiction or nonfiction) that students have already read. Briefly summarize the reading. Model each of the "quick" ways students may respond to the text. You may wish to model each one separately over several days and guide students as they practice in between. Be sure to think aloud as you model each one.

Quick Draw—Use a piece of butcher paper or the overhead projector. Think aloud as you sketch a main character, scene, or collage of words or visual images from the text. Select big ideas to represent.

Quick Drama—Act out a scene or highlight from the text. Model how to freeze in a tableaux (frozen scene), to pantomime, role play, or interview a character. Think aloud and share why you chose the material you did to act out.

Quick Write—Model and think aloud the steps for writing a quick poem, new ending, or different setting to the reading material. Or write a response to the literature by writing a new verse to a familiar tune such as Twinkle Twinkle, This Old Man, Old MacDonald, and so forth.) (Hoyt, 1999; McLaughlin & Allen, 2002).

References Adapted from *Revisit, Relect, Retell* by Linda Hoyt, Heinemann, 1999; from McLaughlin, Maureen & Allen Mary Beth, (2002); *Guided Comprehension: A Teaching Model for Grades 3–8*. Newark: DE International Reading Assn. Reprinted with permission.

Guide the Strategy/Cooperative Groups or Pairs

- After you have modeled the quick responses for students, ask them to reflect on the steps you used to arrive at quick, meaningful products.

- Work with the class to guide students through the creation of each of the quick responses. Discuss steps involved and the social skills necessary (no put downs, sharing, listening to all ideas, working together to create an agreed upon plan).

- Allow each cooperative group or pairs to create a quick drama, draw, or write of their choice to share with the class.

Box 7.4. Model—Practice—Apply the Strategy in Different Classroom Structures

Guided Reading	Literature Circles
After reading a text in a guided reading group, invite students to either pantomime from one of the pages for other students to guess which page the scene is from or to show a quick draw and the group guesses the page or scene. Provide white boards for the quick draws. After each page is correctly identified, the group reads the page or paragraph in unison. Students each draw a quick draw from a page in the book on a white board. The other students guess which page the student has drawn.	The student who is the passage picker (Daniels, 1994) in the group selects a page to either draw or act out and the group guesses which passage and scans for the page. When they guess the right selection, the group reads the text together again either in unison, partners, or they follow along as the passage picker reads aloud from the selected portion of text. Literature circles "Choose a quick one" to perform for the class as a response to their book.

continued

Whole Class	Independent Work
After reading a social studies or science lesson or chapter, students summarize the learning by creating quick draw, quick dramas, or quick writes. They organize their quick responses in only a few minutes and then perform them for the class.	Individual students or pairs use independent work time to prepare their quick drama, drawing, or writing. They may also write out their plan for a quick drama. Students share their work during whole class sessions. Drawings and writing responses are displayed on a bulletin board.

Reflect on the Strategy/Assess the Strategy

- Ask students to reflect on how the quick responses assist them in understanding the reading material. How does a quick response deepen their comprehension and help them remember what they have read? Keep a check list to keep track of which quick ones students have already chosen and encourage them to try different responses for their next quick one.

- Observe students as they perform or share their quick responses.

Quick Drama—What kinds of ideas or events are they selecting to act out? Are they choosing main ideas or details? If they choose details, try modeling and discussing main ideas or important events.

Quick Draw—Are students drawing one select event or idea or putting together a "splash" of themes and bigger ideas or events from the reading? If students need help representing a synthesis, guide the class and groups in creating murals that reflect a synthesis of materials read as a group.

Quick Write—Are students writing about just literal events or details in a text, or are they incorporating larger themes and big ideas? If students need help, guide groups to write examples that incorporate main ideas and themes from the reading.

Choose A Quick One

Team Members _____

Title of Book/Text/Author _____

Work with a team and choose a quick draw, quick drama, or quick write to show your synthesis of your reading. Practice and present the final product to the class.

Quick Draw
• Get a large piece of paper and work quickly to sketch a collage of scenes, symbols, characters, and important words from the reading.
- Make it colorful.
- Add quotes or words.
- Plan how to present the quick draw to the class.
We plan to sketch _____

_____

Quick Write
• Write a quick
- poem
- new ending, new beginning, different setting
- song to the tune of a song you know like
Twinkle, Twinkle, Little Star
Row, Row, Row, Your Boat
If You're Happy and You Know It
This Old Man
We plan to write_____

Quick Drama
• Choose a scene from the reading. Act it out using one of the following formats:
-tableaux, or frozen scene, where nobody moves
-pantomime, with no talking
-act out a scene with talking
-interview a character

We will act out the scene where

_____

The type of quick drama we choose is

_____

Quick Combo
• Combine any of the quick responses using a quick draw, drama, or write.

We will combine

_____

Here is our plan

_____

_____

_____

Strip Poem

Objective: Students will first write an independent response to a reading on a strip of paper then collaborate with a small group to combine their strips for a poem that is a synthesis of their reading. Groups share and also discuss the revisions students made to the order of the strips as they worked on their poems.

Materials: Colored strips of paper in four different colors (optional), and Strip Poem form.

Introduce/Model the Strategy

- Tell students that when they write and discuss with others what they have learned from the reading, they form a synthesis, or big picture of what the reading is about.

- Review main ideas from a book, article, or chapter from a book the class has already read.

- Using a strip of paper, think aloud as you model how to write both poetic and factual type responses. The poem doesn't have to rhyme. Write responses on at least four strips. You may wish to use a frame sentence for younger children. (Example: In the rainforest, the animals sing their noisy, squawking tune as they howl, chirp, and hiss through the dense sticky air; In the rainforest, there are many species of birds like the . . . .)

- After writing the four strips, model and think aloud as you decide how you will order them into a poem. What sounds good at the beginning, middle, and end? Why? Read the poem aloud.

- Invite students to respond to your strip poem. Ask them to tell if they would have ordered the strips differently. Why?

- Ask the class to assist you in listing the steps involved in creating the strip poem.

Guide the Strategy/Cooperative Groups or Pairs

- Review a book, article, chapter, or story the class has read. Then discuss key vocabulary and concepts and create a key vocabulary chart to use when students write their strips.

- Pass out at least four different colored strips. Ask students to write a brief response on their strip. You may opt to use a frame sentence for students to complete. (Examples: Friendship is . . . , The revolutionary war . . . , Martin Luther King was a man who...)

- After students write on their strips, invite students to form groups with others who have the same colored strips. The colored strips serve as a means for forming collaborative groups. Students in each group work to order their sentences into a poem. They decide on and practice a mode for presenting the poem to the class (choral reading, parts, in unison, acting out, singing, etc.).

Box 7.5. Model—Practice—Apply the Strategy in Different Classroom Structures

Guided Reading	Literature Circles
After reading with a guided reading group, pass out strips and ask students to write a one-sentence response. Place in pocket chart, read, and as a group select the order for the poem. Use strips to summarize and respond to the reading with fiction or nonfiction.	The summarizer (Daniels, 1994) in the group can pass out strips and lead the circle in writing a strip poem. Each student quickly writes a one-sentence response and the group orders the poem to share with the entire class.
Whole Class	**Independent Work**
Use strip poems for summarizing chapters in the social studies or science units. Ask groups or pairs to write strip poems to summarize their learning in a content area. Students can write a creative, descriptive response or a fact they learned. Groups perform and share.	Provide strips during independent work time and allow students to work alone or with a partner to produce strip poems. Illustrate, share, and display the poems.

Reflect on the Strategy/Assess the Strategy

- Ask students to reflect on how creating a strip poem helps them synthesize and remember what they read. How do the strip poems differ for fiction and nonfiction?

- Collect strip poems and if students have initialed their responses, you can informally observe the contributions of individual students.

- Check to see if students are accurately synthesizing information from the reading.

- Are the students representing literal events or facts, or are they moving to more inferential thinking?

- If some students misrepresent the information from the text, consider meeting with individuals or students to guide them in rereading and creating additional strips for a poem.

- To guide students to "go deeper" and past literal responses, you may wish to guide and model an additional strip poem with a small group.

- For further assessment suggestions refer to the Appendix on page 223–234.

Strip Poem

1. Think about what you have read. Write a strip for a strip poem. Either write a descriptive piece of writing, or a fact that you learned.
2. Meet with your group. Take turns reading your strips.
3. Arrange all of the group members' strips into several different orders until you find the poem you want. What sounds best to you?
4. Practice reading and acting out the poem. Share with the class. Tell how you decided on the order of your poem.

My life is coming to a end.

Kristina

Joey's dirty and ripped up pants and the sad look on Mary Alice's face gave a clue to their life.

Ravinder

You could feel the sadness, and depression from the Japanese in manzanar.

Adrian

A place they were trapped in life filled with sadness.

Adrian

the smiles turned upside down as sadness crossed faces.

Lacy

My life is coming to a halt.

Kristina

We read different books. We decided not to be so specific and to figure out a connection to all of them.

Strip Poem

1. Think about what you have read. Write a strip for a strip poem. Either write a descriptive piece of writing, or a fact that you learned.
2. Meet with your group. Take turns reading your strips.
3. Arrange all of the group members' strips into several different orders until you find the poem you want. What sounds best to you?
4. Practice reading and acting out the poem. Share with the class. Tell how you decided on the order of your poem.

Super Six Comprehension Strategies: 35 Lessons and More for Reading Success by Lori Oczkus

Synthesis Starters

Objective: Using sentence starters as discussion prompts, students reflect on their synthesis of what they have read.

Materials: The synthesis starter sentences—possibly cut apart for students to "draw" from an envelope, can or pile, and Synthesis Starters form

Introduce/Model the Strategy

- Inform students that they form a synthesis or big picture as they read. These synthesis starters may guide their thinking as they discuss their synthesis with others.

- Select reading material that all of the students have read. Review the material briefly.

- Model and think aloud from each of the synthesis starters in response to the text. You may opt to do so in writing on sentence strips or on the overhead projector. Make sure you model how to give evidence of your thinking with examples from the reading material.

- Call on a few students and invite them to discuss several of the synthesis starters in a literature circle in front of the class. Or model with a partner how to discuss a synthesis starter.

Guide the Strategy/Cooperative Groups or Pairs

- Ask students to reflect on what they witnessed in the modeling portion of the lesson. How did you comment on each synthesis strip by using evidence from the text? How did the students who modeled the strips work together to discuss the strips?

- Guide the class in a synthesis strip discussion by presenting one strip at a time and then allowing each table to briefly discuss the strip. One student serves as a scribe in each group. Invite each table to share a written response on a completed strip. Post strips.

- Once you have guided the class in discussions and have modeled how to respond to each synthesis starter using a think-aloud, allow groups to cut strips apart and then members draw strips from an envelope, pile, or can. The student who draws the strip leads the discussion for the group.

- After all the groups have discussed the strips, call on one group to model for the rest of the class as they discuss one of the strips.

Box 7.6. Model–Practice–Apply the Strategy in Different Classroom Structures

Guided Reading	Literature Circles
After reading a selection, invite students to draw a synthesis starter to respond to. Provide white boards for the responses or allow students to illustrate their ideas. Each student shares or if time is limited, students share with partners. Students may also write their responses at their desks and bring their ideas to the next guided reading session to discuss and share.	The discussion director leads the group as each student draws a synthesis starter and gives a response. Then the discussion director invites the group to pass the strips to the left and to once again give their unique response to the new strip. Continuing passing the strips until each group member responds to all of the strips.
Struggling Readers	Independent Work
Model in a small group setting how to respond to each synthesis starter. Show students how to reread the prompt and how to reread the material while thinking about the prompt. Guide and practice in material at the groups' instructional reading level.	Students write responses in a journal or directly on strips in preparation for a discussion with peers or the teacher. They may also illustrate their responses.

Reflect on the Strategy/Assess the Strategy

- Ask students to reflect on synthesis starters. How do these discussion starters help them deepen their understanding of the text? How does their thinking change while reading the text? How does discussing other's ideas strengthen their comprehension?

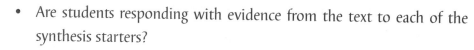

- Are students responding with evidence from the text to each of the synthesis starters?

- If students are unable to provide evidence from their thinking and the text, model using texts that are easier to read. Then move back into more difficult grade level texts. Also try selecting one synthesis starter at a time and guide a small group to share their individual responses.

- For further assessment suggestions refer to the Appendix on page 223–234.

Synthesis Starters

1. Choose one of the synthesis sentence starters to finish. Either choose one or draw one out of a container.
2. Share with others your synthesis sentence.
3. Talk about how you create a synthesis for your reading using your background combined with the book to come up with a new idea.

At first I thought and now I think . . . .

At first I felt, now I feel . . .

I have been changed by this book (chapter, article) in this way . . .

From reading this text, I will remember . . .

The theme in this text was . . .

An "aha" I got from the reading was . . .

A light bulb went on in my head and I realized . . .

My opinion on this topic now is . . .

I will remember the visual I built in my mind for . . .

Super Six Comprehension Strategies: 35 Lessons and More for Reading Success by Lori Oczkus

Teachers As Readers

Reflecting on Our Experiences as Adult Readers

As we read we are building a big picture or synthesis of our understanding of the text that includes themes, lessons, morals, and other deeper meanings associated with the author's purpose. We also quite naturally summarize not just at the end of every chapter but all along the reading road to understanding. By reflecting on our own summarizing and synthesis in our personal reading, we can come to grips with ways to help our students become aware of these two powerhouse strategies to improve their own enjoyment and comprehension of texts.

My Reflections on Summarizing and Synthesizing

Oprah Winfrey's Magazine has a frequent article called, "Books That Made A Difference" where celebrities share their all-time favorite books. Some of the reads these famous readers share might be new and others classics but all are books that had a powerful impact on the life of the celebrity. When I reflect on summarizing and synthesizing I think of my own list of all time favorites which include The Red Tent *(Diamant, 1997),* Gone with the Wind *(Mitchell, 1936), several nonfiction books by Ann Lamott, and* The Poisonwood Bible *(1998), by Barbara Kingsolver. For each of those special books, I suppose I could be forced to write a brief summary, but I might need to page through the books for a moment to refresh my memory. And my synthesis for each book? I guess each one has left a permanent impression that I won't ever forget (unlike other books I've read and two years later can't remember what they were about). The strong emotions, visual images, and incredible writing are all factors for these candidates to be on my best books list.*

The book I'd like to briefly focus on as I reflect on summarizing and synthesis is The Poisonwood Bible *by Barbara Kingsolver. I am choosing this epic book because I thoroughly enjoyed Kingsolver's writing, which is loaded with visual images and metaphors not because I was particularly enthralled by the sad story. The book is the story of a missionary who takes his four daughters and wife to the Belgian Congo to save souls. Each chapter is written in the voice of a different daughter as they weave their tale of woe and hardships that span from their harsh environment to their distant father. I constantly summarized the story line to keep up and even though, it was obvious which daughter was "talking" I often reread to make sure I understood what that daughter was implying.*

My synthesis was definitely like a jigsaw puzzle (Harvey & Goudvis, 2000) that I slowly pieced together with each unveiling chapter. I inferred a feeling for what life in the Belgian Congo would have been like at that time. I also learned what the role of women was and felt their oppression. The message? Well, I won't spoil it for you. But if you read this book, you'll walk away with Kingsolver's message and a few of your own.

My favorite book list grows each year. I've taken Regie Routman's (2000) advice and I keep a reading log of the books I read each month and year. As I glance over the list from the past few years, I can't help but notice that the favorites are the ones that have left the strongest synthesis or impressions with me. I can't wait to see if one of the books in the big "to read" pile next to my bed make it onto my list. I certainly hope so!

Your Reflections on Summarizing and Synthesizing

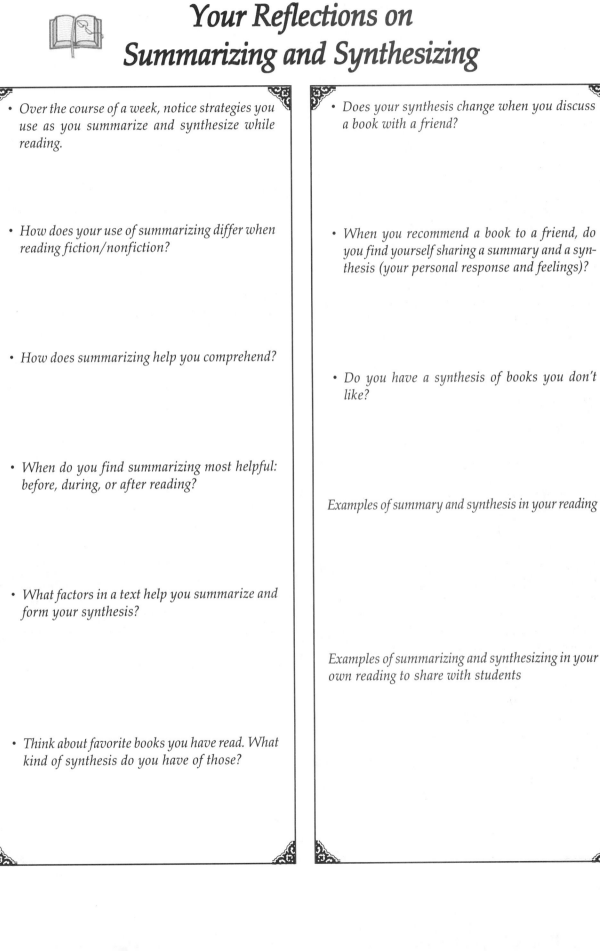

- *Over the course of a week, notice strategies you use as you summarize and synthesize while reading.*

- *How does your use of summarizing differ when reading fiction/nonfiction?*

- *How does summarizing help you comprehend?*

- *When do you find summarizing most helpful: before, during, or after reading?*

- *What factors in a text help you summarize and form your synthesis?*

- *Think about favorite books you have read. What kind of synthesis do you have of those?*

- *Does your synthesis change when you discuss a book with a friend?*

- *When you recommend a book to a friend, do you find yourself sharing a summary and a synthesis (your personal response and feelings)?*

- *Do you have a synthesis of books you don't like?*

Examples of summary and synthesis in your reading

Examples of summarizing and synthesizing in your own reading to share with students

Summarizing

References

Armbruster, B. B., Anderson, T. H., & Ostertag, J. (1987). Does text structure/summarization instruction facilitate learning from expository text? *Reading Research Quarterly, 22,* 331–346.

Brown, A. L, & Day, J. D. (1983). Macrorules for summarizing texts: The development of expertise. *Journal of Verbal Learning and Verbal Behavior, 22* 1–14.

Williams, J. P. (2002). Using the theme scheme to improve story comprehension. In C. C. Block, & M. Pressley (Eds.), *Comprehension instruction: Research-based best practices* (pp. 126–139). New York: Guilford Press.

Evaluating

> *"Expert readers and writers continuously consider their own success. They evaluate the text to determine genre and purpose for reading, and they consider the quality of the text and how much they like it."* **Marge Lipson**, *in* Developing Skills and Strategies in an Integrated Literature-Based Reading Program, *p. 8.*

> *"Good readers are also highly evaluative of the text, deciding whether a text is interesting or the arguments made in it are credible. They make evaluations of the style of the text (e.g., the quality of the writing), as well as its content."* **Michael Pressley,** *in* What Research Has to Say About Reading Instruction, *p. 290.*

Thoughts on Evaluating

As I sat down to look over the newspaper articles I had given the fourth and fifth graders to highlight, I was blinded by page after page of yellow. The articles looked as if they had been spray painted rather than highlighted. This pretest yielded exactly what I needed to know: could the students evaluate and determine which facts are the most important? Like most students, they needed more modeling and practice to help them sort out main ideas in a text.

Teachers everywhere complain that students have a hard time selecting main ideas when reading. Students have difficulty using the structure of the text to help them decide which ideas are most important in fiction and nonfiction texts. Determining importance is a particularly helpful strategy when learning to sort key points from less important ones when reading a nonfiction text.

Determining important ideas from unimportant ones (Harvey & Goudvis, 2000) is a critical reading strategy that is part of a bigger strategy: evaluation.

Imagine the reader stepping up to scales throughout the reading process to evaluate or weigh important ideas, opinions, arguments, the author's craft, and even his own progress as a reader. When students become evaluators they judge, argue, select, rate, prove, recommend, and criticize.

Besides determining important ideas, good readers also give a thumbs up or down to the text, the author, and their engagement with the text. When I taught fifth grade, we spent one morning a month giving videotaped book reports. The tiny newscasters sat behind an anchor desk, donned a suit coat, and a microphone while a huge spot light (the overhead projector) shined brightly in on them. The captive audience never budged for over 90 minutes, spell bound by their peers comments, criticisms, and recommendations for exciting texts to read. I was always amazed at their creativity and insights as they evaluated the morning away.

Although, evaluation is at the top of the critical thinking scale, it is a reachable goal for all students. This chapter contains some lessons that will help you

Evaluating

to make evaluation very explicit for your students by scaffolding experiences where they learn, determine important ideas in texts, judge the texts they read, and evaluate their progress as readers. By helping your students to think more deeply and evaluate as they read, they improve their comprehension and enjoyment of text.

How Does Evaluating Help Students Comprehend?

Good readers continuously evaluate the reading material as well as their own performance during reading. When readers evaluate, they judge and back their opinions of the text, rank important ideas, critique the author's craft, rate the book, and decide if they did well as a reader. Harvey and Goudivis (2000) emphasize teaching children to decipher between important and unimportant information, especially in nonfiction text.

Lipson and Cooper (2002) encourage teachers to explicitly teach students to think metacognitively, or think about their own reading progress and whether they liked the text or not. These researchers also ascertain that many students need explicit instruction in author's craft. Explicit lessons in determining importance in text, evaluating ideas in a text, critiquing the author's craft, and monitoring one's own progress as a reader all contribute to improving comprehension. Given its complexity, evaluation warrants specific lessons to guide students to reach the highest levels of critical thinking as they comprehend text.

Evaluate: Determining Importance In Text

The National Reading Panel (2000) has recommended that children receive explicit instruction in text structures to improve comprehension. Working with text structure before, during, and after reading gives students tools for determining main ideas.

In fiction, knowledge of story elements such as, characters, problem, and key events assist students in determining what is important. A story map or other story organizer provides students with the structure they need to summarize the reading material and to guide their reading while reading. Also, it is helpful to teach students what to expect in various genres such as fantasy, folk tales, mysteries, and realistic fiction.

When reading nonfiction, students need to learn how to utilize text features such as, headings, captions, charts, maps, and graphs to navigate their way through the content and to determine key ideas to remember. Harvey and Goudvis (2000) suggest working with a two-column chart and categorizing facts learned from a nonfiction text as either interesting or important. I often use the interesting and important chart (Harvey & Goudvis, 2002) with first guide students in determining which facts are important and from there I work with students to circle the most important ideas to create a summary.

By teaching students to use text features and graphic organizers, we can provide supportive structures that students rely on as they evaluate and determine importance in both fiction and nonfiction texts.

Evaluation: Promoting Critical Thinking—Debating Issues

Whether reading a fairy tale with first graders or a newspaper article with sixth graders, you can look for a controversial two-sided issue for students to evaluate. A primary example might include discussing whether students think that Goldilocks should have entered the bears house or not and why. Or perhaps after reading Susan Meddaugh's *Tree of Birds* (1990) the students debate whether the boy in the story should have taken care of the injured bird or not. When reading a history text, fifth graders take sides and debate the advantages or disadvantages King Ferninand and Queen Isabella of Spain considered before deciding to fund the voyage of Columbus. By asking students to discuss some issue in the reading that they may agree or disagree with, we can promote critical thinking and guide students in developing their ability to evaluate. You can also encourage students to rank the words, characters, and ideas presented in the text and give reasons for their rankings.

Evalution, Considering Author's Craft

Many students need instruction in evaluating the author's craft (Lipson & Cooper, 2002). As good readers read, they evaluate if the author has done a good job constructing a text that is understandable, creating an interesting text, and engaging the reader. If we ask our students to pause throughout the reading and to evaluate and respond to the author's craft we can deep their comprehension and enjoyment. (Lipson & Cooper, 2002) Some of the devices author's use that students can discuss include use of graphics, humor, imagery, poetic language, suspense, characters, and plot. We can ask, "Do you think the author did a good job with . . . and why do you think so?" Before reading, we can prepare students to evaluate by asking them to be on the lookout for how a certain aspect of author's craft develops and to be ready with examples. One example is when we read *The Great Kapok Tree* by Lynn Cherry (1990) I ask students to watch for the persuasive language that the author builds into the arguments of the animals.

Evaluation, Promoting Self-Evaluation

Another way good readers evaluate, is by reflecting on their own progress as they read the text. They ask, "Did I understand what I read? Do I remember the text? Did I make connections? Did I like the text or not? If it was too easy, hard, or boring for me, what made it that way? Would I recommend it to a friend or not? How does this title compare to other books the author has written?" This kind of thinking about one's own thinking, or self-evaluation is called metacognition (Paris, Wasik, & Turner, 1991) and promotes self-monitoring and strategy use.

Evaluation is sort of the mother of all critical thinking strategies because good readers judge, critique, and value, ideas, the author's craft, and their own reading through self-assessment.

Evaluating

Box 8.1. Teaching Evaluation

Before Reading Evaluating	During Reading Evaluating	After Reading Evaluating
Fiction Is the book interesting? What supports in the text or illustrations help me to predict what it will be about? What do I know about this genre? **Nonfiction** What do I think this will be about? What are the text features I can use to guide my reading? **Author's Style, Craft** So far, what do I notice or predict about the author's craft and style? How is the author helping me understand what the book will be about? What is the author or illustrator doing well or not so well so far? **Self-evaluation** What attracts me to this text? What do I think I will like about it? Is it like other books I have read and understood? Do I have background in the topic? Can I make predictions? Might this book be too hard, easy, or boring for me? Why do I think so?	**Fiction** What is the book about so far? What are the main ideas? Are there any ideas that I agree with, disagree with? Is the book like other books in the genre? **Nonfiction** What are the main ideas so far? What should I remember? What is important? What isn't important? What are the ideas in the text to agree or disagree with? Are the text features helping me understand the text? **Author's Style, Craft** What is the author doing well? What would I like to ask the author about? What is the author doing to support my understanding? **Self-evaluation** Do I still like the text or not? Why? Is the text difficult, easy, or boring at this point? Why? Am I getting the main ideas? Why or why not? Am I stopping to figure out any parts or words that are confusing? How? What?	**Fiction** What was the book about? Are there any ideas or character actions I agree or disagree with? Is the book like the others in the genre? **Nonfiction** What are the main ideas? How is the text organized? What is a summary of the main ideas? Did the text features and organization help me? Is there anything I agree or disagree with I the text? **Author's Style, Craft** What did the author do well? What would I like to ask the author about? What other books does this remind me of? How would I rate the author's style? **Self-evaluation** Did I like the text or not? Why? Was the text difficult, easy, boring, or just right? Why? Did I learn what I thought I would? Why? Why not? Did I get the main ideas? Why or why not? How did I do as a reader when I got stuck? How would I rate myself as a reader in this text?

Evaluating

Super Six Comprehension Strategies: 35 Lessons and More for Reading Success by Lori Oczkus

Evaluating Classroom Vignettes

Primary or Intermediate/Evaluating "Should there be Zoos?" "Agree or Disagree?"

"Are zoos good or bad? " probes Miss Wright.

"I think zoos are bad because the animals look so bored," explains Ryan.

"I think zoos help animals from becoming extinct," defends third grade Christina.

"Who else has an argument for or against zoos?" inquires Miss Wright, the reading specialist in her weekly visit to the classroom.

The room is quiet so Miss Wright directs the students to open their copies of *Should There Be Zoos?* by Tony Stead (Mondo, 2000) to review the persuasive arguments for and against zoos. Partners huddle in discussion, as they pour over the pages in the clever text that was written by a fourth grade class with their teacher.

After leading a discussion of the arguments both for and against zoos, and creating a chart to display the arguments, Miss Wright asks the students to form two lines, across from each other so they can debate in pairs. When she signals, she designates that one line take the "for zoos" arguments and the other the "against zoos." She rings a bell and students who are lined up across from each other begin the debate choosing arguments from the chart or what they remember from the book. Miss Wright signals and students switch partners as one line moves one step to the right. This time the sides switch arguments. The process continues until students have debated for and against zoos for several turns. They return to their desks to write and illustrate a persuasive poster for or against zoos including at least two arguments.

The result? These third grade students are experiencing evaluation by debating real world issues. Just wait until they hit the high school debate team!

Intermediate/"Get the Facts" Race

The fifth grade students are positioned in their natural disaster teams, which include earthquakes, lightning, tornadoes, fires, floods, and hurricanes. Each group of five students is equipped with three or four reference books or materials from the internet, a large piece of butcher paper, and markers. The task is to gather at least eight important facts about their chosen natural disaster, to record those facts on the chart, and to prepare a presentation to the class all in less than 20 minutes! Mrs. Le, gives the signal and they all dive into their books and begin recording facts. After a few minutes the fires group appears stuck, so Mrs. Jones kneels on the floor with them.

"We can't find anything important to write down," admits Adria.

Mrs. Le reviews how to skim and scan over the headings, illustrations, and texts to search for information that may be important. She guides the group as they begin to record their facts. Once on a roll, she slips away from them to visit other groups.

She passes out a copy of the *Kid's Survival Handbook* by Claire Llewellyn (2001) to every group. Each group incorporates the suggestions for surviving their chosen natural disaster. When she calls time, the groups beg for a few more minutes, which Mrs. Le happily provides. After the lively presentations, she asks the class to reflect on their techniques for determining which facts were important enough to make the cut for their posters. The "disaster lesson" proves to be a success!

Get the Facts!

Objective: Students skim, scan, and read quickly to jot down as many facts as they can gather in a short time frame. They sort the ideas collected into either important or more important categories to learn to determine importance.

Materials: Nonfiction texts, butcher paper (optional), the Get the Facts sheet, other paper to sort strips on, scissors, markers or pencils, and self-stick notes.

Introduce/Model the Strategy

- Tell students that sometimes when they read nonfiction they may need to quickly read and decide which facts are the most important to remember. Today they will do an activity called "Get the Facts!" where they will practice reading for important facts and taking notes in their own words.

- Model, "Get the Facts" using a nonfiction source that all students can see.

- Read aloud from the text stopping to think aloud about important facts as you write them into your own words.

- As you read you may want to mark with self-stick notes the eight points in the text and then reread and write the points on the "Get the Facts" sheet. Think aloud as you decide which eight facts are the most important to include.

- After recording the eight facts in front of students on the "Get the Facts" sheet, model any of the following:

  - writing the eight facts on a butcher paper and illustrating the facts with words and quick drawings

  - cutting the "Get the Facts" strips apart and grouping them in one of two ways: by *Important Facts/Most Important Facts* or by *What I Already Knew/What I Learned.*

Guide the Strategy/Cooperative Groups or Pairs

- Guide the class as they read a nonfiction article, chapter, or book together. Stop at various points throughout the text and invite coopera-

Evaluating

tive groups or pairs to reread and select important facts to record. Groups share with the class. Continue to work your way through the text.

- After reading a text as a class and selecting important facts, invite cooperative groups to decorate a butcher paper poster with their facts. Display posters and groups circulate around the room, studying each other's posters.

- Invite each group to write their facts on sentence strips or adding machine tape. Then the students sort the strips into Important Facts/Most Important Facts or What We Already Knew/What We Learned. Groups share their findings with the class.

- Students may wish to race to gather at least the eight important facts. Their facts must be readable.

Box 8.2. Model—Practice—Apply the Strategy in Different Classroom Structures

Struggling Readers	Literature Circles
As students read a nonfiction text silently, invite them to hunt for one or two facts they think are important. They write their facts on strips and after reading share. Guide the group to share the facts into two columns, Important Facts, More Important Facts. Guide students as they give reasons for their facts.	The summarizer may bring facts that he/she has gathered and recorded on strips. The summarizer dumps the facts in the middle of the group and invites each student to take a turn and draw one fact strip and then each student shares the fact. As a group they discuss which facts belong in the Important Facts column and which go in the More Important Facts column.
Cross-Age Tutors	**Independent Work**
Older buddies invite younger buddies to review a nonfiction text and record facts on strips. The older buddy records the fact and the younger buddy illustrates with a small drawing directly on the strip. The two collect a set amount of strips. They rotate to other pairs of buddies and share their findings.	A "Get the Facts" center can be stocked with strips, markers, and various nonfiction books to use for gathering facts. Students work independently or in pairs. Students may illustrate facts.

Evaluating

Reflect on the Strategy/Assess the Strategy

- Ask students to discuss how the various aspects of this activity builds comprehension.

- Discuss collecting the facts in a short amount of time, rereading to determine which facts to remember and record, writing the facts in one's own words, and sorting the facts into categories of important and more important or known facts, new facts.

- If students have difficulty selecting facts, practice in smaller teacher-led groups. Model rereading and pulling out main ideas. Model how to paraphrase by circling or highlighting key words and then thinking of other words with the same meaning.

- Save students "Get the Facts" sheets and date to show growth and to determine which students need additional modeling in a small group.

- For further assessment suggestions refer to the Appendix on page 223–234.

Get the Facts!

1. Choose a topic. Gather at least three books, articles, or other sources on the topic. Work on a team or in a pair to gather as many facts as you can in a set amount of time. (10–30 minutes). Try to gather at least eight facts.

2. Read and write your facts as fast (and neatly) as you can. Be sure to use your own words. Choose one of the following ways to write your facts
   - a piece of butcher paper (each person writes on a section of the paper with markers—also illustrate)
   - or this sheet then cut apart and combine in an order that makes sense.
   - you could order your facts in two columns, Important Facts, Most Important Facts or Facts We Already Knew, Facts We Learned

3. Share your facts with the class.

Facts We Collected

Super Six Comprehension Strategies: 35 Lessons and More for Reading Success by Lori Oczkus

Think Of Three

Objective: Students will listen to or read a text and think of three important facts or ideas, they should remember after reading a text. Students practice determining importance in a text by comparing facts they have recorded.
Materials: Nonfiction or fiction texts and Think of Three form.

Introduce/Model the Strategy

- Tell students that as they read texts, they gather important ideas that they need to remember to understand the text.

- In this activity, students will be asked to focus on listening for three ideas to remember. Then they will compare the ideas they have selected to the ideas others have chosen.

- Read aloud from a brief portion of nonfiction or fiction text. Ask the students to listen as you read and to think about the three most important facts or ideas in the text. Read the text again and this time invite students to raise a finger (until they have three raised) each time they hear what they think is an important fact.

- Stop and think aloud as you select three important ideas, concepts, events, or facts from the text. Write the three on a piece of paper.

- Ask the students if they agree with your three points. Survey the class and ask students to raise their hands after you read each point to see if they also had selected that point.

- Encourage students to discuss any other points they choose. Share with students why you thought your points were important.

Guide the Strategy/Cooperative Groups or Pairs

- Read aloud from a text and ask students to listen for three main ideas. Read the text again and ask students to write three ideas on a paper (no names—saves embarrassment!).

- Collect the papers and read some of them. The class helps you tally main ideas from papers. Which ideas occur the most?

- Lead the class in a discussion as each group shares the three main ideas from the papers they collected. Which ideas occur the most? Does the class agree those are the main ideas of the text? Why or why not?

- Ask pairs of students to work together to find three main ideas. Then pairs rotate around the room sharing their ideas with other pairs. On cue, pairs switch. Discuss afterward with the entire class, which ideas occurred most often. Do the students agree or not? Why?

Box 8.3. Model—Practice—Apply the Strategy in Different Classroom Structures

Struggling Readers	Literature Circles
Read with a small group of students in a nonfiction picture book. Read a text together and list important facts after every page on a chart together. At the end of the text, study the list and circle the three main ideas. Also, practice finding three main ideas and then comparing findings with others. Illustrate findings.	The summarizer (Daniels, 1994) asks each student to "Think of Three" important events or facts from the reading. Students write their three and then the summarizer tallies the responses. Which responses show up most often?
Cross-Age Tutors Older buddies practice finding the main ideas in a text with peers in their class-room before meeting with the younger buddies. Older buddies ask younger buddies to hold up a finger for each important fact they hear.	**Independent Work** Students read high-interest nonfiction texts and write and illustrate three important facts they read to share later with classmates. Students who read the same text, discuss which facts they agree are most important.

Evaluating

Evaluating

Reflect on the Strategy/Assess the Strategy

- Ask students to reflect on "Think of Three" and tell how they go about selecting the most important facts when reading. What happens to their comprehension of the text when they discuss important facts with others?

- Collect "Think of Three" sheets with student names on them and evaluate. Are students choosing minor details or main important facts, ideas, or events?

- If students are having difficulty selecting important ideas, meet with small groups and use high-interest nonfiction or brief articles to practice "Think of Three" with. Practice listing many facts and then circling the three most important ones.

- For further assessment suggestions refer to the Appendix on page 223–234.

Think of Three

- Read a text. As you read try to notice three important points.
- Skim the text again and review what you read. Choose three important points. (If you are reading an article, you may want to highlight your points.)
- Write your points in your own words on the spaces below.
- Exchange and read the three points of others by doing one of the following (Your teacher will tell you which one to check)

  ____Keep a tally as you roam the room and share with one person in the class at a time. Keep sharing until you have reached every one.

  ___ Get into a group and put your papers in a pile and then trade piles with another group.

  ____Your teacher organizes an exchange by mixing up the papers in a hat. Draw one. Read and discuss.

  ____Which ideas were on most think of three lists?

- - - - - - - - - - - - Tear or cut on this line - - - - - - - - - - - - -

Think of Three

1.

2.

3.

Super Six Comprehension Strategies: 35 Lessons and More for Reading Success by Lori Oczkus

Rate and Rank the Reading

Objective: Students will evaluate the text, ideas in the text, and their own reading of the text as they rate and rank various points.

Materials: Nonfiction and fiction texts, Rate form, Rank form.

Introduce/Model the Strategy

- Tell students that when good readers read, they engage in evaluating or judging various aspects of the book, author's style, and even their own progress as readers.

- As you model, you will model for students what you are thinking as you rate and rank the reading.

- Explain the term rate. Survey the children and ask them to rate a food such as licorice or fish. Discuss the rating scale as follows:

  3 =you don't like it

  2= you like it just okay

  1=you love this food

- Also discuss the term rank. Survey the children again and ask them to think of their top 3 favorite foods and then rank order them in order of their favorites.

  1=your first favorite

  2=your second favorite

  3=your third favorite

- Select a text that all can see or choose one that the class is already familiar with. Think aloud as you use the Rate and Rank sheets.

- Model responses for each of the ratings on page 213. Explain your rating of the text, author's style, illustrations, and your own understanding of the text.

- Do the same and model your thinking as you use the ranking sheet for the text.

Guide the Strategy/Cooperative Groups or Pairs

- As you model and after each item, stop and invite students to fill in the same item on their sheets.

- Encourage students to fill out the rate sheet and share with a partner or group.

- Invite students to fill in their ranking sheets and share with a partner or group.

- Gather students and discuss their findings. Do other students have the same or different rankings? Do students agree on some items and not others?

Box 8.4. Model—Practice—Apply the Strategy in Different Classroom Structures

English Language Learners	Literature Circles
Guide English language learners as they rate and rank the texts you read together. Try using a thumbs up, sideways, and thumbs down as a physical response as students rate various aspects of the reading.	The discussion director can select one item off of the Rate and Rank sheet and ask each member of the group to respond individually and then share with the group.
Cross-Age Tutors	**Independent Work**
Older buddies survey their younger buddies after reading a book aloud to them. Together they find examples for their answers.	Students make book Rate and Rank posters for books they've read. As a class come up with a rubric or scoring guide for what the requirements are for a poster that is done well.

Reflect on the Strategy/Assess the Strategy

- Ask students to reflect on rating and ranking processes. How do they help the students understand the text? Which is harder: rating or ranking? Is it harder to rate and rank a fiction text or a nonfiction one?

- Try analyzing data and graphing the class ratings and rankings.

Evaluating

- Collect student samples of rating and ranking and see if they are backing up their answers with logical reasons. If students are having difficulty rating and ranking, then model more and bring in real-world examples from the newspaper (sporting events, movie reviews, restaurant reviews, etc.).

- When working with English Language Learners, you may wish to use some concrete examples of ranking such as favorite television programs, books, or flavors of ice cream. Encourage students to give reasons for their rankings. Then try rating and ranking ideas from texts you have read together.

- For further assessment suggestions refer to the Appendix on page 223–234.

Rate the Reading

Circle one answer for each box and explain your choice with examples from the reading.

Rate the text overall.

3	2	1
I didn't like it.	It was okay.	I loved it!

Explain/ Examples _____

_____

Rate the author's style.

3	2	1
I didn't like it.	It was okay.	I loved it!

Explain/ Examples _____

_____

Rate the illustrations.

3	2	1
I didn't like them.	They were okay.	I loved them!

Explain/ Examples _____

_____

Rate how well you understood the text.

3	2	1
I didn't understand it.	I understood it okay.	I really got it!

Explain/ Examples _____

_____

What else could you rate? Find something to rate in the reading.

Super Six Comprehension Strategies: 35 Lessons and More for Reading Success by Lori Oczkus

Rank the Reading

Put in order your top three in each category. #1 is the most important, #3 is your third choice in order of importance.

Rank the three most important words from the reading.

Word	Why this word is important?
1.	
2.	
3.	

Rank the three most important characters from the reading.

Character	Why this character is important?
1.	
2.	
3.	

Rank the three most important ideas/events from the reading.

Ideas/Events	Why these ideas or events are important?
1.	
2.	
3.	

What else could you rank from the reading? Design your own rank order.

Student Samples

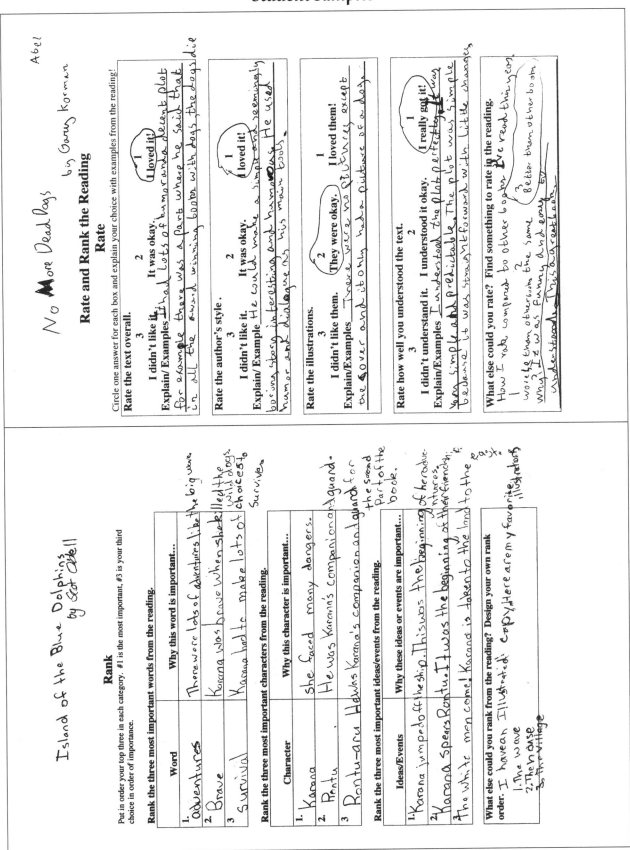

Abel

No More Dead Dogs
by Gordon Korman

Rate and Rank the Reading

Rate

Circle one answer for each box and explain your choice with examples from the reading!

Rate the text overall.

3	2	1
I didn't like it.	It was okay.	I loved it!

Explain/Examples I had lots of humor and a decent plot for example there was a part where he said that in all the award winning books with dogs the dog's die

Rate the author's style.

3	2	1
I didn't like it.	It was okay.	I loved it!

Explain/Example He could make a simple and seemingly boring story interesting and humorous He used humor and dialogue as his main tools

Rate the illustrations.

3	2	1
I didn't like them.	They were okay.	I loved them!

Explain/Examples There were no pictures except the cover and it only had a picture of a dog.

Rate how well you understood the text.

3	2	1
I didn't understand it.	I understood it okay.	I really got it!

Explain/Examples I understood the plot perfectly. It was very simple and predictable. The plot was simple because it was straightforward with little changes.

What else could you rate? Find something to rate in the reading.
How I rate it compared to other books I've read this year

2   3
worse than others   the same   better than other books
why? It was funny and easy to
understand. This was a great book.

Island of the Blue Dolphins
by Scott O'Dell

Rank

Put in order your top three in each category. #1 is the most important, #3 is your third choice in order of importance.

Rank the three most important words from the reading.

	Word	Why this word is important...
1.	adventures	There were lots of adventures like the big wave
2.	Brave	Karana was brave when she killed the wild dogs.
3	Survival	Karana had to make lots of choices to survive.

Rank the three most important characters from the reading.

	Character	Why this character is important...
1.	Karana	She faced many dangers.
2.	Rontu	He was Karana's companion and guard.
3	Rontu-aru	He was Karana's companion and guard for the second part of the book.

Rank the three most important ideas or events are important from the reading.

	Ideas/Events	Why these ideas or events are important...
1.	Karana jumped off the ship.	This was the beginning of her adventures.
2.	Karana spears Rontu.	It was the beginning of their friendship.
3.	The white men come.	Karana is taken to the land to the east.

What else could you rank from the reading? Design your own rank order. I have an Illustrated copy. Here are my favorite illustrations.
1. The wave
2. The house
3. The village

Evaluating

Agree Or Disagree

Objective: Students and the teacher work together to reread the reading material searching for issues with two sides, characters' actions to debate, or even various opinions surrounding the author's craft.

Materials: Nonfiction text or fiction texts and Agree or Disagree sheet.

Introduce/Model the Strategy

- Tell students that as they read they can look for places in the text where they may agree or disagree with an issue brought up in the text, the author's craft, or a character's action.

- Choose a text students are already familiar with and reread or review it together. Select one idea that may have two sides to it and discuss both sides. Also, model whether you agree or disagree with a character's actions and discuss why. Select some aspect of the author's craft that you agree or disagree with and explain your viewpoint.

- Select another text the class is familiar with and review it. Repeat the steps above with this text so students will see that every text may have some idea to evaluate and consider.

Guide the Strategy/Cooperative Groups or Pairs

- Encourage students to work together to discuss controversial or two-sided issues brought out in the texts that you have modeled. Allow partners to discuss first then lead a whole class discussion.

- Assign tables or groups of students' issues to consider as all groups read the same text.

- Ask students to list both sides of each issue they discuss. They can make posters illustrating various viewpoints. Assign to groups:

  - An issue in the text that has two sides. *Should .... What if.... Some people agree that_____ because _____ others may disagree that _____ beacause _____*

  - A character's actions. *Do you think _____ should have _____ ? Why or why not?*

- The author's choice in craft, style, or story line. *Do you agree with the way the author ended, began, and carries on the reading Why or why not?*

Box 8.5. Model—Practice—Apply the Strategy in Different Classroom Structures

Struggling Readers	**Literature Circles**
Guide struggling readers in a small group setting prior to conducting the agree/disagree lesson with the class. Guide the students in finding issues that have two sides. Make a chart listing both sides of each issue discussed. The next day, or later students are prepared to participate in cooperative groups or a whole class discussion.	The discussion director in each circle finds a controversial or two-sided issue to discuss. Groups report on their discussions to the whole class.
Cross-Age Tutors	**English Language Learners**
Older buddies search through picture books for controversial issues to discuss with younger buddies. Ask buddies to consider if they agree with the way the author ended the story or piece. Do you agree with the character's decision to . . . ? Would you have done things differently? Why or why not?	Ask students to act out various two-sided issues that they are evaluating from the text.

Reflect on the Strategy/Assess the Strategy

- Ask students to reflect on evaluating issues in texts? How are they doing? Is it easy to find an issue to evaluate in every text they read? What kinds of issues do they find in nonfiction texts and fiction texts? How do they differ? How are they alike?

- Collect the Agree/Disagree sheets students work on in groups and independently to evaluate their progress. Can students recognize two-sided issues when reading? Are they able to come up with reasons to support their opinions?

- If students need extra support in providing evidence for their viewpoints, guide them in a small group setting using familiar reading materials.

- Work on one agree/disagree example from the form on page 220 at a time in a small group setting. Model, guide, and share students to find examples in both a common text all have read and in texts they have read on their own.

- For further assessment suggestions refer to the Appendix on page 223–234.

Evaluating

Agree or Disagree

1. Explain one idea in the text that has two sides.

   _____

   _____

   Do you ____agree or _____disagree?
   Tell why _____

   _____

2. Is there a character's actions that you might agree or disagree with?

   _____

   _____

   Do you ____agree or _____disagree?
   Tell why _____

   _____

3. Find something about the way the author wrote this text that someone may agree or disagree with.

   _____

   _____

   Do you ____agree or _____disagree?
   Tell why _____

   _____

4. What else can you find in this text to discuss?

   _____

   _____

   Do you ____agree or _____disagree?
   Tell why _____

   _____

Super Six Comprehension Strategies: 35 Lessons and More for Reading Success by Lori Oczkus

Student Sample

Tuck Everlasting

Agree or Disagree

1. Explain one idea in the text that has two sides.

Should people live forever?

Do you ____agree or __✓__disagree?

Tell why. I disagree because I know that when you die you move to a better life.

2. Is there a character's actions that you might agree or disagree with?

One of the main characters kills the villar

Do you ____agree or __✓__disagree?

Tell why. She could have injured him to prevent him from doing harm instead of killing him.

3. Find something about the way the author wrote this text that someone may agree or disagree with.

Should she have done 1 chapter of description, or go straight to the story?

Do you __✓__agree or ____disagree?

Tell why. There was just too much description for my taste in the beginning.

4. What else can you find in this text to discuss?

Was the book better than the movie?

Do you __✓__agree or ____disagree?

Tell why. The book had more depth and made more sense. Besides it had a better plot.

Evaluating

Teachers As Readers

Reflecting on Our Experiences as Adult Readers

As mature readers, we constantly evaluate whether we like the reading, the character's actions, complex two-sided issues in the text, and our own progress as readers. This high-level strategy is made clearer for students when we share how we read and evaluate.

My Reflections on Evaluating

From the moment I picked up One Thousand White Women *by Jim Fergus (1998), I took on my reading role as evaluator. I imagined myself at a weigh station, considering the many thought-provoking and disturbing ideas in the text. I also stepped up to the platform to critique the author's craft and my own response as a reader.*

The book is loosely based on an event that occurred during the Grant administration. In 1854, a Northern Cheyenne chief asked the U.S. Army for the gift of 1000 white women to marry warriors as a means of assimilating into the white man's society. The real request was rejected, but the author toys with the question, "What if the women had actually been sent?" So begins the story and journal of May Dodd, one of the first women in the "Brides for Indians" secret government mission.

What struck me with the most impact was the author's sneaky ability to make the entire text seem historical from his introduction and epilogue, written by the grandson of May Dodd to the codicil written by an Abbott who ended up with the journal. I knew that the text was fictional but I was led along by the author to believe what could have been. It reminded me of The Bridges of Madison County *(1992) because that author also tried to give the impression that the love story was handed down to a family member. Throughout the book I questioned and evaluated the author's craft. I wondered how a man could write a book from a woman's perspective and so beautifully capture her spirit and voice. I marveled at his ability to skillfully weave the story in the letter genre.*

Besides considering the author's unique craft, I found myself engaged in weighing the many controversial ideas that were presented as the story unfolded. I wanted to engage in a debate or conversation with another reader to discuss whether the government had the right to send women as part of a secret government mission. Was it a prudent idea to send women from penitentiaries, prisons, or even mental institutions as candidates for brides? I wondered if it was a fair deal for either party to allow the women to part with the warrior husband after birthing at least one child? I could imagine two movie critics arguing about the controversial issues embedded in this book along with the author's ability to make the text believable.

Of course, as I read I judged my own reading ability. Considering I do not usually enjoy westerns, I was surprised to find myself completely hooked. I stole reading times all day long, not just at my designated nighttime slot. And then I didn't want the book to end. Isn't that the true test of one's reading enjoyment?

If you decide to read One Thousand White Women*, I suggest a book group, even a small one with one friend. You may find, as I did, that you won't run out of topics to discuss and evaluate!*

Evaluating

Your Reflections on Evaluating

- *Think about how you evaluate as you read. Write down examples of your evaluation of author's craft, controversial ideas in the text, and your own progress in reading?*

- *When reading nonfiction how do you determine importance in text?*

- *When reading fiction what helps you determine importance?*

- *What kinds of thoughts do you have when you encounter issues with two sides in your reading?*

- *Do you ever agree or disagree with a character's actions?*

- *How does your evaluation of a text change after discussing it with a friend who read it too?*

- *How do you evaluate before, during, and after reading?*

- *What is a book that comes to mind, where you were forced to evaluate throughout?*

Examples of evaluation in your reading

Examples of evaluation from your reading to share with students

References

Paris, S., Wasik, B., & Turner, J. (1991). The development of strategic readers. In R. Barr, M. Kamil, P. Mosenthal, and P. D. Pearson (Eds.), *Handbook of reading research* (Vol. 2, pp. 609–640). New York: Longman.

Heller, M. F. (1986). How do you know what you know? Metacognitive modeling in the content areas. *Journal of Reading, 29,* 415–422.

Appendix

Assessment Resources

This appendix includes tools for you to choose from as you assess and observe the progress of your students.

Assessment Tools

Tool	When/How to Use It
Assessment Rubric for the Super Six	-Use as you observe students or to interpret their their responses on the reproducibles in this book. -Use the information to flexibly group students according to need. -Share the rubric information with students so they understand what is expected of them. -Create class rubrics in kid language using examples from their reading.
Class Checklist for the Super Six Strategies	-Use to record observations, scores, and other information from reproducibles and observations in class. -Use one each report card period.
Super Six Strategy Survey	-Use at the beginning year as a baseline to see what students already know about the strategies. -For quality answers, give over several days. -Give several times during the year to see if students are growing in their independent use of the strategies and their metacognition. -Use the information gained to form groups based on need.
Interpreting the Strategy Survey	-Use to help interpret the results of the Strategy Survey. -Use to guide flexible groupings and determining next lessons.

Assessment Rubric for The Super Six

As you model, guide, and work with students using the reproducibles in this book, collect dated samples for each student and use to fill in the rubric. Also use the reflection sections from each lesson to record observations about each student and strategy use.

Making Connections

Collect reproducibles and observations from pages _____ to _____ (attach samples)

____ Student identifies possible connections upon initial contact with the material. Includes either text to self, text to text, and text to world.

____ Before, during, and after reading student can identify connections to self, other texts, and the world.

____ After reading student can reflect on which connections were most useful in understanding the text.

____ Student can define the term making connections and provide specific examples of connections from reading material. (Refer to the Strategy Survey page 230)

Notes /Observations:

Predicting/Infering

Collect reproducibles and observations from pages _____ to _____ (attach samples)

____ Student uses text clues to make logical predictions/inferences.

____ Student uses prior knowledge to make predictions/inferences.

____ Before reading, student can tell what he thinks he will learn or predict what the selection is about.

____ During reading, the student can identify new predictions and tell if he has confirmed or changed predictions.

____ After reading student can talk about confirmation or changed predictions and inferences made using prior knowledge and text clues.

____ Student can define the terms predict and infer and give specific examples from reading material. (Refer to the Strategy Survey page 230)

Notes/Observations:

continued

Asking Questions

Collect reproducibles and observations from pages ___ to ___ (attach samples)

____ Student identifies possible questions upon initial contact with the material.

____ Student asks wonder questions before, during, and after reading.

____ During and after reading, student constructs questions using information from the text using who, what, when, where, and why.

____ During and after reading, student generates inferential questions that require background knowledge and text clues.

____ After reading, student generates main idea questions.

____ Student generates questions for the author.

____ Student can define the term question and provide specific examples of questions he had while reading. (Refer to the Strategy Survey page 230)

Notes /Observations:

Monitoring

Collect reproducibles and observations from pages _____ to _____

____ Student identifies words she doesn't understand.

____ Student identifies ideas she doesn't understand.

____ Student describes what she is visualizing as she reads.

____ Student identifies strategies she uses to clarify words she doesn't understand.

____ Student identifies strategies she uses to clarify ideas she doesn't understand.

____ Before reading student identifies possible confusions.

____ Student can define the terms monitor and gives specific examples from reading material. (Refer to the Strategy Survey page 230)

Notes/Observations:

Summarizing/Synthesizing

Collect reproducibles and observations from pages ___ to ___

___ Before reading, the student identifies how the text is organized (Fiction with a problem/solution, nonfiction with headings, etc.).

___ During reading, the student stops to summarize what has happened or been presented so far.

___ After reading, student summarizes using only main points of the text.

___ Student gives main points in order.

___ After reading, student gives the big idea or theme, lesson, or moral the author wanted to convey.

___ After reading. the student reflects on a personal meaning or lesson learned from the reading.

___ Student can define the terms summarize and synthesize and provide specific examples from her reading. (refer to the Strategy Survey page 230)

Notes /Observations:

Evaluating

Collect reproducibles and observations from pages _____ to _____ (attach samples)

___ Student tells why she choose the text.

___ During reading student judges her own progress. Is the book too hard, easy, or just right?

___ After reading student tells whether she likes the text or not and why.

___ Student tells if she agrees with the character's actions and why.

___ Student discusses controversial or two-sided issues from the text.

___ Student rates author's style.

___ Student can define the terms evaluate and gives specific examples from reading material. (Refer to the Strategy Survey page 230)

Notes/Observations:

Class Checklist for The Super Six Strategies

Take notes from reproducibles in each strategy chapter and/or observe students. Include at least two dated observations or samples to show growth. Use this information to form flexible strategy groups that meet to work on an area of need. Duplicate as necessary for the number of students in your class.

Student Name	Connections	Predict/ Infer	Ask Questions

Super Six Comprehension Strategies: 35 Lessons and More for Reading Success by Lori Oczkus

Student Name	Monitor	Summarize/Synthesize	Evaluate

Super Six Strategy Survey

Please think about what each strategy means and tell about it. Then give specific examples from your reading and tell how the strategy helps you.

Name _____

Making Connections

When I read I make connections. This means I _____

_____

_____

Some examples from my reading

_____

_____

_____

Making connections helps me understand what I read because _____

_____

_____

_____

_____

Predicting/Inferring

When I predict I _____

_____

_____

Some examples from my reading

_____

_____

_____

Predicting helps me understand what I read because _____

_____

_____

_____

_____

Questioning

When I read I question. This means I _____

_____

_____

_____

Some examples from my reading

_____

_____

_____

Asking questions helps me understand what I read because _____

_____

_____

Monitoring

When I monitor I _____

_____

_____

_____

Some examples from my reading

_____

_____

_____

Monitoring helps me understand what I read because _____

_____

_____

Summarizing/Synthesizing

When I read I summarize. This means I _____

_____

_____

_____

_____

When I read I synthesize. This means I _____

_____

_____

_____

_____

Some examples from my reading

An example of summarizing_____

_____

_____

_____

_____

An example of synthesis._____

_____

_____

_____

_____

Summarizing helps me understand what I
read because _____

_____

_____

_____

Synthesizing helps me because

_____

_____

_____

_____

Evaluating

When I evaluate I _____

_____

_____

_____

_____

_____

_____

_____

_____

Some examples from my reading

_____

_____

_____

_____

_____

_____

_____

_____

Evaluating helps me understand what I read
because _____

_____

_____

_____

_____

_____

_____

Interpreting the Strategy Survey

The purpose of the strategy survey is to measure how metacognitive or aware of their thinking about the strategies students are. The goal is for students to become aware of each strategy and be able to call on that strategy during reading for optimal understanding. You can administer the survey one strategy at a time. In fact, that is advised so students don't tire. You may also wish to use the survey as a baseline before teaching the strategies to see what the students know about the strategies before teaching them. If they can define and give examples from their reading for a particular strategy that has been taught well in other grades, then you can continue reinforcing that strategy strength while focusing on other needed strategies.

Give the strategy survey every few months to see if students are growing in their awareness of their strategy use. Continue modeling during reading lessons how to define and talk about strategy use using think-alouds. Use multiple measures to help you evaluate and assess strategy use. Collect written student samples from the reproducibles in this book to help you measure strategy use and growth. Use the reflection suggestions in each lesson as you observe students. Also, use the assessment rubric on page 225 to evaluate students. Use the chart on the next page to help you interpret the strategy survey.

Connecting	Predicting/Inferring
Defining the strategy.	**Defining the strategy.**
Does the student	- include information about using text clues such as illustrations
- include all three connections text to self, text to text, and text to world.	- include using ones' own background information
- use any words that indicate understanding of the strategy like "what I know," "reminds me of," etc.	- refer to confirming or changing predictions
Giving examples from reading.	**Giving examples from reading.**
- Does the student give examples from one or more connections?	- Can the student give an example that is a logical prediction or inference and that uses clues from the text?
Telling how the strategy helps with . understanding	**Telling how the strategy helps with understanding**
- student cites usefulness such as keeps him interested or makes him think of his life	Does the student give usefulness of strategy reasons
- student uses background knowledge and connections to help him understand the new information in the text	- predicting/inferring makes reading interesting, and keeps student interested
	- helps student know what is coming next

continued

Super Six Comprehension Strategies: 35 Lessons and More for Reading Success by Lori Oczkus

Questioning

Defining the strategy.

Does the student

- mention the word wondering
- refer to questioning throughout the reading process before, during, and after
- mention teacher questions like main idea
- mention inferential questions
- give reference to any question words
- refer to actually answering one's own questions

Giving examples from reading.

- Does the student give examples of both literal and inferential questions?
- Can the student give examples of when he had these questions—before, during, and after reading?

Telling how the strategy helps with . understanding

Does the student give reasons for the usefulness of questioning.

- helps keep one engaged throughout the reading process
- is fun after reading to ask each other questions
- helps the student remember what was read
- during reading the student begins to identify parts of text that would make good questions

Monitoring

Defining the strategy.

Does the student

- mention asking if the reading makes sense.
- discuss words that may be difficult
- mention confusing ideas
- ways to fix up words
- ways to clear up confusing ideas

Giving examples from reading.

- Does the student give examples of both ideas and words that were confusing during reading?

Telling how the strategy helps with understanding

Does the student give usefulness of strategy reasons

- discusses figuring out and clarifying difficult words or ideas
- discusses strategies for clearing up problems
- refers to making sense of reading

continued

© 2004 Christopher-Gordon Publishers, Inc.
Super Six Comprehension Strategies: 35 Lessons and More for Reading Success by Lori Oczkus

Summarizing/Synthesizing	Evaluating
Defining the strategy.	**Defining the strategy.**
Does the student	Does the student
- mention giving main events	- mention that evaluating includes an opinion of the text and the author's style
- discuss ordering logical and main events	- tell about controversial ideas or character actions that might be evaluated in the text
- a synthesis as the theme, lesson, and moral of the story	- talk about his own progress in the text
- a synthesis as a personal interpretation of the reading	
Giving examples from reading.	**Giving examples from reading.**
Does the student	Does the student
- give an actual summary	- give examples of a general opinion or evaluation of a text he has read
- give examples of summarizing during or after reading?	- include whether he agrees or disagrees with ideas in a text or character actions
- give an example of a synthesis—lesson, moral, and so on for a synthesis	- provide a reflection of his own
- tell how his ideas may change during and after reading	- reflect on the author's craft
Telling how the strategy helps with understanding.	**Telling how the strategy helps with understanding.**
Does the student give usefulness of strategy reasons	Does the student give usefulness of strategy reasons
- summarizing helps the reader keep track and know what is going on in the text	- discusses how evaluating keeps one interested in the reading
- synthesis helps stay engaged and in remembering the text	- helps one decide what is important to remember from the text
- synthesis helps the student think about what he will take away from the reading	- gives one ideas to debate and discuss after reading
	- makes one really think about the reading

References

Bibliography of Professional Resources on Comprehension

Allington, R. L., (1998). *Teaching struggling readers: Articles from The Reading Teacher.* Newark, DE: International Reading Association.

Allington, R. L. (2001). *What really matters for struggling readers: Designing research based programs.* New York: Addison Wesley Longman

Almasi, J. (2003). *Teaching strategic processes in reading.* New York: Guilford.

American Heritage Dictionary. (1985). 2nd college edition. Boston: Houghton Mifflin.

Anderson, R. C., & Pearson, P. D. (1984). A schema-theoretic view of basic processes in reading comprehension. In P. D. Pearson, R. Barr, M. L. Kamil, & P. Mosenthal (Eds.), *Handbook of reading research* (pp. 255-291.). New York: Longman.

Armbruster, B. B., Anderson, T. H., & Ostertag, J. (1987). Does text structure/summarization instruction facilitate learning from expository text? *Reading Research Quarterly, 22,* 331–346.

Atwell-Vasey, W. (1998). *Nourishing words: Bridging private reading and public teaching.* Albany, NY: State University of New York Press.

Baltas, J., & Nessel, D. (1999). *Easy strategies & lessons that build content area reading skills.* New York: Scholastic.

Beck, I. L., McKeown, M. G., Worthy, J., Samdora C. A., & Kucan, L. (1996). Question the author: A year-long classroom implementation to engage students with text. *Elementary School Journal, 96,* 385–xxx

Bisplinghoff, B. S. (2002b). Under the wings of writers: A teacher reads to find her way. *The Reading Teacher, 56,* 242-252.

Blachowicz, C., & Ogle, D. (2001). *Reading comprehension strategies for independent learners.* New York: Guilford.

Block, C., & Pressley, M. (2000). *Comprehension instruction: Research-based best practices.* New York: Guilford.

Boyle, O., & Peregoy, S. (1998). Literacy scaffolds: Strategies for first and second-language readers and writers. In M. Opitz, ed., *Literacy instruction for culturally and linguistically diverse students,* (pp. 150-156). Newark, DE: International Reading Association.

Brown, A. L, & Day, J. D. (1983). Macrorules for summarizing texts: The development of expertise. *Journal of Verbal Learning and Verbal Behavior, 22,* 1-14.

Burke, J. (1999). *I hear America reading.* Portsmouth, NH: Heinemann.

Campbell Hill, B., Johnson, N., & Schlick Noe, K. (2001*). Literature circles resource guide.* Norwood, MA: Christopher-Gordon.

Campbell Hill, B., Johnson, N., & Schlick Noe, K. (Eds.). (1995*). Literature circles and response.* Norwood, MA: Christopher Gordon.

Cassidy, J., & Cassidy, D. (2003). What's hot, what's not for 2003. *Reading Today. Vol. 20, number 3.* Newark, DE: International Reading Association.

Clay, M. M. (1985). *The early detection of reading difficulties* (3rd ed.) Portsmouth, NH: Heinemann.

Commeyras, M., Shockley, B., & Olson, J. (2003*). Teachers as readers: Perspectives on the importance of reading in teachers' classrooms and lives .* Newark, DE: International Reading Association.

Cooper, J. D. (1993). *Literacy: Helping children construct meaning* (2nd ed.). Boston: Houghton Mifflin.

Cooper, J. D., Boschken, I., McWilliams, J., & Pistochini, L. (1999). *Soar to success: The intermediate intervention program.* Boston: Houghton Mifflin.

Cooper, J. D., Boschken, I., McWilliams, J., & Pistochini, L. (1997). A study of effectiveness of an intervention program designed to accelerate reading for struggling readers in the upper grades. *Final Report.* Unpublished.

Costa, A., & Garmston, R. (1994). *Cognitive coaching: A foundation for renaissance schools.* Norwood, MA: Christopher Gordon Publishers.

Cunningham, J. (1982). Generating interactions between schemata and text. J. A. Niles & L. A. Harris (Eds.), *New inquiries in reading research and instruc-*

tion (pp. 42–47). Rochester, NY: National Reading Conference.

Daniels, H. (1994*). Literature circles: Voice and choice in the student-centered classroom.* York, ME: Stenhouse.

Dole, J. A., Duffy, G. G., Roehler, L. R., & Pearson, P. D. (1991*).* Moving from the old to the new: Research on reading comprehension instruction. *Review of Educational Research, 61* (2), 239–264.

Donahue, P. L., Voeklkl, K. E., Campbell, J. R., & Mazzeo, L. (1999*). The NAEP reading report card for the nation and the states.* Washington, DC: U.S. Department of Education, Office of Educational Research and Improvement, National Center for Education Statistics (NCES) report no. 1999-500.

Duffy, G. (2003). *Explaining reading.* New York: Guilford.

Duffy, G. G., Roehler, L. R., & Herrmann, B. A. (1988). Modeling mental processes helps poor readers become strategic readers. *The Reading Teacher, 41,* 762–767.

Duffy, G. G., Roehler, L. R., Sivan, E., Rackliffe, G., Book, C., & Meloth, M. (1987). Effects of explaining the reasoning associated with using reading strategies. *Reading Research Quarterly, 22,* 347–348

Duffy, G G., & Roehler, L. R. (1987). Improving reading instruction through the use of responsive elaboration. *The Reading Teacher, 40,* 514–521

Duke, J., & Pearson, P. D. (2002). Effective practices for developing reading comprehension. In A. Farstrup and J. Samuels, Eds.,*What research has to say about reading instruction.* Newark, DE: International Reading Association.

Durkin, D. (1978/1979). What classroom observations reveal about reading comprehension instruction. *Reading Research Quarterly, 14,* 481-533.

Fielding, L., & Pearson, P. D., (1991). Comprehension instruction. In R. Barr, M. L. Kamil, P. B. Mosenthal, & P. D. Pearson (Eds.), *Handbook of reading research* (Vol. 2, pp. 815–860). New York: Longman.

Fountas, I. C., & Pinnell, G. S. (1996). *Guided reading: Good first teaching for all children.* Portsmouth, NH: Heinemann.

Fountas, I. C., & Pinnell, G. S. (2001). *Guiding readers and writers grades 3–6: Teaching comprehension, genre, and content literacy.* Portsmouth, NH: Heinemann.

Freeman, D., & Freeman, B. (2000) *Teaching reading in multilingual classrooms.* Portsmouth, NH: Heinemann.

Garcia, G. (Ed.). (2003*). English learners: Reaching the highest level of English literacy.* Newark, DE: International Reading Association.

Graves, M., & Graves, B. (2003). *Scaffolding reading experiences: Designs for student success, 2nd ed.,* Norwood, MA: Christopher-Gordon.

Hacker, D., & Tenent, A. (2002). Implementing reciprocal teaching in the classroom: Overcoming obstacles and making modifications. *Journal of Educational Psychology Vol. 94,* 699–718.

Hansen, J. (1981). The effects of inference training and practice on young children's reading comprehension. *Reading Research Quarterly 16,* 391–417.

Hansen, J., & Pearson, P. D. (1983). An instructional study: Improving the inferential comprehension of good and poor fourth grade readers. *Journal of Educational Pschology, 75,* 821–829.

Harvey, S. (1998). *Nonfiction matters.* York, ME: Stenhouse.

Harvey, S. & Goudvis, A. (2000). *Strategies that work: Teaching comprehension to enhance understanding.* York, ME: Stenhouse.

Heimlich, J. E., & Pittelman, S. D. (1986). *Semantic mapping: Classroom applications.* Newark: DE: International Reading Association.

Herrell, M., & Jordan, M. (2004) 50 strategies for teaching English language learners. Upper Saddle River, NJ: Pearson Education.

Hiebert, E. H., & Taylor, B. (Eds). (1994). *Getting reading right from the start: Effective early literacy interventions .* Boston: Allyn & Bacon.

Hiebert, E. H., Pearson, P. D., Taylor, B. M., Richardson, V., & Paris, S. G. (1998). *Every child a reader.* Ann Arbor, MI: Center for the Improvement of Early Reading Acheivement. (CIERA).

Heller, M. F. (1986). How do you know what you know? Metacognitive modeling in the content areas. *Journal of Reading, 29,* 415–422.

Hoyt, L. (2002). *Make it real: Strategies for success with informational texts.* Portsmouth, NH: Heinemann.

Hoyt, L. (1992.) Many ways of knowing. *The Reading Teacher, 45,* 580–584.

Hoyt, L. (1999). *Revisit, reflect, retell: Strategies for improving reading comprehension.* Portsmouth, NH: Heinemann.

Hoyt, L., Mooney, M., & Parkes, B. (2003). *Exploring informational texts.* Portsmouth, NH: Heinemann.

Hubbard, R., Power, B. (1999). *Living the questions. A guide for teacher researchers.* Portsmouth, NH: Heinemann.

Jobe, R., & Sakari, D. (2002). *Info-kids: How to use nonfiction to turn reluctant readers into enthusiastic learners.* York, ME: Stenhouse

Kagan, S. (1989). *Cooperative learning: Resources for teachers.* Laguna Nigel, CA: Resources for Teachers.

Keene, E., & Zimmerman, S. (1997). *Mosaic of thought: Teaching comprehension in a reader's workshop.* Portsmouth, NH: Heinemann.

Lipson, M. W. (2001). *A fresh look at comprehension.* Paper presented at the Reading/Language Arts Symposium, Chicago.

Lipson, M. W. (1982). Learning new information from text: The role of prior knowledge and reading ability. *Journal of Reading Behavior, 14,* 243–261.

Lipson, M. W. (1996). *Developing skills and strategies in an integrated literature-based reading program.* Research paper for Houghton Mifflin, Invitations to Literacy. Boston: Houghton Mifflin.

Lipson, M. W., & Cooper, J. D. (2002) *Understanding and supporting comprehension development in the elementary and middle grades.* Research paper for Houghton Mifflin Reading Language Arts Program. Boston: Houghton Mifflin.

Lubliner, S. (2001). *A practical guide to reciprocal teaching.* Bothell, WA: Wright Group/McGraw Hill.

Mantione, R., & Smead, S. (2003). *Weaving through words. Using the arts to teach comprehension strategies.* Newark, DE: International Reading Association.

Marriott, D. (2002). *Comprehension right from the start. How to organize and manage book clubs for young readers.* Portsmouth, NH: Heinemann.

McCormack, R., & Paratore, J. (2003). *After early intervention, then what? Teaching struggling readers in grades 3 and beyond.* Newark, DE: International Reading Association.

McKoon, G., & Ratcliff, R. (1992). Inference during reading. *Psychological Review, 99,* 440–466.

McLaughlin, M., & Allen, M. B. (2002). *Guided comprehension in action lessons for grades 3–8.* Newark, DE: International Reading Association.

McLaughlin, M., & Allen, M. B. (2002). *Guided comprehension a teaching model for grades 3–8.* Newark, DE: International Reading Association.

Miller, D. (2002). *Reading with meaning: Teaching comprehension in the primary grades.* York, ME: Stenhouse.

National Reading Panel. (2000) *Teaching children to read: An evidence-based assessment of the scientific research literature on reading and its implications for reading instruction.* Washington, DC: National Institutes of Health.

National Reading Panel. (2000) *Putting reading first.* Washington, DC: National Institutes of Health.

Neuman, S. (1998). Enhancing children's comprehension through previewing. In J. Readence & R. S. Baldwin (Eds.), *Dialogues in literacy research* (37th Yearbook Of the National Reading Conference, pp. 219–224). Chicago, IL: National Reading Conference.

Northwest Regional Lab. (1999). *Seeing with new eyes.* Portland, OR: Northwest Regional Laboratory.

Oczkus, L. (2004). *Super six comprehension strategies: 35 lessons and more for reading success.* Norwood, MA: Christopher-Gordon.

Ogle, D. (1986). K-W-L: A teaching model that develops active reading of expository text. *The Reading Teacher, 39 (6),* 564–570.

Opitz, M., & Ford, M. (2001). *Reaching readers: Flexible and innovative strategies for guided reading.* Portsmouth, NH: Heinemann.

Osmundson, E. (2003). *Personal communication. Observation Protocol. UCLA CRESST MSA Evaluation.* Los Angeles: University of California Los Angeles.

Palincsar, A. S., & Brown, A. L. (1984). Reciprocal teaching of comprehension-fostering and monitoring activities. *Cognition and Instruction, 1,* 117–175.

Palincsar, A. S., & Brown, A. L. (1986). Interactive teaching to promote independent learning from text. *The Reading Teacher, 39,* 771–777

Palincsar, A. S., Brown A. L., & Martin, S. M. (1987). Peer interaction in reading comprehension instruction. *Educational Psychologist, 22,* 231–253.

Baltas, J. & Nessel, D. (1999). *Easy strategies & lessons that build content area reading skills.* New York: Scholastic

Paris, S., Wasik, B., & Turner, J. (1991). The development of strategic readers. In R. Barr, M. Kamil, P. Mosenthal, and P. D. Pearson (Eds.), *Handbook of reading research* (Vol. 2, pp. 609–640). New York: Longman.

Pearson, P. D., & Fielding, L. (1991). Comprehension instruction. In R. Barr, M.Kamil, P. Mosenthal, and P. D. Pearson. (Eds.), *Handbook of Reading Research* (Vol. 2, pp. 815–860. New York: Longman.

Pearson, P. D., Roehler, L. R., Dole, J. A., & Duffy, G. G. (1992). Developing expertise in reading comprehension. In J. Samuels & A. Farstrup (Eds.), *What Research Has to Say About Reading Instruction*. Newark, DE: International Reading Association.

Pehrsson, R. S., & Robinson, H. A. (1985). *The semantic organizer approach to writing and reading instruction*. Rockville, MD: Aspen Systems Corp.

Pikulski, J. (1994). Five successful reading programs for at-risk students. *The Reading Teacher, 48*, 30–39.

Pinnell, G., Rodgers, E. (2002). *Learning from teaching in literacy education: New perspectives on professional development*. Portsmouth, NH: Heinemann.

Polselli-Sweet, A. & Snow, C. (2003). *Rethinking reading comprehension*. New York: Guilford

Pressley, M. (2002). *Reading instruction that works: The case for balanced teaching*. New York: Guilford.

Pressley, M. (1997). Imagery and children's learning: Putting the picture in developmental perspective. *Review of Educational Research, 47*, 586–622.

Pressley, M., Block, C., & Gambrell, L. (2003). *Improving comprehension instruction. Rethinking research, theory, and classroom practice*. Newark, DE: International Reading Association.

Pressley, M., El-Dinary, P. B., Gaskins, I., Schuder, T., Gergman, J., Almasi, L., & Brown, R. (1992). Beyond direct explanation: Transactional instruction of reading comprehension strategies. *Elementary School Journal, 92*, 511–554.

Pritchard, R., Spangenberg-Urbschat, K. (1994). *Kids come in all languages: Reading instruction for ESL students*. Newark, DE: International Reading Association

Quindlen, A. (1998). *How reading changed my life*. New York: Ballantine.

Rinehart, S. D., Stahl, S., & Erickson, L. G. (1986). Some effects of summarizing training on reading and studying. *Reading Research Quarterly, 21*, 422–438.

Robb, L. (2000). *Redefining staff development. A collaborative model for teachers and administrators*. Portsmouth, NH: Heinemann.

Rosenblatt, L. M. (1978). *The reader, the text, and the poem: The transactional theory of the literary work*. Carbondale, IL: Southern Illinois University Press.

Rosenshine, B., Meister, C., & Chapman, S. (1996). Teaching students to generate questions: A review of the intervention studies. *Review of Educational Research, 66(2)*, 181–221.

Routman, R. (2000). *Conversations: Strategies for teaching, learning and evaluating*. Portsmouth, NH: Heinemann

Routman, R. (2003). *Reading essentials: The specifics you need to teach reading well*. Portsmouth, NH: Heinemann.

Rumelhart, D. E. (1982). Schemata: The building blocks of cognition. In J. Guthrie (Ed.), *Comprehension and teaching: Research reviews* (pp. 3–26). Newark, DE: International Reading Association

Rummel, M. K., & Quintero, E. P. (1997). *Teachers' reading/ teachers' lives*. Albany: State University of New York Press.

Samway, K. D., Wang, G., & Pippitt, M. (1995). *Buddy reading: Cross-age tutoring in a multicultural school*. Portsmouth, NH: Heinemann.

Samway, K. D., & Wang, G. (1996). *Literature study circles in a multicultural classroom*. York, ME: Stenhouse.

Schulman, M., & DaCruz, P. C. (2000). *Guided reading: Making it work*. New York: Scholastic.

Schwanenflugel, P. J., Stahl, S. A., & McFals, E. L. (1997). Partial word knowledge and vocabulary growth during reading comprehension. *Journal of Literacy Research, 29*, 531–553

Seely-Flint, A. (1999). *Professional's guide literature circles*. Westminster, CA: Teacher Created Materials, Inc.

Singer, J., & Donlan, E. (1982). Active comprehension: Problem-solving schema with question generation for comprehension of complex short stories. *Reading Research Quarterly, 17*, 166–168.

Snow, C. E., Burns M. S., & Griffith, P. (Eds.) (1998). *Preventing reading difficulties in young children*. Washington, DC: National Academy Press.

Spandel, V. (2001). *Creating writers through 6 trait instruction*. New York: Addison Wesley Longman.

Strickland, D., Ganske, K, & Monroe, J., (2002) *Supporting struggling readers and writers: Strategies for intervention*. York, ME: Stenhouse.

Sweeney, D. (2003). *Learning along the way. Professional development by and for teachers*. York, ME: Stenhouse.

Taylor, B. (1982). Text structure and children's comprehension and memory for expository material. *Journal of Educational Psychology, 74*, 323–340.

Vasquez, V. (2003). *Getting beyond "I like the book": Creating space for critical literacy in k-6 classrooms*. Newark, DE: International Reading Association.

Vygotsky, L.S. (1978). *Mind in society: The development of higher psychological processes.* Cambridge, MA: Harvard University Press.

Vogt, M. E., & McLaughlin, M. (2000). *Creativity and innovation in content area teaching.* Norwood, MA: Christopher-Gordon.

Whisler, N., & Williams, J. (1990). *Literature and cooperative learning: pathway to literacy.* Sacramento, CA: Literature Coop.

Williams, J. P. (2002). Using the theme scheme to improve story comprehension. In C. C. Block & M. Pressley (Eds.), *Comprehension instruction: Research-based best practices* (pp. 126–139). New York: Guilford.

Wood, S. S., Bruner, J. S., & Ross, G. (1976). The role of tutoring in problem solving. *Journal of child Psychology and Psychiatry, 17,* 89–100.

Children's Literature Cited

Allard, H. (1977). *Miss Nelson is missing.* Boston: Houghton Mifflin.

Brenner, B. (1997). *Thinking about ants.* New York: Mondo.

Brown, M. (1995). *D. W. the picky eater.* New York: Little Brown.

Brown, M. (1947). *Goodnight moon.* New York: Harper & Row.

Bunting, E. (1994) *Flower garden.* New York: Harcourt Brace.

Cherry, L. (1990). *The great kapok tree.* New York: Harcourt Brace.

Creech, S. (2000). *The wanderer.* New York: Harper Collins.

Cullen, E. (1996). *Spiders.* New York: Mondo.

Cummings, P. (1991). *Clean your room, Harvey Moon!* New York: Simon & Schuster.

Dahl, R. (1964) *Charlie and the chocolate factory.* New York: Bantam.

deGroat, D. (1996). *Roses are pink, your feet really stink.* New York: Mulberry.

Di Camillo, K. (2000). *Because of Winn Dixie.* New York: Scholastic.

DuTemple, L. (1999). *Whales. Soar to success.* Boston: Houghton Mifflin.

Gardiner, J. R. (1980). *Stone Fox.* New York: Harper Collins.

Gibbons, G. (1988). *Sunken treasure.* New York: HarperCollins.

Hale, B. (2001). *The big nap.* New York: Harcourt Brace.

Harris, N. (1999). *Owlbert. Soar to success grade 5.* Boston: Houghton Mifflin.

Houghton Mifflin. (1999). *America will be. Houghton Mifflin social studies.* Boston: Houghton Mifflin.

Houghton, Mifflin. (1991). *Oh, California. Houghton Mifflin social studies.* Boston: Houghton Mifflin.

James, S. (1996). *Meet the octopus.* New York: Mondo.

Konigsburg, E. L. (1968). *From the mixed-up files of Mrs. Basil E. Frankweiler.* New York: Athenium.

Levin, G. C. (1999). *Dave at night.* New York: Harper Trophy.

Lewis, C. S. (1978). *The lion, the witch, and the wardrobe.* New York: Harper & Row.

Llewellyn, C. (2001). *Kid's survival handbook.* New York: Tangerine Press.

Lobel, A. (1971) *The garden. Frog and toad together.* New York: Harper & Row.

Meddaugh, S. (1990). *Tree of birds.* Boston: Houghton Mifflin.

Mora, P. (1997). *Tomas and the library lady.* New York: Random House.

Peck, R. (1998). *A long way from Chicago.* New York: Puffin.

Pilkey, D. (1993). *Dogzilla.* New York: Harcourt.

Polacco, P. (2001). *Thunder cake. In delights anthology Houghton Mifflin reading (2003).* Boston: Houghton Mifflin.

Pullman, P. (1995). *The golden compass.* New York: Knox.

Rothman, N. P. (1997). *Ruby the copycat.* New York: Scholastic.

Rowling, J. K. (1999). *Harry Potter and the prisoner of Azkaban.* New York: Scholastic.

Rylant, C. (1982). *When I was young in the mountains.* New York: Dutton.

Say, A. (1993). *Grandfather's journey.* Boston: Houghton Mifflin.

Sendak, M. (1963) *Where the wild things are.* New York: Harper & Row.

Silverstein, S. (1964). *The giving tree.* New York: HarperCollins

Soto, G. (1990). *Baseball in april and other stories.* Orlando, FL: Harcourt.

Stead, T. (2000). *Should there be zoos?* New York: Mondo.

Stefoff, R. (1998*). Ant.* New York: Benchmark.

Tabakas, A. (2001). At the opening ceremony. Olympics. *Reading Safari Magazine.* New York: Mondo.

Van Allsburg, C. (1981). *Jumanji.* Boston: Houghton Mifflin.

Van Allsburg, C. (1990). *Just a dream.* Boston: Houghton Mifflin.

Wilcox, C. (1999). Mummies and their mysteries. *Houghton Mifflin soar to success.* Boston: Houghton Mifflin.

Wheeler C. (1994). *Bookstore cat.* New York: Random House.

White, E.B. (1952). *Charlotte's web.* New York: Harper Collins.

Adult Level Books to Read and Discuss
(Books Cited in this Text)

Chevalier, T. (1999). *Girl with a pearl earring.* New York: Plume.

Cooper, S. (2000*). Sticks and stones.* New York: Three Rivers Press.

Diamant, A. (1997). *The Red Tent.* New York: Picador.

Fergus, J. (1998). *One thousand white women.* New York: St. Martin's-Griffin.

Grisham, J. (2001). *Skipping Christmas.* New York: Doubleday.

Kingsolver, B. (1998) *The poisonwood bible.* New York: Harper Collins.

Lamott, A. (1993). *Operating instructions: A journal of my son's first year.* New York: Fawcett/ Columbine.

Marcus, L. (Ed.). (1998). *Dear genius: The letters of Ursula Nordstrom.* New York: HarperCollins.

Mitchell, M. (1936). *Gone with the wind.* New York: Macmillan

Pennac, D. (1999). *Better than life.* York, ME: Stenhouse.

Vreeland, S. (1999). *Girl in hyacinth blue.* New York: Penguin.

Waldman, A. (2001). *The big nap.* New York: Penguin.

Waller, R. J. (1992*). Bridges of Madison County.* New York: Warner Books.

Winfrey, O. (2001). Books that made a difference. *Oprah Magazine.*

Photo by Kate Burkart

Lori Oczkus is a nationally recognized literacy consultant and popular speaker at state and national conferences. She is in constant demand as a literacy coach/demonstration teacher and has trained over 10,000 teachers in California and across the country. Lori has extensive experience teaching struggling readers/writers, bilingual students, and gifted and talented students. Her first book *Reciprocal Teaching at Work: Strategies for Improving Reading Comprehension* published by the International Reading Association was selected as the IRA book of the month for October 2003.

Lori Oczkus lives in Orinda, California and works in classrooms in the San Francisco Bay Area and throughout the United States. She can be reached at loczkus52@earthlink.net.

Index